European
Market
Information

A Handbook for Managers

European
Market
Information

A Handbook for Managers

DAVID MORT

FINANCIAL TIMES

PITMAN PUBLISHING

Pitman Publishing
128 Long Acre, London WC2E 9AN

A Division of Longman Group UK Limited

First published in 1992

©Longman Group UK Ltd, 1992

British Libarary Cataloguing in Publication Data
A CIP catalogue record for this book can be obtained from the British Library

ISBN 0 273 037366

Printed and bound in Great Britain by
Biddles Ltd, Guildford and King's Lynn

CONTENTS

INTRODUCTION

Published statistical data is an important business information resource with statistical time series providing useful indicators for a range of subjects. These include national economic and financial trends, demographic characteristics, business conditions, economic activity and industrial structures, the production and markets for specific products and services, labour market data, and social trends.

In Western Europe, major producers of statistics are national statistical offices in specific countries publishing 'official statistics', the statistical office of the European Communities and other organisations such as trade associations, professional bodies and economic research institutes publishing 'non-official statistics'.

The general subject areas and sectors covered by published statistics are basically the same from one country to another but differences occur in the nature of the statistics produced, the amount of detail published and the coverage of the statistics, and also in the general approaches to the collection and publishing of statistical data. The aim of this book is to provide a guide to published statistics and statistical activity across Western Europe and in the specific countries of Western Europe, concentrating particularly on business statistics such as industrial structure data, production and external trade data and service sector statistics.

A chapter is devoted to each Western European country, each starting with a general description of the organisation of official statistics in that country and an outline of general sources of statistics. The bulk of the chapter provides a review of industrial structure, production, trade and service sector statistics with a description of sources in specific key sectors. The main statistical titles from official sources are included plus, for the main countries, selected titles from trade associations, economic research institutes and related organisations. Where available, details are also given about the industrial and trade classifications used in each country and the methods used for compiling the statistics.

An opening chapter (Chapter 2) looks at pan-European statistical information, concentrating on the role of **Eurostat**, the statistical office of the EC, and its main publications. This chapter also examines the attempts to produce standardised international statistical information and the development of internationally agreed classifications and definitions of statistical data.

An index provides details of all the statistical publishers mentioned in the book and there is also a subject index and an index, by country.

This book does not attempt to be a comprehensive guide to sources of statistical information in Western Europe. Its purpose is to review the organisation and extent of statistical activity in Western Europe with references to the major business statistics titles published and it offers a practical guide to all those needing European statistical data on a regular basis.

1 BACKGROUND TO EUROPEAN STATISTICAL PUBLISHING

EUROPEAN STANDARDISATION

By the end of 1992, the creation of a Single Market involving the 12 member states of the European Community is set to become a reality producing another step in the growing internationalisation of markets and industries. As more countries, such as Sweden and Austria, look to join the EC and growing links are forged between the EC and other groups of nations like the **European Free Trade Association (EFTA)** and the East European countries, the Single European Market is likely to expand.

As the European market develops, business users will increasingly need pan-European data and be looking for standardised data sources from one country to the next. To satisfy these user demands, standardised statistical sources across a range of topics and countries are needed but different approaches to statistical collection, analysis and publishing in the individual European countries means that a Single European Market in statistical information is still some way off. International organisations, including the EC through its statistical office **Eurostat** and the United Nations, are working to create international co-operation and harmonisation in the compilation and publishing of statistics but the process remains relatively slow and gradual.

A general outline of European statistical publishing is given in this chapter followed by a chapter describing pan-European statistical sources. Detailed information by country is given in the remaining chapters.

NATIONAL STATISTICAL PUBLISHING

In all the Western European countries, the main sources of statistics are Central Government departments and most countries have a national statistical office which co-ordinates government statistical activity and publishes statistical publications. These statistics are known as 'official statistics'. Other producers and publishers of statistics are 'non-official' organisations outside central government such as trade associations, professional bodies, banks and research institutes. In some instances, these non-official sources are simply repackaging, analysing and simplifying official data and this is a useful exercise in itself. Other non-official sources are producers of original data which can often be more detailed and up-to-date than the official sources.

Official statistics

In most developed countries, the general subject areas covered by official statistics are the same from one country to the next and these main subject areas are listed in Table 1.1.

National economic & financial conditions & trends

Demographic characteristics, trends & projections

Social trends & characteristics

Labour Market

Economic sector activity, e.g:
   Agriculture, forestry, fishing
   Mining, quarrying, energy
   Manufacturing
   Services
   Construction
   Transport
   Public sector & public utilities

External Trade

Table 1.1 General subject areas of official statistics

The problem is that, although the same general subject areas are covered in each country, the amount and nature of the data collected and published on these subjects can vary considerably from one country to another. The example of production statistics emphasises this point.

All countries publish statistics on the production of specific products in their country but it is still difficult to compare one country's production figures with another. First, each country has its own industrial classification scheme and each country has its own set of products and product definitions which it collects data on. These product lists and definitions will vary from country to country and will reflect the importance of specific products in particular countries. The samples used to collect results, the questions asked and the way in which the questions are asked are likely to vary in each country. The frequency of the surveys and the frequency of publication of results is also likely to vary. In some countries, legislation obliges respondents to participate in official surveys but, in other instances, the surveys are voluntary. Some countries publish annual production statistics, others publish quarterly or monthly data and some a combination of these. The published statistics might refer to manufacturers' sales of products, production, deliveries or shipments and the quantities are sometimes expressed in national currency values or physical volumes, or both. The different languages used in each country add an extra complication when trying to compare one country's statistics with another and, finally, different countries devote differing amounts of resources to statistical activity. Production statistics are just one example but similar problems exist in most other subject areas.

On a general level in Western Europe, the basic rule is that as you move northwards, the better official statistics become. For example, the Scandinavian countries, notably Denmark and Sweden, have particularly good official statistics and they have been actively involved in the international attempts to improve statistical provision. Statistics in countries such as the Netherlands, France and Germany are fairly good while UK statistics are reasonable although not as comprehensive or reliable as they were some years ago. However, the real problem areas are in Southern Europe in Italy, Spain and Portugal although, in the latter two countries, statistical provision has improved with membership of the EC.

Non-official statistics

At least official statistics follow a similar subject pattern from country to country and the national statistics in each country form part of a growing attempt to produce an international statistical database. In the non-official sector, the collection and publishing of statistics is much more fragmented and the quality and reliability of the data produced can vary considerably from one source to the next. The major non-official publishers of regular statistics are trade associations.

There are thousands of associations across Europe with some representing broad industrial and service sectors and others concentrating on specific products and services. Some associations are well established while others are relatively new. Most associations do not collect or publish statistics at all while others may collect statistics occasionally. The relatively small number of associations that are regular statistical publishers have different levels of statistical expertise, are using different methodologies to collect the data and may have a specific motive for publishing the data.

In these circumstances, obtaining consistent and reliable figures from one country to the next is almost impossible although, in selected sectors, national associations have come together to form pan-European associations. Some of these are publishing pan-European statistics and working towards standardised European data for their areas of interest. A number of pan-European associations are described in the next chapter and selected trade association publishers in specific countries are included in the country chapters.

Accessibility of statistics

A final problem for the potential user of European statistics is that few statistical series are accessible via on-line systems or in other machine readable formats such as CD-Rom, so scanning pages and pages of statistical tables is still often the only way to track down data. A great deal of national economic and financial data is available in machine readable format along with import and export data but in other areas such as industrial structure and production data, demographic data and social statistics, most of the information is still only available in traditional printed publications.

Official statistics are gradually being incorporated into machine readable systems and on-line services but most of the data from non-official sources remains outside this new information technology. A selection of on-line systems, and PC-based systems, containing statistical time series are described in the chapters that follow.

2 PAN-EUROPEAN STATISTICS

INTRODUCTION

The preceding chapter emphasised the problems of comparing statistics produced in different countries and the difficulties involved in creating pan-European statistical series. Nevertheless, some progress has been made largely through the work of international organisations such as the **European Communities** (EC), **United Nations** (UN) and the **Organisation for Economic Co-operation and Development** (OECD). All these organisations collect and publish statistics covering a range of countries and details of their main publications are given in the sections below. These international bodies are also involved in developing international classification schemes for statistical purposes and in trying to standardise the way statistics are collected, processed and published across various countries.

For example, in some topic areas, such as industrial statistics and external trade statistics, international classification schemes covering activities, sectors and products have been created. These have been adopted by many countries so data from one country is comparable with another and a consistent international picture can be developed. In other areas, such as labour force statistics, family expenditure surveys and population census data, the same questions are asked in surveys in each country and surveys are carried out at approximately the same time and using similar samples. By adopting these internationally agreed approaches, survey and census results from one country are closely aligned to the results from another country and meaningful 'pan-European' data can be produced.

On a lesser scale, regional groupings of countries such as the **Nordic Statistical Secretariat** (Denmark, Sweden, Norway, Finland, Iceland) are also trying to standardise statistical data. In the non-official sector, national trade associations and professional bodies are joining together to form European-wide associations and some publish statistics while market research and specialist research organisations are filling the gap in certain subjects by producing European reports and statistics.

The problem is that the development of consistent and reliable international statistics across a range of subjects is a relatively slow process which depends on the co-operation of individual countries. As the following individual country chapters will show, some countries have adopted the new international classifications and definitions relatively quickly while others have largely ignored them. In other instances, countries have developed amended versions of the international schemes to suit their own particular needs. For the development of pan-European statistics, the result is a mixed bag of some successes and some failures and examples of these will be shown in the sections to follow.

A detailed description is given of the work of **Eurostat**, the EC's statistical office, with briefer descriptions of other international bodies such as the UN, OECD, IMF. This is followed by a description of the key pan-European and international sources.

ORGANISATIONS

European Communities statistical office (EUROSTAT)

INTRODUCTION

Eurostat is the multilingual short formula used to describe the Statistical Office of the European Communities (EC). It is a Directorate General of the Commission and the Commission itself is the main customer for **Eurostat** data. The office is responsible for collecting and publishing statistics on the EC and its constituent countries, developing European definitions, concepts and classifications and harmonising data collection methods and procedures across the EC.

A Statistics Division of the European Communities was established in 1958 and, in 1959, it had 58 staff and a budget of 64 million Belgian francs. By 1989, **Eurostat** had 376 staff in its Luxembourg office, a small staff team in Brussels and a budget of ECU 38 million (£25.6 million). In addition, there are approximately 140 statisticians and other specialists employed on short-term contracts. The office is divided into five directorates, A to E, with directorate D responsible for business statistics. Directorate A deals with dissemination and computer processing, B covers economic statistics and national accounts, C is responsible for international trade statistics and E deals with social statistics.

Eurostat
Commission of the European Communities
Batiment Jean Monnet
381907 Luxembourg

Eurostat has grown as the European Community has grown but the above staffing levels still represent only 1 per cent of the total number of statisticians employed in all the national statistical offices of the 12 EC member states. Given its relatively small size, **Eurostat** does not undertake many of its own statistical surveys and most of its published output is based on data supplied by national statistical offices.

Some statistics are supplied to **Eurostat** by national statistical offices on a voluntary basis while, in other cases, the supply of statistics is governed by directives and other forms of EC legislation. The nature and type of statistics to be collected are based on statistical programmes developed by **Eurostat** every few years. The latest programme covers the period 1989–92 and is, for the first time, a legal commitment. The programme is approved by the Commission, adopted by the EC Council and European Parliament and it will be updated each year before a committee chaired by the Director General of **Eurostat** and consisting of representatives of the statistical offices of each member state.

Eurostat publications

Statistical publications are produced monthly, quarterly, annually and occasionally and **Eurostat** also has a number of on-line, disc and magnetic tape services. Many publications are available in the nine key languages of the EC – English, French, German, Italian, Spanish, Danish, Dutch, Portugese and Greek – while some are only published in English, French and, sometimes, German.

Publications can be obtained from the Office for Official Publications of the European Communities in Luxembourg or through sales offices in individual member countries. Sales offices in the United Kingdom are **HMSO Books** and **Alan Armstrong** and a list of all the offices in Europe, North America and Japan is given at the back of the **Eurostat Catalogue** published annually. Up to 1990, **Eurostat News**, published quarterly, had details of the range of EC publications along with articles and news items on statistical developments. After a gap of 12 months, **Eurostat News** was replaced by a new publication, **SIGMA – the bulletin of European Statistics**, with the first issue published in October 1991. This first issue has general articles on statistical developments but few references to specific publications.

The published statistics are classified by nine statistical themes, each with its own number and colour code, and the publications in each theme have the number and colour on their covers for easy identification:

Theme 1 General statistics (dark blue)
Theme 2 Economy & finance (purple)
Theme 3 Population & social conditions (yellow)
Theme 4 Energy & industry (light blue)
Theme 5 Agriculture, forestry & fishing (green)

Theme 6	Foreign trade (red)
Theme 7	Services & transport (orange)
Theme 8	Environment (turquoise)
Theme 9	Miscellaneous (brown)

Brief details of the main publications in themes 1–3 are given in the relevant subject sections below and this is followed, under the individual sector headings, by a more detailed look at the organisation and dissemination of statistics in themes 4, 6 and 7. Details of the prices and languages of specific publications are given in the annual **Eurostat Catalogue**.

Eurostat also offers six statistical databanks known as **Cronos**, **Comext**, **Sabine**, **Regio**, **FSSRS** and **IOT**. FSSRS and IOT are specialist databanks, the former contains the results of a survey of agricultural holdings and **IOT** is a databank of input-output tables. The remaining four are general industrial, trade and economic databases and they are described in more detail below.

Cronos contains 1.5 million time series, or over 100,000 indicators per country, dating back to the 1950s with various series updated annually, half-yearly, quarterly or monthly. The indicators cover the 12 member states and the EC in total and the data is shown in a world context, compared with the data for the main developed countries, i.e. the United States and Japan, and the Community's main trading partners. Information can be supplied on-line via host systems **WEFA**, **GSI-ECO** and **Datacentralen/DC Host Centre** (*see* organisation index for further details) or in magnetic tape or disc form. Details of magnetic tape services are available from **Eurostat** while disc products are distributed by a specialist host, **DSI** (*see* organisation index). The databank is divided into 23 separate subject domains, each with its own identifying code, and brief details of each of these are given below:

General statistics

ICG	Short-term economic data
ZPVD	Developing countries data

National accounts

SEC1	National accounts aggregates
SEC2	National accounts, goods & services
AMP1	National accounts, institutional sectors
FINA	Financial accounts
ZBP1	Balance of payments, geographical data
GBOP	Balance of payments, global data
BIF1	Banking & financial statistics

Industrial statistics

INDE	Annual industrial survey
BISE	Sector statistics
SIDR	Iron & steel industry
ZEN1	Energy

Agricultural statistics

ZPA1	Agricultural products
PRAG	Agricultural prices & price indices
COSA	Agricultural accounts
FISH	Fisheries statistics
RICA	Farm accountancy data network

External trade

FRIC	External trade – products & trading partners
ZCA1	ACP external trade

Social statistics

SIPS	Integrated social security system
SOCI	Social statistics

Miscellaneous

ZRD1	Research & development

Comext is a databank of the Community's external trade and intra-Community trade. It has data for individual product headings and individual EC countries plus statistics from the United States, Canada and Japan. Quarterly statistics cover the last three years with monthly data for the last 18 months. Available on-line from **WEFA** and also in magnetic tape and disc format. **Eurostat** has also recently introduced a CD-Rom of detailed external trade statistics updated on a regular basis.

The **Sabine** system of databanks houses all the relevant classifications used for statistical purposes such as **NACE**, **NIMEXE**, **HS** and **CN**. Available on magnetic tape or disc.

Regio is a databank of EC regional economic and social data. Data covers the size of regions, population, accounts of various sectors of the economy, unemployment, employment market and industrial structures. Data is either updated monthly or annually. Available on-line via **WEFA** and in magnetic tape and disc format.

Benelux

Benelux is an economic union involving Belgium, the Netherlands and Luxembourg. It publishes some statistics for the individual countries and others covering **Benelux** as a whole. A regular statistical compilation published twice a year is **Statistiques**.

> **Benelux**
> Rue de la Regence 39
> B-1000
> Brussels
> Belgium

European Free Trade Association (EFTA)

EFTA, based in Geneva, only publishes a few statistical titles and the major one is an annual review of **EFTA** trade.

> **European Free Trade Association**
> **EFTA**
> 9–11 rue de Varembe
> CH-1211 Geneva 20
> Switzerland

Nordic statistical secretariat

The Secretariat was created in 1969 and provides data on Denmark, Finland, Norway, Sweden and Iceland on behalf of the Nordic Council of Ministers. The aim is to facilitate comparisons between the statistical output of the member countries and develop co-operation in statistical activities between countries. Publications are prepared with the help of the central statistical offices and other bodies in each country. The major publication is the **Yearbook of Nordic Statistics** although there are other titles on specialist areas and a series of specialist statistical committees.

> **Nordic Statistical Secretariat**
> PO Box 2550
> DK-2100 Copenhagen
> Denmark

Organisation for Economic Co-operation and Development (OECD)

Regular **OECD** statistics are published on the main western developed economies. Most of the statistics come from the Economics and Statistics Department based in the OECD's offices in Paris. Many statistics are collected from national statistical offices but some statistical and forecasting activities are carried out by the OECD in Paris.

Economics and Statistics Department
OECD
2 rue Andre-Pascal
F-75775 Paris Cedex 16
France

United Nations (UN)

United Nations membership covers most of the countries of the world and the **UN** publishes a range of statistics on these countries. A statistical office is based in the UN's headquarters in New York and there is also a European statistical office in Geneva.

UN Statistical Office
Room DC2-853
United Nations
New York
NY 10017
USA

The **UN** has developed an international classification of economic activities, **ISIC**, and a classification of international trade known as **SITC** and both of these are described in later sections.

GENERAL STATISTICAL TITLES

Compilations

Three annuals from **Eurostat** provide general data on the 12 member states. **Eurostat Review** gives data, for each of the main statistical themes, for the last 10 years. Comparative information is also provided for the United States and Japan. **Basic Statistics of the Community** is a pocket-book with summary data on the EC and its countries plus the United States, Japan and ACP countries.

The Community's involvement in regional policy and regional financial assistance is reflected in the third publication, **Regions Statistical Yearbook** with data on the economic and social life of the EC's standard regions.

All the above are traditional statistical publications with pages of standard statistical tables. A break from this usual presentation of statistics comes in **Europe in Figures**, with diagrams, tables and illustrations in full colour together with a brief commentary.

The UN publishes the **Monthly Bulletin of Statistics** with statistics from over 200 countries, including all the European countries. As well as general economic and social data, there are regular monthly figures on major industries and special quarterly and annual statistical features. The UN's **Statistical Yearbook** is another compilation of international data although the figures are a few years out-of-date by the time the publication appears. The 1987 volume, for example, was published in 1990.

The **Yearbook of Nordic Statistics** is published in English by the Nordic Statistical Secretariat and is a compilation of statistics on the Nordic countries. **Statistiques** is a twice-yearly compilation covering the Benelux countries.

A number of private publishers have general compilations of European statistics and these include the annuals **European Marketing Data and Statistics** published by **Euromonitor** and **European Market and Media Fact** from **Zenith Market and Media Fact**. A new report is the **Eurodata Report** published for the first time in 1991. The report from the **Reader's Digest** is based on a comprehensive sample survey of demographic trends and consumer purchases, habits, attitudes and ownership levels in specific European countries.

Economic data

Monthly economic data on EC countries, plus the United States and Japan, is included in **Eurostatistics: data for short-term economic analysis. Euro-statistics** is published by **Eurostat** in three languages – English, French and German and is divided into four sections: the 'in brief' section analyses recent trends; graphs illustrate the main series in the EC, its countries, the United States and Japan; Community tables give data for all member states harmonised by **Eurostat** on the basis of common criteria; country tables provide a selection of the main economic indicators.

The **EC**'s Directorate General for Economic and Financial Affairs also publishes the monthly **European Economy** in two parts. **Supplement A** has commentary and statistics on recent economic trends while **Supplement B** includes summary results from the regular business trend surveys and consumer opinion surveys carried out in EC member states. These surveys are described in detail in the section headed 'Trend Surveys and Opinion Surveys'. on page 20.

The monthly **Main Economic Indicators** from **OECD** has regular economic data, in tables and graphs, on 19 European countries and aggregate figures in most tables for the EC and OECD-Europe. The quarterly **OECD Economic Outlook** has trends and projections for the major European economies and **OECD Economic Surveys** provide annual surveys of economic developments in individual member countries. **Economic Survey of Europe** is an annual from the **UN**'s office in Geneva with analysis and statistics on economic trends. A quarterly **Economic Bulletin for Europe** is also published.

Most of the economic time series are available on magnetic tape and disc systems from the individual international organisations and many of the series have been incorporated into economic databases offered by the major hosts such as **DRI**, **WEFA** and **IP Sharp**.

Demographic and social statistics

The **Eurostat** yearbook, **Demographic Statistics**, includes data for each member country and for the total Community. Chapters cover population structure, movements, fertility, marriages, deaths, foreign residents and population projections. From the 1990 issue onwards, two new chapters have been added on 'The Community and its Regions' and 'The European Community in the World'. An EC Council Regulation requires member states to carry out regular sample surveys of the labour force and comparative results are published in EC **Labour Force Sample Surveys**.

Family Budgets: comparative tables are a series of reports giving standardised results, derived from national surveys on family budgets within the EC. The **UN**'s annual **Demographic Yearbook** has data on 216 countries, including all the European countries, and a particular demographic issue is covered in each annual volume.

Sector data

General industrial statistics

Published international statistics on industrial activity, production and external trade are available from **Eurostat**, **UN** and the **OECD**. They are essentially compilations of data supplied by individual national statistical offices and can be considerably out-of-date where many countries are involved. **Eurostat** publications are based on the **NACE** classification of economic activities while **UN** and **OECD** titles are usually arranged according to the **ISIC** classification. These classifications, along with other attempts at international standardisation, are described here before considering the specific publications.

EC Classifications of Economic Activity and Products

A major objective of **Eurostat**, from its establishment in 1958, has been the development of harmonised European industrial structure statistics and European production statistics for specific products. In addition, the aim is to harmonise the production statistics with external trade statistics covering specific products.

The problem is that each country has developed its own unique industrial classification and product nomenclature (these are described in more detail in the individual country chapters) and other areas such as the sample sizes, levels of detail, frequency of surveys and the units measured also vary from country to country.

In 1970, **Eurostat** introduced a classification of economic activities, known as the **Nomenclature generale des activites economique Communautes europeenes (General Industrial Classification of Economic Activities within the European Communities)** or, as it is more commonly known, **NACE**. The idea of **NACE** was to offer a European-wide classification, of sectors and products, which could be adopted by member countries with the ultimate aim of producing a harmonised and standardised set of industrial statistics across the EC.

NACE covers mining, public utilities, manufacturing, construction and services and comprises a series of 1-digit codes (divisions) for broad sectors, 2-digit codes (classes) covering the main sectors, a 3-digit code for sub-sectors (groups), a 4-digit code for general product areas (sub-groups) and some 5-digit codes for specific items. For example, **NACE** heading 34 covers Electrical engineering and, within this heading, 346 covers domestic-type electric appliances and 3403 covers domestic electric refrigerators. Details of the main classes of **NACE** in the manufacturing, mining, construction and public utilities sectors are given in Table 2.1. Details of the services sector are described in the 'Services – General' section on page 39.

Individual EC countries have been relatively slow to embrace **NACE** although gradually, some countries are starting to amend their individual classification schemes to link them to **NACE**. For example, the latest revision of the UK Standard Industrial Classification (**SIC**) is closely linked to **NACE**. By the end of the 1980s, however, the ideal of a harmonised European statistical system was still some way off particularly at the product level.

In 1987, harmonised EC-wide manufacturing data was available for seven sectors and approximately 450 product headings with harmonization work in progress in four other sectors. Table 2.2 lists these sectors. Even where harmonised statistics exist, they are usually only available for a small number of EC member states while, to be truly comprehensive, the data needs to cover between 7,000 and 10,000 product headings.

Code	Description
11	Extraction & briquetting of solid fuels
12	Coke ovens
13	Extraction of petroleum & natural gas
14	Mineral oil refining
15	Nuclear fuels industry
16	Production/distribution of electricity, gas, steam & hot water
17	Water supply; collection, purification & distribution of water
21	Extraction & preparation of metalliferous ores
22	Production & preliminary processing of metals
23	Extraction of minerals other than metalliferous & energy-producing minerals; peat extraction
24	Manufacture of non-metallic mineral products
25	Chemical industry
26	Man-made fibres industry
31	Manufacture of metal articles
32	Mechanical engineering
33	Manufacture of office machinery & data processing machinery
34	Electrical engineering
35	Manufacture of motor vehicles & parts/accessories
36	Manufacture of other means of transport
37	Instrument engineering
41/42	Food, drink & tobacco industry
43	Textile industry
44	Leather & leather goods industry (excl. footwear & clothing)
45	Footwear & clothing industry
46	Timber & wooden furniture industries
47	Manufacture of paper & paper products; printing & publishing
48	Processing of rubber & plastics
49	Other manufacturing industries
50	Building & civil engineering

Table 2.1   NACE classes and groups (see Appendix 1)

Sectors covered:
Chemical fibres, textiles, clothing   (106 products)
Leather & footwear   (69 products)
Pulp, paper & board   (42 products)
Office & data processing equipment   (17 products)
Household electrical appliances   (18 products)
Mechanical engineering, including industrial robots   (153 products)
Electrical & electronic engineering   (47 products)

Harmonization work in progress:
Medical & surgical equipment
Measuring, checking & precision instruments & apparatus
Optical instruments & photographic equipment
Watches & clocks

Table 2.2   Harmonised EC statistics

With only a small percentage of products covered by harmonised data, **Eurostat** seems to have accepted the failure of this harmonisation attempt and has turned to a completely new product classification known as **PRODCOM** (PRODucts of the European COMmunity). With the Single Market approaching, the idea behind **PRODCOM** is to create a comprehensive list of product headings in as short a period of time as is possible. The **PRODCOM** product list should be in use by 1993 or 1994. The reason why it can be developed relatively quickly is because it is based on the existing classification of overseas trade product data, the HS classification, which is used by most countries and is described in more detail in the section headed 'Classifications of International Trade' on page 19. By linking **PRODCOM** to the existing international trade classification, industrial statistics and international trade statistics should be directly comparable for the first time.

UN Classification of Economic Activity and Products

The latest revision (revision 3) of the **UN**'s economic activity classification, **International Standard Industrial Classification of all Economic Activities** or **ISIC** was approved in February 1989. This revision attempts to reflect the increasing importance of the service industries.

A	Agriculture, hunting, forestry
B	Fishing
C	Mining & quarrying
D	Manufacturing
E	Electricity, gas & water supply
F	Construction
G	Wholesale & retail trade; repair of motor vehicles, motorcycles & personal & household goods
H	Hotels & restaurants
I	Transport, storage & communications
J	Financial intermediation
K	Real estate, renting & business activities
I	Public administration & defence; compulsory social security
M	Education
N	Health & social work
O	Other community, social & personal service activities
P	Private households with employed persons
Q	Extra-territorial organisations & bodies

Table 2.3   ISIC tabulation categories (see Appendix 2)

ISIC covers agriculture, forestry and fishing, mining, manufacturing, public utilities, construction, distribution and services, public services, private households and extra-territorial organisations. The classification comprises 17 broad 'tabulation categories' and 60 'divisions' within these categories. For example, 'D' is the tabulation category for manufacturing and, within this, there are 23 divisions covering specific manufacturing sectors. All the categories of **ISIC** are listed in Table 2.3 and the specific divisions within the manufacturing category are shown in Table 2.4. There is a further breakdown into 3-digit and 4-digit headings for product and service groups and specific products and services.

Division	Description
15	Manufacture of food products & beverages
16	Manufacture of tobacco products
17	Manufacture of textiles
18	Manufacture of wearing apparel; dressing & dyeing of fur
19	Tanning & dressing of leather; manufacture of luggage, handbags, saddlery, footwear
20	Manufacture of wood & wood & cork products, except furniture; manufacture of articles of straw & plaiting materials
21	Manufacture of paper & paper products
22	Publishing, printing & reproduction of recorded media
23	Manufacture of coke, refined petroleum products & nuclear fuel
24	Manufacture of chemicals & chemical products
25	Manufacture of rubber & plastics products
26	Manufacture of other non-metallic mineral products
27	Manufacture of basic metals
28	Manufacture of fabricated metal products, excl. machinery & equipment
29	Manufacture of machinery & equipment not elsewhere classified
30	Manufacture of office, accounting & computing machinery
31	Manufacture of electrical machinery & apparatus not elsewhere specified
32	Manufacture of radio, television & communication equipment & apparatus
33	Manufacture of medical, precision & optical instruments, watches & clocks
34	Manufacture of motor vehicles, trailers & semi-trailers
35	Manufacture of other transport equipment
36	Manufacture of furniture; manufacturing not elsewhere classified
37	Recycling

Table 2.4 ISIC manufacturing category 'D'

ISIC is used in the industrial statistics publications from the **UN** described in the sections below and is also used as the basis for a number of national country classifications. In some instances, countries are still using the old **ISIC** classification and not the latest revision. **ISIC** and **NACE** are not comparable but, since 1974, there has been a programme to improve harmonisation of the activity classifications of the UN and EC.

Classifications of International Trade

A number of internationally recognised trade classification schemes have been developed over the years and the existence of more than one classification can be confusing to users. The newest is known as the **Harmonised System (HS)**. This came into force in 1988 and is now the internationally accepted classification of traded products covering over 5,000 product headings. The classification known as the **Combined Nomenclature (CN)** extends the **HS** to meet European needs and covers approximately 9,500 product headings. An EC regulation makes it compulsory for all member states to use the **CN** and it replaces the old **NIMEXE** classification, covering approximately 7,990 product headings, used in the EC prior to 1987.

Another well established trade classification is the **Standard International Trade Classification (SITC)** of the UN. The latest version of this is **SITC rev.3** covering 1,033 product groups with 720 of these further subdivided into 2,805 headings. The **SITC** headings are basically aggregations of headings used in the **HS** and correlation tables are published by the **UN** and **Eurostat** identifying the links between the two classifications. Trade statistics, using both the **CN** and **SITC** classifications, are published by **Eurostat** while the **UN** and **OECD** publish **SITC**-based trade statistics.

Trend Surveys and Opinion Surveys

In the EC, harmonisation has been more successful in the area of business surveys and industrial trends surveys where business managers are asked a series of questions, usually qualitative in nature, about factors such as production trends, order books, stocks and employment. The questions are kept simple and the respondents are asked to comment on the present situation and their expectations of future trends. These surveys are a relatively recent development in Europe with the first survey being conducted in Germany in 1949. France and Italy soon followed and, from 1962, the growth of business surveys in Europe has largely taken place within the framework of the harmonised programme of the EC.

Currently, the EC is involved in a regular industry survey, an investment survey, a building survey and a retail trade survey. There are also well advanced plans to harmonise a number of national business surveys in the service sector with a quarterly harmonised survey proposed. As well as these sector surveys, there is also a regular survey of consumer opinion.

The same questions are asked in each of these surveys in individual EC countries, usually at the same time, and the EC publishes the results in regular monthly publications which are described in the relevant sections later in the chapter. Brief descriptions of each of the surveys are given below.

Industry and investment surveys

The harmonised industry survey is conducted monthly throughout the EC, except in Denmark where it is quarterly. The surveys are conducted using a nomenclature based on **NACE** and there are results for specific industry sectors. The surveys are carried out on the Commission's behalf at national level and, in some cases, official statistical offices are involved while, in other cases, the work is carried out by industry federations or polling organisations. A list of the relevant bodies in each country is given in Table 2.5 .

Belgium	Banque Nationale de Belgique (BNB)
Denmark	Danmarks Statistik (DS)
France	Institut National de la Statistique et des Etudes Economiques (INSEE)
Germany	Ifo-Institut fur Wirtschaftsforschung
Greece	Institute of Economic & Industrial Research (IEIR)
Ireland	Confederation of Irish Industry (CII) & Economic & Social Research Institute (ESRI)
Italy	Istituto Nazionale per lo Studio della Congiuntura (ISCO)
Luxembourg	Service Central de la Statistique et des Etudes Economiques (Statec)
Netherlands	Centraal Bureau voor de Statistiek (CBS)
Portugal	Instituto Nacional de Estatistica (INE)
Spain	Ministerio de Industria y Energia (MIE)
United Kingdom	Confederation of British Industry (CBI) & Central Statistical Office (CSO)

Table 2.5 EC industry surveys – national organisations responsible for undertaking the survey

Questionnaires are sent by post to a sample in each country which is usually made up of several thousand firms, although the number of companies and the distribution of the firms in the various member countries depends on the relative size and concentration of different industries. Individual replies and the results for each sector are weighted to take account of the structure of the sector.

The survey questionnaire is made up of a monthly section and a quarterly section and the questions usually require an answer of 'up', 'down' or 'unchanged' or 'above normal', 'below normal' or 'normal'. The monthly section is designed to establish the production trend and the factors determining that trend and the six questions asked are:

1. Production trend observed in recent months
2. Assessment of order-book levels
3. Assessment of export order-book levels
4. Assessment of stocks of finished products
5. Production expectations for the months ahead
6. Selling price expectations for the months ahead

The quarterly questions are designed to pinpoint the elements determining the production trend and to assess the situation of the factors of production. The eight questions are:

7   Employment expectations for the months ahead
8   Limits to production
9   Assessment of current production capacity
10 Duration of production assured by current order books
11 New orders in recent months
12 Export expectations for the months ahead
13 Current level of capacity utilisation
14 Assessment of stocks of raw materials

The investment survey is carried out every six months in March/April and October/November. Questionnaires are generally sent to the firms in the monthly survey although this survey also includes the extractive industries and, in some countries, public enterprises. The number of firms surveyed in some sectors is also increased to obtain a more accurate picture of the movement of investment. The investment survey asks quantitative questions on the change in the firm's investment expenditure and it also includes questions covering the purpose of the investment.

Building Survey
Harmonised building surveys were started in the late 1960s and, currently, a postal questionnaire is sent to approximately 12,000 firms in the Community and it is a monthly survey in most countries. Quarterly surveys are carried out in Denmark, Greece, France, Ireland and the United Kingdom but there are plans to switch to a monthly survey in these countries as well. In most countries, the organisations carrying out the survey are those identified in Table 2.5 but, in four countries, different organisations specifically concerned with building and construction are responsible:

Ireland	Construction Industry Federation (CIF)
Netherlands	Economisch Instituut voor de Bouwnijverheid (EIB)
Portugal	Associacao de Empresas de Construcao e Obras Publicas do sul (Aecops)
United Kingdom	Building Employers Confederation (BEC)

Retail Trade Survey
The survey began in January 1984 in just four countries – Belgium, France, Germany and the United Kingdom. Participation has been gradually extended and the survey now includes Italy (from 1985), Netherlands (from 1986), Spain (from 1988) and Portugal (from 1989). The survey is undertaken every month except in France and Italy where it takes place every two months. France and Italy have agreed to move to a monthly survey in the near future. Replies are usually received from approximately 7,350 firms across the EC countries covered. Most countries carry out a postal survey although telephone surveys are conducted in the Netherlands and Spain and the published results cover six

main retail sectors. The organisations involved in the survey in the specific countries are listed in Table 2.6

Belgium	Banque Nationale de Belgique (BNB)
Germany	Ifo-Institut fur Wirtschaftsforschung
France	Institut National de la Statistique et des Etudes Economiques (INSEE)
Italy	Istituto Nazionale per lo Studio della Congiuntura (ISCO)
Netherlands	Nederlands Instituut voor de Publieke Opinie en het marktonderzoek (NIPO)
Portugal	Instituto Nacional de Estatistica (INE)
Spain	Intergallup SA
United Kingdom	Confederation of British Industry (CBI)

Table 2.6 EC retail trade survey – National organisations responsible for carrying out the survey

The questionnaire has four simple monthly questions on the present business conditions, present stock, orders with suppliers over the next three months, business trends over the next six months and a quarterly question on employment trends over the next three months.

Consumer Survey

The first harmonised consumer survey took place in May 1972 with five countries taking part – Belgium, France, Germany, Italy and the Netherlands. Denmark, Ireland and the United Kingdom have participated from 1974, Greece since 1982 and Spain and Portugal from 1986. Originally, the survey was carried out three times a year but, since July 1986, the EC has obtained monthly results. In each country, a sample of approximately 2,000 households is contacted, with the exception of Ireland where 1,250 households make up the sample.

PUBLICATIONS PRODUCED BY EUROPEAN ORGANISTIONS

General industry and trade

Structure and Activity of Industry, Annual Inquiry (EC)

Following an EC Council Directive of 6 June 1972, a co-ordinated annual inquiry on the structure and activity of industry, based on the **NACE** classification, is carried out by the member states of the EC. The basic sampling unit for the inquiry is the enterprise and the general cut-off point is organisations employing 20 or more people. Below the basic unit of the enterprise is a smaller descriptive unit known as the 'kind of activity unit' or KAU and this comprises all those parts of an enterprise carrying out the same activity. The problem is that the KAU is a term used only in certain countries: the United Kingdom, Italy, Spain, Portugal and Greece do not use the KAU in their statistical surveys and Germany uses a different version of the KAU to other EC countries.

The cut-off point of 20 employees produces varying results from country to country and from industry to industry. In the handicrafts, food and construction sectors, for example, companies employing less than 20 people are major employers while, in Southern European countries, smaller enterprises are more common and are an important part of the economy. A more comprehensive survey, including organisations with fewer than 20 employees, is carried out every five years.

The basic results of the inquiry are published in the **Structure and Activity of Industry Annual Inquiry – Main Results** which contains the main results, at **NACE** 3-digit level, from the last two year's inquiries. Statistics are included on the number of enterprises, size, employees, labour costs, production value and gross value added. A separate section has statistics by KAU.

Unfortunately, the EC directive does not stipulate a deadline date for the submission of the data so there is an inevitable time delay in collecting and publishing the statistics from all the member countries. The latest data in the annual published in 1990, for example, only covers 1986 and 1987. Data from Spain and Portugal is not yet fully co-ordinated into the EC system so there are gaps and divergences in the data for these two areas while data for Greece lags behind the other countries. In the above volume, for example, Greek statistics are only available up to 1984 and 1985.

Every two years, the **Structure and Activity of Industry – Data by Size of Enterprise** is published. The 1990 edition has statistics for 1985 to 1987. A volume presenting the data by region is also published.

Industry Statistical Yearbook (EC)
The yearbook brings together statistics on the industrial structure of the Community, its member states, the United States and Japan. The data is collected from various sources with full references to more detailed sources of data.

Industrial Production Quarterly Statistics (EC)
Statistics of the production of selected products in the EC as a whole and in the member countries of the EC. The publication is split into two sections with one section (Part A) covering products where harmonised data is available (*see* Table 2.2) and a second section (Part B) covering a selection of products where harmonised data is not available. Although the publication is quarterly, there are only a few instances where the data is actually updated quarterly. Even in the

harmonised tables, there are many gaps and omissions with few countries providing quarterly data up to the latest quarter available. More typically, the data is available annually, as the extract in Table 2.7 shows. The extract is taken from the fourth quarter 1990 issue but data for most countries is only available up to 1987 and 1988.

Industrial Trends Monthly Statistics (EC)

Monthly indices, in graphs and tables, of industrial activity in the EC. The first section gives indices for production, turnover, new orders, employees, wages and salaries. Statistics are available for each **NACE** class and for industry as a whole. A second section gives indices for the building and civil engineering sector and a final section has producer price indices for manufacturing. Occasionally produced statistics are sometimes included as an annex or another section. The data is taken from the **CRONOS** databank between the 20th and 25th of each month and the bulletin appears at the beginning of the following month.

Results of the Business Survey Carried Out Among Managements in the Community (EC)

The results of the harmonised business survey, described earlier, are published in detail in this monthly publication with data for industry in total and by major industrial sectors. The industry sectors are based on the **NACE** classification but given a number code from 1 to 20. Domestic electrical appliances, for example, are included in Section 15 and the contents page refers readers to the relevant **NACE** classification code, i.e. 346.

Summary results from the business surveys are published in the monthly **European Economy: Supplement B**.

Panorama of EC Industry (EC)

In an attempt to widen its coverage of manufacturing and service sectors and to move away from the traditional statistical publications noted above, **Eurostat** began publishing the **Panorama of EC Industry** in 1989. The volume combines statistical data with expert commentaries on specific sectors. Many of the statistics are taken from the annual inquiries in each country but this data is supplemented with information from industry bodies, trade associations and some private companies.

Individual chapters cover specific **NACE** sectors with a total of 180 sectors included. Each chapter has basic historical data for the main indicators, more up-to-date statistics on key areas and a detailed commentary on trends and the outlook for the sector. Where data from trade associations or private companies is used, a full reference to the original source is included. For a general review of EC industry and services, the book is useful although the range of sources used means that the reliability and currency of the data varies from chapter to chapter.

HAUSHALTSGEFRIER- UND- TIEFKUEHLMOEBEL
DOMESTIC DEEP-FREEZERS
CONGELATEURS MENAGERS
3407* — 1000 ECU

	1984	1985	1986	1987	1988	1989	II	III	IV	1990 I	II
EUR											
B											
DK	138402	153306	142682	132156			29302	38588			
D	182111	193962	212205	202097	215506	211954	55576	58212	43934	54229	58719
GR											
E			32921056	28303472							
F											
IRL											
I		215625	273943	268619	33412		8691	9517			
NL											
P											
UK	27922	28689	26575	27813							

HAUSHALTSGEFRIER- UND -TIEFKUEHLMOEBEL
DOMESTIC DEEP-FREEZERS
CONGELATEURS MENAGERS
3407* — STUECK / PIECES / PIECES

	1984	1985	1986	1987	1988	1989	II	III	IV	1990 I	II
EUR											
B											
DK	763756	771342	731199	665558			144022	192477	164968	198016	206276
D	787550	844764	861780	786792	837302	791248	208916	219348			
GR			219000	210000							
E											
F											
IRL											
I	1550000	1201041	1498744	1433283							
NL											
P											
UK	159000	153000	154000	179000	191000		49000	54000			

ELEKT. HAUSHALTSWASCHMASCHINEN U. TROCKNER
DOMESTIC ELEC. WASHING MACHINES AND DRYERS
MACH. ELEC. A LAVER ET SECHER LE LINGE
3409 — 1000 ECU

	1984	1985	1986	1987	1988	1989	II	III	IV	1990 I	II
EUR											
B	11545	9557	7359	7870	7433	5642					
DK											
D	881252	981545	1123376	1273226	1415001	1527108	417837	407969	293823	407632	442219

GR	:	:	:	:	:	:	:	:	:	:	:
E	226672	228610	238014	263146	:	:	:	:	:	:	:
F	:	:	:	:	:	:	:	:	:	:	:
IRL	:	:	:	:	:	:	:	:	:	:	:
I	:	:	:	:	:	:	:	:	:	:	:
NL	:	:	:	:	:	:	:	:	:	:	:
P	:	6800	6157	7757	:	:	:	:	:	:	:
UK	:	:	:	:	:	:	:	:	:	:	:

3409

ELEKT. HAUSHALTSWASCHMASCHINEN U. TROCKNER — DOMESTIC ELEC. WASHING MACHINES AND DRYERS — MACH. ELEC. A LAVER ET SECHER LE LINGE

STUECK — PIECES — PIECES

EUR	:	:	:	:	:	:	:	:	:	:	:
B	157238	123975	113142	109276	108424	87467	:	:	:	:	:
DK	:	:	:	:	:	:	:	:	:	:	:
D	2511268	2810204	3050247	3276409	3604600	3818289	1070871	1016161	725680	1005577	1047194
GR	:	:	:	:	:	:	:	:	:	:	:
E	1102000	1085000	1220000	1407000	:	:	:	:	:	:	:
F	:	:	:	:	:	:	:	:	:	:	:
IRL	:	:	:	:	:	:	:	:	:	:	:
I	3275000	3058021	3991200	4140481	:	:	:	:	:	:	:
NL	:	:	:	:	:	:	:	:	:	:	:
P	:	32165	27291	30528	:	:	:	:	:	:	:
UK	1350000	1433000	1317000	1343000	1351000	:	303000	286000	:	:	:

3411*

ELEKT. WASCHMASCH. TROCKEN. FASSUNG. <6KG — DOMESTIC WASHING MACH. DRY-LINEN CAP. <6KG — MACH. A LAVER ELEC. DE CAPACITE <6KG

1000 ECU

EUR	:	:	:	:	:	:	:	:	:	:	:
B	:	:	:	:	:	:	:	:	:	:	:
DK	:	:	:	:	:	:	:	:	:	:	:
D	714609	753917	864630	965207	1011311	1116551	294279	294198	212220	316272	344272
GR	:	:	:	:	:	:	:	:	:	:	:
E	226427	228354	226730	221479	:	:	:	:	:	:	:
F	288068	297305	271692	293691	312091	:	113700	98537	:	:	:
IRL	:	:	:	:	:	:	:	:	:	:	:
I	:	654324	861836	913517	:	:	:	:	:	:	:
NL	:	:	:	:	:	:	:	:	:	:	:
P	:	:	:	:	:	:	:	:	:	:	:
UK	355573	390577	372369	367955	414643	:	96847	90341	:	:	:

Table 2.7 Harmonised EC production statistics – selected entries for refrigerators and washing machines

Industrial Statistics Yearbook (UN)

Published annually in two volumes. Volume 1 is subtitled General Industrial Statistics with individual country sections. Where available, information is given, by sector, on the number of establishments, persons employed, wages and salaries, supplements to wages and salaries, operatives, hours or days worked by operatives, output, value added, gross fixed capital formation and the value of stocks. Indices of industrial production are also included, where available. Additional data, such as the costs of goods and services consumed and the costs of materials and fuels is available on a magnetic tape version available from the UN. Volume 2 is subtitled **Commodity Production Statistics** and has production figures for 556 industrial commodities broken down by country.

Inevitably, it takes time to collect the data from individual national statistical offices with the 1988 Yearbook published in 1991. This delay means that although a revised **ISIC** classification was adopted in 1989, this publication still uses the old **ISIC** classification.

Industrial Structure Statistics (OECD)

The 7th edition of this annual publication was published in 1991 with the title **Industrial Structure Statistics 1988**. Included are statistics on value added, production, establishments, investment, employment, wages and salaries, supplements to wages and salaries and imports and exports for specific industrial sectors in individual OECD countries. The sector breakdowns are by the 2-digit and 3-digit levels of the **ISIC**, and in some cases, by the 4-digit level.

Indicators of Industrial Activity (OECD)

A quarterly publication with monthly and quarterly indices of output, deliveries, prices and employment in mining, manufacturing and utilities and quarterly data from surveys of business conditions.

External Trade – Statistical Yearbook (EC)

General details of community trade, in total and by country, and details of EC and world trade with some commodity data based on the **SITC** classification of trade. An introductory section has comments on Community trade in recent years, together with charts illustrating trends and structures.

External Trade – Monthly Statistics (EC)

Short-term trends in the external trade of the Community and the member states, based on the **SITC** sections, plus data on the Community's share of the trade of the major non-Community countries.

External Trade – Analytical Tables (EC)

The analytical tables are published annually and provide detailed published data, at product level, of Community trade and the trade of individual countries. Product data is based on the lowest level of the **CN**, with figures given in value and volume, and the published data consists of two series of twelve volumes (one series for imports and one series for exports) giving the latest annual import and export figures for specific products. Extracts from typical pages showing imports, by quantity and value in ECUs, are included as Tables 2.8 and 2.9. In addition, there are two volumes arranged by countries showing imports and exports.

Detailed external trade statistics, by product and country are now also available on a regularly updated CD-Rom from **Eurostat**:

CN – Products – Countries (EC)
CN – Countries – Products (EC)
SITC – Countries – Products (EC)
SITC – Products – Countries (EC)

These four sets of quarterly microfiche update the annual product import and export data.

Monthly Statistics of Foreign Trade, Series A (OECD)

General trends in the external trade of the main countries and country groupings in the OECD area.

Foreign Trade by Commodities, Series C (OECD)

An annual publication with tables of trade between OECD countries and partner countries for commodity groups at the 1- and 2-digit levels of the **SITC**.

Series B: Trade by Country (OECD)

Series C: Trade by Commodities (OECD)

Two sets of microfiche files with detailed annual trade figures by country and commodity respectively. In **Series C**, figures are given down to the 5-digit level of the **SITC** and there are separate fiches for imports and exports. Separate subscriptions can be taken out to these.

Commodity Trade Statistics (UN)

A series of reports (approximately 25–30 per year) published throughout the year, as data becomes available, with statistics on the commodities imported and exported by the major trading countries. The commodities are classified by the **SITC**. This series is also available on microfiche.

Value – Valeurs: 1000 ECU

Reporting country – Pays déclarant

Origin / Consignsent
Origins / Provenance
Comb. Nomenclature
Nomenclature comb.

8418.10-90

Code	Nomenclature	EUR-12	Belg.-Lux	Danmark	Deutschland	Hellas	Espagne	France	Ireland	Italia	Nederland	Portugal	U.K.
008	DANEMARK	19616	282		79	524	7224	3114	415	3682	716	7	3573
009	GRECE	1299			113		661			511	14		
011	ESPAGNE	8934	83		799	1030		2928	54		463	3549	28
030	SUEDE	24981	72	2865	3300		4626	5512		2108	1228	88	5182
032	FINLANDE	893		734							89		68
038	AUTRICHE	1254			699	30	14	2	10	57	442	16	505
048	YOUGOSLAVIE	17937	17	373	1562	55	2728	11332	67	1178	104	1	2327
056	U.R.S.S.	5459	2676		389			11	21		34		252
064	HONGRIE	4156	163		303			3383	31				252
400	ETATS–UNIS	18195	364	219	2222	3726	24	4479		3283	766	755	1553
624	ISRAEL	553				323	827	211	51				19
1000	M O N D E	445534	12192	9042	33757	15876	84632	147599	7716	21045	37029	11111	65535
1010	INTRA–CE	370057	8873	4846	25179	11523	76370	122222	7586	14126	34066	9886	55388
1011	EXTRA–CE	75474	3319	4195	8577	4353	8261	25377	130	6919	2964	1225	10154
1020	CLASSE 1	64144	469	4192	7855	3836	8224	21653	79	6904	2750	860	7322
1021	A E L E	27508	88	3600	4056	30	4640	5786	10	2172	1786	88	5252
1030	Classe 2	1216	11		2	360	14	212		1	6	354	252
1040	Classe 3	10114	2839	4	719	157	24	3511	51	14	207	12	2588

8418.21 Réfrigérateurs ménagers, a compression, (non repr. sous 8418.10)

8418.21-10 Réfrigérateurs ménagers, a compression, capacite >340 L, (non repr. sous 8418.10-10 ET 8418.10-90)

Code	Nomenclature	EUR-12	Belg.-Lux	Danmark	Deutschland	Hellas	Espagne	France	Ireland	Italia	Nederland	Portugal	U.K.
004	RF ALLEMAGNE	3760	237	116		122	2366	234		118	203	113	251
005	ITALIE	1210	97	7		2245	6425	600			291	238	734
006	ROYAUME-UNI	874	44		796	262		1	18	8		2	
008	DANEMARK	2539	293		1399		269	237	23				79
009	GRECE	649	104	19	19	1029	3	1					283
011	ESPAGNE	1487								54	134	131	
038	AUTRICHE	628	2		14					56		402	
048	YOUGOSLAVIE	931	28		742	16	136			1	220	6	385
400	ETATS–UNIS	16954	707	1	1027	697	9661	3712		517	335	16	281
1000	MONDE	43601	1617	199	5560	5256	19651	4992	41	1242	1486	1129	2428
1010	INTRA–CE	23011	857	123	3767	3783	9565	1104	41	270	856	1007	1638
1011	EXTRA-CE	20591	759	76	1793	1473	10087	3888		972	630	123	790
1020	CLASSE 1	19870	759	76	1793	791	10085	3863		972	630	111	790
1021	AELE	1204	24	75	23	1	136	23		52	295	95	480

8418.21–51 REFRIGERATEURS MENAGERS, A COMPRESSION, CAPACITE = <340 L, MODELE TABLE, (NON REPR. SOUS 8418.10–10 ET 8418.10–90)

Code		1	2	3	4	5	6	7	8	9	10	11
002	BELG.-LUXBG.	688			45		22	196	36	249	10	140
003	PAYS-BAS	851	262				2					135
004	RF ALLEMAGNE	16064	5182	450	9394		3	720	497	8438		756
005	ITALIE	31731	1865	2	400		597	8749		8744	21	2057
011	ESPAGNE	531						17	126	100		110
048	YOUGOSLAVIE	5206			306			2948	149	560		
056	U.R.S.S.	11207	1484		1256			5622	294	1365		9
058	RD. ALLEMANDE	7885			2442		284	4682	2234	959		
060	POLOGNE	2801	434		749			562		795		10
062	TCHECOSLOVAQ	2408	617					1626				261
064	HONGRIE	8320						2501		1814	165	
066	ROUMANIE	5669	316	431	3467	104	3	2391	2660	237		64
1000	MONDE	95302	10417	896	17822	829	891	30245	6168	24061	34	3648
1010	INTRA-CE	50680	7437	452	9876	385	601	9825	734	17777	32	3270
1011	EXTRA-CE	44620	2980	444	7946	445	289	20420	5434	6284	1	377
1020	CLASSE 1	5749	1	12	1270	2	284	2949	245	949	1	37
1030	CLASSE 2	551	102		17	339	2	87				4
1040	CLASSE 3	38317	2876	431	6658	104	3	17385	5188	5335	1	336

8418.21–59 REFRIGERATEURS MENAGERS, A COMPRESSION, CAPACITE = <340 L, A ENCASTRER, (NON REPR. SOUS 8418.10-10 ET 8418.10–90)

Code		1	2	3	4	5	6	7	8	9	10	11
001	FRANCE	1271	244	4	750			5	29	24		220
003	PAYS-BAS	3115	1597		728				72			713
004	RF ALLEMAGNE	71227	7821	1246	12929		107	24143	2986	18325	524	13793
005	ITALIE	36064	1034	15	128	2017	60	10563		1884	649	8846
035	SUISSE	790	16			123	1	610		22		3
048	YOUGOSLAVIE	880			185	35			10	51		1
400	ETATS-UNIS	689	1		93	334	16		44	144		1
732	JAPON	1515			1466			49	1			1
1000	MONDE	116855	10763	1270	16448	2690	204	36243	3162	20934	974	23606
1010	INTRA-CE	112527	10701	1268	14481	2141	186	34941	3105	20670	973	23599
1011	EXTRA-CE	4326	62	2	1967	548	17	1302	57	264	1	7
1020	CLASSE 1	4042	40	2	1967	372	17	1224	57	257	1	6
1021	AELE	954	39	2	223	2		610	11	62	1	3

8418.21–91 REFRIGERATEURS MENAGERS, A COMPRESSION, CAPACITE = <250 L, (NON REPR. SOUS 8418.10-10 A 8418.21–59)

Code		1	2	3	4	5	6	7	8	9	10	11
001	FRANCE	5069			87	65		253	124	31	225	4188
002	BELG.-LUXBG.	3470	330	55	2696	19	5		7	343	7	91
004	RF ALLEMAGNE	23481	2525	761		590		2826	6141	4601	570	456
005	ITALIE	133058	7000	4834	63473	2193	590	15786	6141	6529	1468	29188
006	ROYAUME-UNI	1749	175	83	76	6		297	17	121	31	
008	DANEMARK	1176	61		416	157		87	113	125		162
010	PORTUGAL	5441			52				89	38		3
011	ESPAGNE	3346	7		128	4474		785	129	136	602	56
030	SUEDE	1849	189	988	96	7		1722	282	11	72	186
032	FINLANDE	1663		1617	5					36		3
036	SUISSE	1004	48	2	884	2			44	16	1	3
038	AUTRICHE	1560	675		422	3		18	91	298		4

Table 2.8 EC imports of refrigerators – selected product headings (value figures)

Origin / Consignment
Origins / Provenance
Comb. Nomenclature
Nomenclature comb.

Reporting country – Pays déclarant

Code	Name	EUR-12	Belg.-Lux	Danmark	Deutschland	Hellas	Espagne	France	Ireland	Italia	Nederland	Portugal	U.K.
048	YOUGOSLAVIE	14256	394	527	1743	1407	861	2221	72	3520	517	279	2715
056	U.R.S.S.	7771	347	221	1467	530		1270	479	634	192	1	2630
058	RD. ALLEMANDE	4555	1145	429		75	1547	68	21	214	34		1022
060	POLOGNE	1486	80			664		576	127		23	16	
062	TCHECOSLOVAQ	654			32	405		137	62	3	15		
064	HONGRIE	5804		251	741	63		1745			58	11	2932
066	ROUMANIE	5859	3		505	346	196	1449		265	12	114	2960
208	ALGERIE	673			405	646	6	264				4	
400	ETATS-UNIS	906			56			2		88	49	40	9
728	COREE DU SUD	1095			2	134	1		10				958
732	JAPON	590			112	2	25	54			32		365
1000	MONDE	227820	13181	9774	73487	11635	10093	29584	3402	11820	13293	3497	48054
1010	INTRA– CE	177292	10221	5734	67009	6700	7445	21759	2595	6619	12000	2948	34262
1011	EXTRA– CE	50520	2960	4041	6478	4935	2648	7818	807	5200	1293	548	13792
1020	CLASSE 1	22196	1363	3139	3321	2377	902	2307	118	4026	959	402	3282
1021	AELE	6075	913	2612	1410	27	9	21	36	419	361	84	193
1030	CLASSE 2	1879	9		410	166	3	265		57		4	965
1040	CLASSE 3	26443	1588	901	2748	2392	1743	5245	689	1117	334	142	9544

8418.21-99 REFRIGERATEURS MENAGERS, A COMPRESSION, CAPACITE <250 L MAIS = <340 L, (NON REPR. SOUS 8418.10-10 A 8418.21- 59)

Code	Name	EUR-12	Belg.-Lux	Danmark	Deutschland	Hellas	Espagne	France	Ireland	Italia	Nederland	Portugal	U.K.
001	FRANCE	1373	227		1	47	24			39	24	990	21
004	RF ALLEMAGNE	23864	2300	281		2097	1466	2835	10	8301	5334	1167	73
005	ITALIE	31790	2428	7	2256	2471	8528	10117	304		3896	1462	321
006	ROYAUME–UNI	846	77		11			238	472	170	81	34	
008	DANEMARK	4196	265		383	27	21	317	40	156	228	1	2837
010	PORTUGAL	3313					2885	323	10	101			
011	ESPAGNE	1439	20					1453	68	153			52
030	SUEDE	4350		1079	185		183	1221		480	24	823	763
048	YOUGOSLAVIE	2628	390		252	21	352	2285	67	102	40	183	183
056	U.R.S.S.	4773	175		51				556	864	596		245
060	POLOGNE	788				117			671				
400	ETATS-UNIS	2535	319		19	11	2	2	14	1507	29	17	615
1000	MONDE	85340	6990	1410	3268	4867	13678	19211	2223	12130	11318	4803	5442
1010	INTRA–CE	67820	5450	288	2719	4668	12947	13897	915	9069	9958	4566	3343
1011	EXTRA–CE	17521	1541	1122	549	199	731	5314	1308	3061	1360	237	2099
1020	CLASSE 1	11288	1183	1083	497	38	716	2847	81	2167	591	231	1854
1021	AELE	5223	1183	1083	225	160		1546		557	522	214	893
1040	CLASSE 3	6172	358	39	51			2459	1227	864	769		245

Table 2.8 EC imports of refrigerators – selected product headings (value figures) (cont.)

Quantity – Quantités: 1000 kg

Origin / Consignment
Origine / Provenance
Comb. Nomenclature
Nomenclature comb

Reporting country – Pays déclarant

8418.10–90

Nomenclature comb	EUR-12	Belg-Lux.	Danmark	Deutschland	Hellas	Espagne	France	Ireland	Italia	Nederland	Portugal	U.K.
008 DENMARK	4492	73	.	18	122	1755	804	115	502	194	2	907
009 GREECE	326			29		170			123	4		4
011 SPAIN	2263	28	641	200	243		817	17	520	117	833	8
030 SWEDEN	5847	19	164	789		1066	1313			316	21	1162
032 FINLAND	307									21		11
038 AUSTRIA	6791			177	7	2		4	15	102		242
048 YUGOSLAVIA	3541	6	104	571	25	943	4325	29	494	46	6	1484
056 SOVIET UNION	1565	1797		223			7	8		22		110
064 HUNGARY	3140	54		110		5	1273	13				273
400 USA		57	27	414	764	144	657		568	105	131	
624 ISRAEL	128				80		44					4
1000 WORLD	107770	4101	2111	7120	3424	19010	38837	1851	3538	8847	2574	16357
1010 INTRA-EC	85732	2164	1175	4819	2458	16845	31106	1798	1907	8113	2322	13025
1011 EXTRA-EC	22036	1937	936	2301	965	2165	7730	53	1631	734	252	3332
1020 CLASSE 1	16440	83	936	1962	800	2160	6360	33	1624	637	158	1687
1021 EFTA COUNTR.	6410	20	805	975	7	1068	1355	4	537	444	22	1173
1030 CLASS 2	280	2			91		44			1	90	51
1040 CLASS 3	5318	1851		339	74	5	1327	20	7	96	5	1594

8418.21 COMPRESSION–TYPE REFRIGERATORS, HOUSEHOLD TYPE (EXCL. 8418.10)
8418.21–10 HOUSEHOLD REFRIGERATORS, COMPRESSSION–TYPE, CAPACITY >340 L, (EXCL. 8418.10–10 TO 8418.10–90)

Nomenclature comb	EUR-12	Belg-Lux.	Danmark	Deutschland	Hellas	Espagne	France	Ireland	Italia	Nederland	Portugal	U.K.
004 FR GERMANY	782	61	23	214	25	517	33	11	16	35	25	47
005 ITALY	2527	23	1	155	495	1405	171	21		40	58	109
006 UTD. KINGDOM	186	10		238	56	68	65					18
008 DENMARK	477	32		5		1			13	39	33	50
009 GREECE	167	26			214				18		93	
011 SPAIN	325									56		99
038 AUSTRIA	159			3	6				5			1
048 YUGOSLAVIA	213	11		144	6	47			70	46	2	
400 USA	2994	104		134	139	1843	617					39
1000 WORLD	8872	290	37	911	1347	4156	967	32	191	242	277	422
1010 INTRA-EC	4783	169	23	628	816	2148	272	32	52	129	248	266
1011 EXTRA-EC	4089	122	13	283	531	2008	695		139	114	29	155
1020 CLASS 1	3728	122	13	283	181	2008	688		139	114	25	155
1021 EFTA COUNTR.	275	6	13	4	1	31	7		8	68	23	114

8418.21–51 HOUSEHOLD REFRIGERATORS, COMPRESSION–TYPE, CAPACITY = <340 L, TABLE MODEL, (EXCL. 8418.10–10 TO 8418.10–90)

Nomenclature comb	EUR-12	Belg-Lux.	Danmark	Deutschland	Hellas	Espagne	France	Ireland	Italia	Nederland	Portugal	U.K.
002 BELG-LUXBG.	289			6	3							38
003 NETHERLANDS	302	69		154							7	49
004 FR GERMANY	3235	792	104				156	23	101	1923		155
005 ITALY	8593	448		2483	72	183	2699	4		2172		535

Table 2.9 EC imports of refrigerators – selected product headings (volume figures)

Quantity – Quantités: 1000 kg

Reporting country – Pays déclarant

Origin / Consignment / Origine / Provenance / Comb. Nomenclature / Nomenclature comb		EUR-12	Belg-Lux.	Danmark	Deutschland	Hellas	Espagne	France	Ireland	Italia	Nederland	Portugal	U.K.
011	SPAIN	90						2	11	25	22		25
048	YUGOSLAVIA	2142			519			1245		71	209	5	2
056	SOVIET UNION	9645	1334		1279		96	5615		215	1202		
058	GERMAN DEM.R	4247						2577		1162	504		4
060	POLAND	1375	226		364			278			373		
062	CZECHOSLOVAK	1443	322					1029			92		134
064	HUNGARY	3428						1095			741		
066	ROMANIA	3213	165	181	1372	28	1	1326		1519	169		34
1000	WORLD	38507	3419	286	6193	212	281	16252	60	3156	7646	12	990
1010	INTRA-EC	12732	1346	104	2656	83	184	3044	60	169	4262	12	812
1011	EXTRA-EC	25775	2073	182	3537	129	97	13208		2987	3384		178
1020	CLASS 1	2263		1	522		96	1245		90	304		5
1030	CLASS 2	166	20		1	101		43					1
1040	CLASS 3	23344	2052	181	3014	28	1	11920		2897	3080		171

8418.21-59 HOUSEHOLD REFRIGERATORS, COMPRESSION–TYPE, CAPACITY = <340 L, BUILDING-IN TYPE (EXCL. 8418.10-10 TO 8418.10-90)

		EUR-12	Belg-Lux.	Danmark	Deutschland	Hellas	Espagne	France	Ireland	Italia	Nederland	Portugal	U.K.
001	FRANCE	213	42		124					6	5		36
003	NETHERLANDS	484	233		130			1		17			103
004	FR GERMANY	13581	1483	233	2760	365	9	4907	50	540	3303	91	2600
005	ITALY	7788	240	11	21	22	19	2373	42		414	108	1799
036	SWITZERLAND	139	3		70			110		1	3		
048	YUGOSLAVIA	296			10	12		182		15	17		
400	USA	98							6				
732	JAPAN	171			166	59	1	5			22		1
1000	WORLD	23071	2010	246	3315	509	33	7671	102	586	3857	199	4543
1010	INTRA-EC	22238	2000	245	3038	388	32	7329	96	569	3801	199	4541
1011	EXTRA-EC	833	11		278	121	1	342	6	17	56		1
1020	CLASS 1	729	7		31	1	1	296	6	17	52		1
1021	EFTA COUNTR.	163	7			1		110		1	12		1

8418.21-91 HOUSEHOLD REFRIGERATORS COMPRESSION–TYPE, CAPACITY = <250 L. (EXCL. 8418.21-10 TO 8418.21-59)

		EUR-12	Belg-Lux.	Danmark	Deutschland	Hellas	Espagne	France	Ireland	Italia	Nederland	Portugal	U.K.
001	FRANCE	1203	62	11	17	9	5			59	7	74	970
002	BELG-LUXBG.	422			284	4	3	47		2	60		11
004	FR GERMANY	4916	560	177		951	113	618	20		1039	110	89
005	ITALY	34098	1635	1238	15715	222	715	4286	352	1239	1752	398	7785
006	UTD. KINGDOM	385	41	21		33		31	216	2	28		
008	DENMARK	293	15		102			24	8	28	34		28
010	PORTGUAL	1533			15		54	281		25	11		1
011	SPAIN	859	1		28	109	1200	484		35	40	151	6
030	SWEDEN	395	47	213	13			3	5	73	6	11	29

Code	Partner											
032	FINLAND	320		314	1						4		1
036	SWITZERLAND	162	8								3		
038	AUSTRIA	363	176		145	5	387			20	67	5	
048	YUGOSLAVIA	5804	149	177	86	458		907		1772	207	105	992
056	SOVIET UNION	5644	296	121	622	419	682	911	258	490	147		1972
058	GERMAN DEM. R	2147	579	198	1030	34		38	10	116	20		470
060	POLAND	781	51			359		295	59		11	6	
062	CZECHOSLOVAK	357			18	211		81	38	3	6		
064	HUNGARY	2402	2	94	294	22	87	682			28	4	1276
066	ROMANIA	3250	5		330	207		758		150	9	67	1637
208	ALGERIA	348			196			150				2	
400	USA	144					1		1	6	5	6	1
728	SOUTH KOREA	361			8	32							329
732	JAPAN	54			8	1	3	4			3		35
1000	WORLD	66759	3696	2563	18940	3536	3252	9605	1008	4036	3507	971	15645
1010	INTRA-EC	43848	2352	1447	16187	1338	2092	5772	610	1390	2994	765	8901
1011	EXTRA-EC	22912	1345	1116	2753	2198	1161	3833	398	2645	514	206	6743
1020	CLASS 1	7411	408	704	884	717	391	918	33	1878	294	127	1057
1021	EFTA COUNTR.	1241	231	527	245	5	1	4	4	100	79	16	29
1030	CLASS 2	733	4		197	40		150		9		2	331
1040	CLASS 3	14768	933	412	1672	1441	770	2765	364	759	220	77	5355

8418.21-99 HOUSEHOLD REFRIGERATORS, COMPRESSION-TYPE, CAPACITY >250 L BUT = <340 L. (EXCL. 8418.10-10 TO 8418.21-59)

Code	Partner											
001	FRANCE	457	59	65		10	9		5	9	6	361	3
004	FR GERMANY	5339	567	1	570	375	313	640	82	1851	1252	259	12
005	ITALY	8060	634		3	555	2027	2702	176		1069	359	61
006	UTD. KINGDOM	274	18		99	6	4		6	35	21	20	
008	DENMARK	1114	77					80	3	40	64		
010	PORTUGAL	922					781	115	17	23			738
011	SPAIN	337	6					78		32		200	4
030	SWEDEN	989		233	28		43	418	28	97	10	43	117
048	YUGOSLAVIA	1135	146		76	7	119	645	290	49	14		51
056	SOVIET UNION	3200	132		33			1615	319	515	425		190
060	POLAND	374				55			6				
400	USA	394	54		9					220	5	3	97
1000	WORLD	23701	2008	315	842	1042	3410	6487	938	2922	3145	1276	1316
1010	INTRA-EC	16774	1392	66	693	951	3142	3645	295	2022	2520	1224	824
1011	EXTRA-EC	6929	616	250	149	90	268	2843	643	901	625	52	492
1020	CLASS 1	3039	389	234	116	11	264	1124	34	380	136	50	301
1021	EFTA COUNTR.	1158		16	32		43	437		111	117	47	137
1040	CLASS 3	3873	227		33	79	43	1715	609	515	489		190

Table 2.9 EC imports of refrigerators – selected product headings (volume figures) (cont.)

International Trade Statistics Yearbook (UN)

Published in two volumes each year with Volume 1 subtitled, **Trade by Country** and Volume 2 subtitled, **Trade by Commodities**. Includes 153 countries with product data classified by the **SITC**.

EFTA Trade

An annual review of general trends in trade in the EFTA area.

TRADSTAT Database

For more up-to-date external trade statistics than those available from published sources, the **Tradstat** on-line database is available from **Data-Star**. Each month, product import and export statistics are supplied from 21 countries, including EC and EFTA countries. The data is arranged by the **HS** classification and the statistics can be retrieved in various report formats offering various manipulations, rankings and calculations of the data.

Construction

Annual Bulletin of Housing Statistics for Europe

Published by the **UN**, there are specific country sections including data on industry structure, production, starts, dwelling stock, etc. Tables, where possible, include data for the latest five years.

Construction Statistics in Europe

Published regularly by the **European Construction Industry Federation** with members in 18 European countries.

Food and drink

Both the EC and the UN have a strong interest in the agricultural sector and this is reflected in the number of publications on this sector produced by these two organisations. Some of these publications include extensive statistics on food and drink. Selected titles from the **EC** include the **Agricultural Situation in the EC** and **Agriculture – Statistical Yearbook**, both published annually. There are also titles on specific areas such as the quarterlies, **Animal Production and Crop Production**.

The European office of the **UN** produces an annual **Agricultural Review for Europe** in six volumes. The first two volumes provide general data and the remaining volumes concentrate on the **Grain Market** (Volume III), the **Livestock and Meat Market** (Volume IV), the **Milk and Dairy Products Market** (Volume V) and the **Egg Market** (Volume VI).

Agra Europe Reports

A series of monthly, fortnightly and weekly reports on food markets and specific foods in Europe published by **Agra Europe**. The weekly **Agra Europe** has news items and statistics on the production and markets for specific foods and other publications look at specific food areas such as milk and milk products, potatoes and fish. On-line services are also produced by the company.

EC Dairy Facts and Figures

An annual compilation of statistics on milk and dairy products from the **Milk Marketing Board** in the United Kingdom. Statistics for specific countries are given.

Statistical Bulletin of the IOCCC

Annual statistics from the **International Office of Cocoa, Chocolate and Sugar Confectionery (IOCCC)**. The statistics are compiled from data supplied by national associations of chocolate, sugar confectionery and biscuit manufacturers.

Monograph Statistique

CAOBISCO, the European association for confectionery, biscuits and pastries, publishes annual data on production, consumption, sales and foreign trade trends in the main European countries. The report includes English translation of table headings.

Chemicals and chemical products

Annual Review of the Chemical Industry

Production statistics, by country, for general sectors and specific products published by the **UN**. The 1988 yearbook was published in 1990.

Annual Bulletin of Trade in Chemical Products

Import and export statistics, by country and area, published annually by the **UN**.

Chemfacts

A series of individual reports on specific countries with statistics on the production of and trade in over 100 organic and inorganic chemicals. Historical statistics are included. The reports are published by **Chemical Intelligence Services** and other services available include data on specific chemical companies and standard reports in machine readable format. On-line services are also accessible via **Dialog** and **Datastream**.

General statistics on the European chemical industry are also available from the **European Chemical Industry Federation**.

AIS Statistical Tables

Annual statistics on the European soap and detergent industry from the

Association Internationale de la Savonnerie et de la Detergence (International Association of the Soap and Detergent Industry). An English language version is produced with sections on toilet products, household and industrial soaps, washing products, surface cleaners and scourers. Based largely on data from national trade associations.

Textiles and clothing

Recueil statistique
An annual report from **AEIU**, the **European Association of Clothing Industries**. Clothing production, markets and trade are covered for specific countries based on a combination of original data and **Eurostat** statistics.

Bulletin de Comitextil
The **Coordinating Committee for the Textile Industries in the EC** publishes regular statistics and some appear in the above journal published six times a year.

Some statistics on the wool industry are available from the **Committee of the Wool Textile Industry in the EC**.

Electrical and mechanical engineering

Annual Bulletin of Steel Statistics for Europe
Published by the **UN** with statistics for specific countries. The UN also publishes the annual **Steel Market in Europe** with commentary and statistics.

Iron and Steel Statistical Yearbook
Iron and Steel Monthly Statistics
Two regular publications from **Eurostat** and external trade data for iron and steel products is also available on microfiche.

Annual Review of Engineering Industries and Automation
Published annually in two volumes by the European office of the **UN**. The first volume provides an analysis of trends and the second volume concentrates on the detailed statistics.

CECIMO, the European Committee for Cooperation of the Machine Tool Industries publishes some statistics and the **Association of West European Shipbuilders (AWES)** also has some statistics.

Electronics

Yearbook of World Electronics Data, Volume 1: Western Europe

The yearbook has sections on the main electronic sectors and products notably EDP, office equipment, control and instrumentation, medical and industrial products, communications and military products, telecommunications, consumer products and components. The statistics cover production and market trends in 14 countries, excluding Portugal, Luxembourg and Greece, with actual figures for the latest two years available, estimates for the current year and forecasts for selected years. Based largely on an analysis of official and trade association data, the yearbook is published by **Elsevier Advanced Technology** and there is also a version on disc.

VADEMECUM Part II – Statistics

Annual statistics on the sales and costs structures of electrical wholesalers in 14 European countries. Published by the **European Union of Electrical Wholesalers** and based on returns from 14 national associations.

Regular statistics are also produced on the consumer electronics sector by the **European Association of Consumer Electronics** and on domestic electrical appliances by **CECED**, the European Committee of Manufacturers of Electrical Domestic Appliances.

Services – general

Service sectors are included in the **NACE** classification and the main 2-digit **NACE** classes involved are listed in Table 2.10.

Code	Description
61	Wholesale distribution
62	Dealing in scrap & waste materials
63	Agents
64/65	Retail distribution
66	Hotels and catering
67	Repair of consumer goods & vehicles
71	Railways
72	Other land transport
73	Inland water transport
74	Sea transport & coastal shipping
75	Air transport
76	Supporting services to transport
77	Travel agents, freight brokers & other transport agents
79	Communications
81	Banking & finance
82	Insurance, except for compulsory social insurance
83	Activities auxiliary to banking, finance insurance; real estate transactions

Table 2.10 NACE headings relating to service sectors

Code	Description
84	Renting, leasing & hiring of movables
85	Letting of real estate by the owner
91	Public administration, national defence & compulsory social security
92	Sanitary services & administration of cemeteries
93	Education
94	Research & development
95	Medical & other health services; veterinary services
96	Other services provided to the general public
97	Recreational services & other cultural services
98	Personal services
99	Domestic services
00	Diplomatic representation, international organisations & allied armed forces

Table 2.10   NACE headings relating to service sectors (*cont.*)

There are also 3- and 4-digit breakdowns. For example, within class 64 Retailing, 648/649 covers the retail distribution of household equipment, fittings and appliances, hardware and ironmongery and 648.4 is the retailing of household electrical appliances and large domestic appliances.

Traditionally, the service sectors have been poorly covered by statistical sources and **Eurostat** has recently turned its attention to this problem with the publication of a new report described below.

Some Statistics on Services

A first attempt by **Eurostat** to publish pan-European statistics on the service sector. Published in 1991, and with figures up to 1988, it is intended as an annual publication. The first issue had statistics on the distributive trades, hotels and catering, travel agencies, transport activities, credit institutions, insurance and information, commercial and business services. The statistics are non-harmonised and based on a combination of data from national statistical offices, some **Eurostat** surveys and other specialised sources. Inevitably, there are many gaps in the tables but it is hoped that coverage will improve and be extended in future issues.

Retailing and distribution

The above mentioned publication from the EC, **Some Statistics on Services**, includes a section on retailing and wholesaling. In addition, the opinion survey, **Retail Trade Survey**, co-ordinated by the **EC** and described in the introduction to industrial statistics in this chapter is also a major source. Pan-European associations publishing retailing statistics are the **Liaison Committee of European Retailers** with members in 17 countries and the **European Association of Multiple Retailers**.

Financial services

Selected financial service sectors are included in **Some Statistics on Services** described in the 'Services – General' section on pp. 39–40, and a regular source of general data is **Money and Finance**, published quarterly by **Eurostat**.

Activity Report

Published twice a year in English by the **European Savings Banks Group (ESBG)** and based on data supplied by national associations in specific countries. The group also has a monthly journal.

Annual Report

The **EC Mortgage Federation** publishes an annual report with statistics on mortgage credit and its funding in specific EC countries. There are also sections with general economic data and housing construction and property market data.

EVCA Yearbook

The yearbook, published by the **European Venture Capital Association (EVCA)**, includes a statistical overview of the European venture capital industry with commentary on specific countries.

Leisure and tourism

Some statistics on hotels, catering and travel agents are included in **Some Statistics on Services** described in the 'Services – General' section on pp. 39–40.

Tourism – Annual Statistics

Published by **Eurostat** with data on tourism trends and expenditure.

The **World Tourism Organisation** is also based in Spain and publishes the **Yearbook of Tourism Statistics**.

Transportation

Transport sectors are included in **Some Statistics on Services** described in the 'Services – General' section on pp. 39–40 and other publications include the following.

Transport and Communications Annual Statistics

An **EC** publication with a general section followed by sections on railways, road, inland waterways, shipping, aviation, pipelines, post and tele-communications.

Transport Statistics for Europe

Published annually by the **UN** with statistics on specific countries for various types of transport. The difficulties of collecting comparable data across various countries, means that many tables have gaps and omissions. The 1990 yearbook had statistics for the latest three years, where available, up to 1988.

Statistical Trends in Transport

An annual publication from the **OECD** with data on the main transport sectors.

Carriage of Goods

Annual reports from the **EC** with specific reports on particular types of transport such as road, rail and inland waterways.

AEA Yearbook and Statistical Appendices

Published annually in May, the yearbook of the **Association of European Airlines (AEA)** has separate statistical appendices with data on revenue, traffic capacity and production data for each airline. The tables cover the previous calendar year and the two preceding years. Also published in May is a medium-term forecast of European scheduled passenger traffic.

Important international associations based in Europe also include the **International Road Federation** publisher of the annual **World Road Statistics**, the **Union International des Chemins de Fer** with annual railway statistics and the **International Air Transport Association** with a series of monthly and annual titles including **World Air Transport Statistics** published annually.

Advertising and market research statistics

ESOMAR Industry Survey

Annual statistics on market research turnover, by country, with details of the major market research companies and key markets. Published by the **European Society for Opinion and Marketing Research (ESOMAR)** which also publishes statistics on the price of market research every two years.

European Advertising and Media Forecast

Published quarterly by **NTC Publications Ltd** in the United Kingdom with statistics on advertising expenditure in various European countries. The data is drawn together by the Advertising Association in the United Kingdom on behalf of the **European Advertising Tripartite**. In 1991, the Advertising Association also prepared a special report on European direct marketing statistics on behalf of the **European Direct Marketing Association**. The report's title was **Direct Marketing in Europe: An Examination of the Statistics**.

3 AUSTRIA
Business statistics

INTRODUCTION

Austria has a centralised system of official statistics based around the national statistical office, the **Osterreichisches Statistisches Zentralamt**. It is an autonomous office established by the Federal Statistics Act of 1965. Its staffing and budget are the responsibility of the Federal Chancellory and there is a Central Statistical Commission which acts as a link between the consumers and producers of statistics.

The office is based in Vienna at:

Osterreichisches Statistisches Zentralamt
Hintere Zollamtsstrasse 2B
PO Box 9000
A-1033 Vienna
Austria

Publications can be ordered from the above address and from:

Osterreichischen Staatsdruckerei
Remweg 12A
A-1037 Vienna
Austria

The office is split into eight main divisions. Division 3 is responsible for industry and internal trade statistics while Division 4 covers external trade, transport and tourism statistics.

There is a half-yearly list of publications, **Publikationsangebot**, and general inquiries are dealt with by the **Informationsabteilung** (Central Information Service) at the first address above.

All the main economic sectors are also covered by trade association statistics and the currency and reliability of the data is good.

GENERAL STATISTICAL TITLES

Compilations

Statistisches Handbuch fur die Republik Osterreich is the annual statistical yearbook with summary data from a wide range of official series. It also has an international section and the list of chapters and table headings are given in English.

The monthly **Statistische Nachrichten** has commentary and analysis on recent statistical surveys plus regular tables on key indicators.

Economic data

Osterreichisches Institut fur Wirtschaftsforschung (Austrian Institute for Economic Research) publishes the monthly report, **Monatsberichte**, with articles, commentary and statistics on economic trends.

The **Creditanstalt – Bankverein** has the quarterly, **Facts and Figures on Austria's Economy**, available in English with commentary and a statistical appendix. Another quarterly in English, **Report of the Austrian Economy**, includes articles, statistics and forecasts.

Demographic and social statistics

A population census is carried out approximately every 10 years with the latest in 1991. Census reports are published in the series, **Beitrage zur Osterreichischen Statistik.**

Mikrozensus – Jahresergebnisse is an annual collection of demographic data based on a sample survey of the population and an annual volume of general population statistics is **Demographisches Jahrbuch Osterreichs**.

Sector data

General industrial statistics

The Central Statistical Office carries out an annual industrial survey covering all establishments. The results include data on industrial structure and the production of individual products. The framework for the survey is provided by the **Betriebssystematik 1968** (Classification of all Economic Activities 1968) which broadly corresponds to the international **ISIC** classification.

Detailed external trade statistics are based on the **HS** classification but there are also general statistics based on the **SITC** classification.

PUBLICATIONS PRODUCED BY NATIONAL ORGANISATIONS

General industry and trade

Industrie – und Gewerbestatistik

An annual publication with summary commentary and statistics for industry and trade including data on energy use, indices of production and the production of selected products over the last two years.

Industriestatistik

An annual title, in two parts, with structural data at the 2-digit level on specific sectors, including the number of establishments broken down by employment size, establishment size, production, investment, etc. National and provincial data is included. Production data for specific products, at the 4-digit level, is also included. An extract from the production figures is shown in Table 3.1.

Austrian Economic Outlook

A quarterly survey of industry by the **Verein Oesterreichischer Industrielle**. An on-line version of the data is available through **IP Sharp**.

Der Aussenhandel Osterreichs, Series 1A: Spezialhandel nach Waren und Landern

A quarterly publication presenting import and export statistics for specific products broken down by major trading partners. Value and volume figures are given with data for the latest quarter and the cumulative year-to-date figure. The products are broken down by the 8-digit code of the HS classification.

Der Aussenhandel Osterreichs Series 1B: Spezialhandel nach Landern und Waren

A half-yearly title showing the trade between Austria and its individual trading partners. Within each country section, a product breakdown at the 6-digit level of the **HS** classification is given.

Der Aussenhandel Osterreichs Series 2: Spezialhandel nach dem internationalen Warenschema (SITC – revised 3)

A half-yearly publication which is less detailed than the two publications noted above. It gives trade by countries and product groups at the 3-digit level of the **SITC** classification.

Construction

Baustatistik

An annual publication, in two volumes, with structural data on the Austrian building industry.

INDUSTRIE PRODUKTION

PRODUKT	EIN-HEIT	WERT IN MENGE	1000 S 1988	WERT IN MENGE	1000 S 1989
4.1.30 MASCHIENE– UND STAHLBAUINDUSTRIE					
Eisenbahnsicherungsanlagen	T	270	10892	213	8592
Wälzlager u. Wälzlagerbestandteile	T	9463	1169793	11869	1297576
	ST	4538225		4878049	
Getrieberäder bzw.Zahnräder	T	742	81567	909	85877
Getriebe	T	4215	575535	5171	661881
Kupplungen u.sonst.Antriebselemente	T	876	121174	880	161499
Büromaschinen	KG	220	636	67	193
Feuerschutz-u.Feuerlöscheinrichtungen	T	353	20790	276	18293
Maschinen f. d. Akkumulatoren-Industrie	T	158	64717	205	82928
Mech. u.hydr. Steuerelemente, univ.					
verwendbar	T	3268	246928	3724	295540
Waschmaschinen, Zentrifugen,Geschirrsp.; f.					
gew.Zwecke	T	77	15321	80	15577
Einzel-u. Ersatzteile f.Waschmaschinen	T	–	–	3	813
Prüfmaschinen	T	473	288847	316	237953
Sonstige Maschinen	T	4558	1297217	7658	1574136
Sonstige Maschinenteile (ausgen. elektrische)	T	8482	932861	9997	1101952
Groß–,Schnell–,Band–u.Dosierwaagen	T	721	134199	725	142071
Brücken– u. Brückenkonstruktionen	T	3040	153480	1233	67041
Andere Hochbaukonstruktionen	T	46268	1167247	46145	1190285
Weichen, Drehscheiben, Schiebebühnen	T	19307	394598	20739	504697
Stahlwasserbau	T	3037	178601	4512	233811
Sonst.fert.Stahlbaut.u.Konstruktionen					
(a.Wellblechgar.)	T	41524	1584389	63605	1896156
Anlagen z.Nutzg.v.Sonnenenergie,					
einschl.Komponenten	T	10	1133	1	126
Schiffe u. Boote mit motor.Antrieb	T	10202	1295750	3327	146472
Schiffe u. Boote ohne motor. Antrieb	T	460	11500	743	93000
Schiffs– u. Bootsreparaturen	+)	.	72550	.	134405
Großarmaturen	T	12336	461163	14357	544553
Dampf– u.Säurearmaturen	T	4196	488044	2908	610725
Feinarmaturen	T	38	8409	48	10462
Sonderarmaturen	T	1072	114766	1066	156871
Druck– u. Vakuumbehälter	T	5729	290531	4099	226105

Table 3.1 Austrian production statistics – extracts of entries covering machinery.

Food and drink

Ergebnisse der landwirtschaftlichen Statistik

An annual statistical report covering food and agriculture with tables on specific foodstuffs and products.

Jahresbericht

The annual report of the **Fachverband der Nahrungs- und Genuss-mittelindustrie Osterreichs** contains statistics on the Austrian food sector. The association also publishes a journal, **Ernahrung**.

Chemicals and chemical products

Some statistics are produced by the trade association, **Fachverband der Chemischen Industrie Osterreichs** which publishes a monthly journal, **Osterreichische Chemie-Zeitschrift**.

Jahresbericht

An annual report with some statistics on oil and gas production, exploration and trade plus data on the production and consumption of specific products. Published by the **Fachverband der Erdolindustrie Osterreichs**.

Textiles and clothing

Osterreichische Textilindustrie

Statistischer Bericht

The first title is an annual report comprised mainly of text but there are statistics for the last three years on the textile industry. Quarterly statistics on the sector are included in the second title and both publications come from the **Fachverband der Textilindustrie Osterreichs**.

Jahrbuch

A yearbook from the **Verein der Baumwoll Spinner und Weber Osterreichs** which includes statistics on cotton and cotton spinning.

Electrical and mechanical engineering

Some statistics are produced by the engineering and shipbuilding association, **Fachverband der Maschinen- und Stahlindustrie Osterreichs**.

Retailing and distribution

A retailing census took place in the mid 1980s and annual figures are available from:

Gross- und Einzelhandelsstatistik

A statistical yearbook with the results of a sample survey of wholesaling and retailing businesses. Includes actual figures on turnover, employment, goods purchased, etc. and a series of tables with indices.

Financial services

Jahresbericht

An annual report from the **Verband Osterreichischer Banken und Bankiers** with statistics on banking and financial trends.

Leisure and tourism

Der Fremdenverkehr in Osterreich

Annual statistics on tourist trends.

Transportation

Bestandsstatistik der Kraftahrzeuge in Osterreich

An annual publication with data on motor vehicle production, registrations, stocks, etc. with many tables broken down by type and model. Data for local areas is also included.

Monatliche Kraftfahrzeugzulassungsstatistik

Monthly figures on new registrations of motor vehicles.

Jahrbuch

An annual report from the **Fachverband der Fahrzeugindustrie Osterreichs** with statistics on the motor vehicles sector including cars, commercial vehicles and motor cycles.

Zivilluftfahrt in Osterreich

Annual statistics on the civil aviation sector in Austria including data on specific airports and passengers.

Advertising statistics

Advertising expenditure data in total and by product and media type is published in a range of services from **Nielsen Media Research**.

4 BELGIUM

Business statistics

INTRODUCTION

Belgium's central statistical office is the **Institut National de Statistique (INS)** which publishes most of Belgium's official statistics. There are also other government departments and agencies involved in statistical activities and, in 1985, the **INS** was given a co-ordinating role for all the activities of the national statistical system. The **INS** is part of the Ministere des Affaires Economiques (Ministry of Economic Affairs) which provides its budget, and an advisory body is the High Council of Statistics. The main offices of **INS** are in Brussels but there are also sales offices in Charleroi and Liege:

Institut National de Statistique
INS
rue de Louvain 44
B-1000 Brussels
Belgium

INS
Centre Albert
8a etage
Place Albert 1e4
B-6000 Charleroi
Belgium

INS
Boulevard de la Sauveniere 73-75
B-4000 Liege
Belgium

An annual catalogue of publications, with regular updates, is **Catalogue des publications de l'Institut National de Statistique** and an annual report on **INS**'s activities is **Rapport des activites de l'Institut National de Statistique**.

Belgium also has a number of trade associations publishing statistics including various pan-European associations which have located here mainly because of the local presence of the EC administration. Details of the latter are given in Chapter 2. Some of the national trade associations not only collect statistics for themselves but also provide data for official titles. As many sectors are not covered in detail by official statistics, the data from trade associations can be particularly useful.

GENERAL STATISTICAL TITLES

Compilations

The **Annuaire statistique de la Belgique** is the annual statistical yearbook with summary data from all the main official series. **Annuaire statistique de poche** is a small pocket-book of key statistics. Regularly updated statistics are included in the monthly **Bulletin de statistique**. Subscribers to the **Bulletin de statistique** also receive free copies of the weekly bulletin, **Communique hebdomadaire** which contains up-to-date statistics on various topics including industrial production, demographic trends, external trade, commerce and social trends. All the above publications are available from the **INS**.

Economic data

The **Ministry of Economic Affairs** publishes a monthly **Lettre de conjoncture** with commentary, graphs and tables on economic trends and industrial production. **L'Economie Belge en 19– –: Synthese annuelle** from the same department has a detailed commentary, with graphs and tables, on the Belgian economy.

The monthly **Bulletin de la Banque Nationale de Belgique** has a regular commentary on the Belgian economic situation plus a statistical section.

Demographic and social statistics

Censuses of population and dwellings, **Recensement de la population et des logements**, are undertaken every 10 years with the most recent in 1981 and 1991. The results are published in a series of volumes which can take some time to appear. For example, Volume 8 from the 1981 census on the economically active population was not published until 1990.

Statistiques demographiques is published three or four times a year and has general data on population trends and characteristics with each issue usually devoted to a specific demographic topic. **Statistiques sociales** also appears three or four times a year with data on employment, hours and salaries.

Sector data

General industrial statistics

Detailed censuses of industry and commerce take place approximately every 10 years but there is an annual survey of industrial structure plus annual and monthly surveys of industrial production.

The annual survey of industry is based on a regularly updated register of local production units and it generally covers all production units employing 5 or more people. In some sectors, this employment cut-off point is amended to 10 or more people and, in some cases, to 20 or more people. As well as data on industrial structure, the annual survey also obtains production data for approximately 4,000 products. A monthly survey covering the key sectors of industry also collects more up-to-date data on the production of approximately 2,000 products.

The results from the annual and monthly surveys are included in the monthly **Statistiques industrielles** which is described in more detail below.

Overseas trade statistics for specific products are published monthly and cover the customs union of Belgium and Luxembourg. These statistics are based on the European **CN**.

PUBLICATIONS PRODUCED BY NATIONAL ORGANISATIONS

General industry and trade

Production data for selected products is included in the **Annuaire statistique de la Belgique** and the monthly **Bulletin de statistique** and more detailed information is available from the titles described below.

Statistiques industrielles

This monthly publication is the main source of data from the monthly and annual industrial inquiries. It includes general production indices and actual monthly production figures, usually in volume terms, for selected products in key sectors. An example of a production table from the food industry is given in Table 4.1 and a list of the key sectors covered in each issue is given below:

Coal mining, iron ore
Coal deliveries, imports & exports
Extraction of building stone & other non-metallic minerals
Food
Tobacco
Textile mills & other textile industries
Weaving

	PRODUCTION DE BISCUITS, BISCOTTES ET PAINS D'EPICE (EN TONNES)							
	Production de farine (meunière) industrielle (1000T)	Gaufres	Biscuits sucres	Speculoos	Biscottes, toasts et produits similaires autres produits non-sucres	Pains d'epice	Autres produits sucres	Gaufrettes biscuits non sucres et autres produits
1985	78	1674	6447	1378	150	685	497	1780
1986	71	1659	7082	1352	179	695	676	1848
1987	78	1783	7071	1411	178	678	1643	2144
1988	75	1919	7439	1422	239	655	1786	2305
1989	–	2068	7662	1472	256	620	2003	2949
1990								
JANVIER	104	2311	7551	1478	347	592	1080	3049
FEVRIER	91	2326	7980	1354	270	721	1095	2685
MARS	102	2358	8739	1527	349	646	1166	2846
AVRIL	91	2231	8023	1305	313	664	1077	2955
MAI	101	2190	7915	1497	264	621	951	3248
JUIN	93	2139	8366	1237	315	683	1292	3238
JUILLET	81	1694	5898	880	190	516	980	3169
AOUT	97	2198	6190	1719	219	537	1147	3740
SEPTEMBRE	100	2186	8936	1882	397	598	1295	3413
OCTOBRE	74	2671	10423	2160	323	728	1383	3518
NOVEMBRE	63	2065	8467	1814	356	706	1241	3102
DECEMBRE	75	1835	6583	1038	285	558	1881	2443
1991								
JANVIER	67	2336	8175	1623	225	627	2497	3173
FEVRIER	73	2378	7995	1606	220	636	2446	2920
MARS	87	2236	7962	1368	314	735	1386	3212
AVRIL	69	2471	8130	1640	292	614	1430	3065
MAI	64	2334	8204	1280	232	652	1579	3139
JUIN	66	2349	9493	1616	241	663	1359	3292
JUILLET	–	2647	6892	1315	167	539	1227	2520

	INDUSTRIES ALIMENTAIRES DIVERSES : PRODUCTION (EN TONNES)									
	Chicoree En Grains	Chicoree Fine	Malt	Cafe Torrefie (1)	Moutarde	Picca-lilli	Oignons au Vinaigre	Corni-chons au Vinaigre	Mayon-naise et autres sauces condim-entaires	Vinaigre production (en 1000 L) ramene a 8 degre
1985	549	109	39627	5947	384	262	79	191	4055	1583
1986	576	105	40648	5432	389	282	211	201	4204	1750
1987	468	82	41845	5486	394	265	216	265	4611	1684
1988	469	82	42118	5701	384	259	248	297	4703	1728
1990										
JANVIER	531	78	47814	6518	529	294	105	72	4764	1571
FEVRIER	390	89	40965	5861	475	249	89	92	4875	1793
MARS	397	51	47466	6701	482	286	91	57	5646	2209
AVRIL	310	34	48542	6188	443	262	83	74	5392	2252
MAI	391	42	52594	5618	474	264	219	171	6592	2029
JUIN	429	83	49789	7323	517	262	189	243	7589	2333
JUILLET	105	50	49354	4970	460	249	840	297	5046	2750
AOUT	429	46	47895	5037	482	254	1076	427	6494	2415
SEPTEMBRE	347	96	48225	6063	550	250	96	158	7781	2110
OCTOBRE	493	85	49865	7041	568	331	64	117	7103	2059
NOVEMBRE	338	51	49976	6559	557	232	94	54	5790	1527
DECEMBRE	290	62	43696	5536	521	213	55	313	3694	1929
1991										
JANVIER	578	76	42774	8415	615	351	130	81	4721	2005
FEVRIER	520	68	46324	6909	469	273	77	100	4139	1921
MARS	112	55	50874	6194	489	242	83	177	5258	2761
AVRIL	116	63	50625	7011	439	288	90	230	5374	2479
MAI	116	56	49184	5432	418	314	108	233	5307	1956
JUIN	375	49	48481	5542	532	252	89	178	4439	2120

(1) LES CHIFFRES NE COMPRENNENT PAS LES QUANTITES DE CAFE TORREFIE POUR USAGE PROPRE (EX. : PAR LES PERSONNES PARIVEES, L'ARMEE, LES HOPITAUX, ETC.) NON PLUS QUE LA PRODUCTION DES ATELIERS N'OCCUPANT PAS DE PERSONNEL ASSUJETTI A LA SECURITE SOCIALE

Table 4.1 Belgium production statistics – extracts of entries for the food industry

Hosiery
Clothing
Footwear & slippers
Wood & related products
Paper
Leather & rubber
Soap
Chemicals
Petroleum products & derivatives
Gas production, imports, exports
Products of minerals & metals
Iron & steel
Non-ferrous metals
Metal products
Plastic products
Electricity
Water

Industrial structure data from the annual industrial survey is also included with each issue covering a number of specific sectors. Eventually, in a series of monthly issues, all the sectors in a particular annual survey are covered. For example, the first sector report from the 1987 industrial survey appeared in the March/April 1989 issue and 1987 sector reports were still being published in the February 1991 issue. Some monthly issues contain reports from more than one annual survey as the last reports from one year are published and the first reports from the next year start to appear. For example, the August 1991 issue had four sector reports from the 1988 survey and one sector report from the 1990 survey. These reports on specific sectors can also be purchased separately.

Published data from the annual survey includes information on the number of enterprises, employment, wages and salaries, materials, energy and products consumed, taxes, value of stocks, investment and production, deliveries and stocks of selected products. Sometimes, the sector reports also have a regional breakdown and data on equipment used.

Communique hebdomadaire

Although a general weekly publication with a range of statistics, it has a large industrial production section with regular data on the production of selected products and the industrial structure in the major sectors of Belgian industry.

Statistiques du commerce exterieur de l'Union economique belgo-luxembourgeoise

Monthly figures for product imports and exports, by country, arranged by European **CN** codes. Value and volume figures are given with the latest month's and cumulative year-to-date statistics included in each issue.

Construction

Statistiques industrielles

This monthly publication includes a section in each issue showing building permits authorised and building work started. National and regional data is included.

Monthly statistics on building trends are also published by the building confederation, **Confederation Nationale de la Construction (CNC)**.

Food and drink

Statistiques de l'IEA

The **Ministere de l'Agriculture, Administration de la Recherche Agronomique, Institut Economique Agricole (IEA)** publishes an annual statistical review of food and agriculture with data on production and consumption. The review covers specific foods and alcoholic and non-alcoholic drinks.

Guide du Marche des Friandises

CHOBISCO

The first title provides an annual review of the chocolate and sugar confectionery markets while the second title is published 11 times per year and has statistics on the production, sales and trade of biscuits, snacks and chocolate confectionery. Published by the trade association, **CHOBISCO**.

Bulletin Economique des Vins et Spiritueux

A regular bulletin, usually only for members, from the **Federation Belge des Vins et Spiritueux (FBVS)**. General information on the production and distribution of wines and spirits is also available monthly in **Revue Belge des Vins et Spiritueux**.

Chemicals and chemical products

Flash Conjoncture
Flash Commerce Exterieur

Regular bulletins on the chemical industry and external trade in chemicals and chemical products from the **Federation des Industries Chimiques de Belgique (FECHIMIE)**.

AGIM Chiffres-Cles

Basic statistics from the **Association Generale de l'Industrie du Medicament** with data on pharmaceuticals turnover by sector, employment, prescriptions, prices, consumption, etc.

Textiles and clothing

Rapport sur l'exercice

An annual report, with some statistics, on the Belgian textiles sector. Published by the textile association, **Federation de l'Industrie Textile Belge (FEBELTEX)**.

Habillement Belge

Regular statistics on menswear and womenswear from the **Federation Belge des Industries de l'Habillement**. The title is published approximately eight times a year and most of the data is reproduced from official sources.

Rapport

An annual report, in two volumes, from the hosiery trade association, **Comite Centrale de la Bonneterie Belge**. The report is largely text but there is a statistical section with data on production, sales, consumption and external trade by product areas.

Annuaire Rapport & Statistiques

An annual report with statistics from **Textielpatroonsverbond**, the Belgian Carpet and Upholstery Fabric Board.

Some statistics are also produced by the **Federation Belge de l'Industrie du Coton et des Fibres Chimiques (FEBEL)** covering cotton and man-made fibres.

Electrical and mechanical engineering

La Siderurgie Belge en 199–

The **Groupement de la Siderurgie** publishes a yearbook on the iron and steel industries.

L'Industrie Belge des Metaux non Ferreux – Recueil statistique

The **Federation des Enterprises de Metaux non Ferreux** publishes annual production, trade and employment statistics for the non-ferrous metals industry. Summary data is also published monthly in **Recueil Statistique Mensuel** and there is a monthly external trade publication.

Annuaire Statistique

Fabrimetal, the engineering and metal working association, publishes an annual statistical volume plus a monthly bulletin, **Fabrimetal**.

Retailing and distribution

Rapport annuel Exercice

An annual report on the retailing and distributive trades from the **Federation Belge des Enterprises de Distribution (FEDIS)**. The report is mainly a review of the year but there are statistical tables on the number of enterprises, sales, consumption, employment, outlets, etc.

The **Comite Belge de la Distribution (CBD)** also publishes the journal, **Distribution d'aujourd' hui**, which contains regular statistics.

Financial services

Statistiques financieres

Three or four issues a year are published by INS on specific financial topics.

Rapport sur les activites et sur la situation des enterprises d'assurances en Belgique

An annual report from the Office de Controle des Assurances with statistics on the structure of the insurance industry, insurance revenue and some market share data.

L'activite bancaire en 199–
Vade-mecum statistique du secteur bancaire 199–

Two annual publications with banking statistics from the Belgian Bankers Association, **Association Belge des Banques**. The association also publishes an annual report, **Rapport Annuel**, and other reports containing banking data.

Le Marche Belge de L'Assurance

A market profile of the Belgian insurance market from the **Union Professionnelle des Entreprises d'Assurances (UPEA)**. **UPEA** also publishes an annual report, with a summary available in English; **Flash sur l'assurance**, a pamphlet with basic data on the insurance sector plus various one-off reports.

Transportation

Statistique mensuelle des vehicules neufs immatricules en Belgique

Monthly statistics covering new vehicle registrations by make, model, country of manufacture, etc. plus data on vehicle production. Published by the **Federation Belge des Industries de l'Automobile et du Cycle (FEBIAC)**.

Le Radioscope de l'Autocar

An annual compilation of figures on public road transport from the **Federation Belge des Exploitants d'Autobus et d'Autocars (FBAA)**. Most of the data is based on official statistics and a commentary accompanies the data. Other publications are produced on specific types of road transport.

Public sector

Annuaire Statistique

A yearbook for the electricity supply industry from the **Federation Professionnelle des Producteurs et Distributeurs d'Electricite de Belgique**. Statistical data on capacity, production, consumption, imports, exports, equipment and prices with current and historical data.

Annuaire Statistique

Annual statistics from **Federation de l'Industrie du Gaz (FIGAZ)** covering the supply and distribution of gas in Belgium.

Advertising statistics

Regular advertising statistics, for specific products and by media type, are published by the private company, **Advertising Audit Services**.

5 DENMARK
Business statistics

INTRODUCTION

In 1988, Eurostat statisticians described Denmark's official statistics as a 'statistician's dream' because of their good coverage and timeliness. The country has also been one of the most active in Europe in utilising internationally agreed statistical classifications and standards both through its involvement with the EC and through the **Nordic Statistical Secretariat**, based in Copenhagen, which attempts to produce standardised statistics covering the five Nordic countries (*see* Chapter 2).

Most of the official, and non-official, titles have English translations of the table headings and sub-headings and many have English language introductions, notes and indexes.

The central statistical office is **Danmarks Statistics (DS)**, an independent institution separated from government whose activities are governed by the 1971 Statistics Act. **DS** is the responsibility of the Ministry of Economics and Budgetary Affairs with 20 per cent of its budget coming from revenue from users and the remainder coming from the national budget. A Board of Governors controls DS and its budget is recommended by this board.

Danmarks Statistik
DS
Sejrogade 11
DK-2100 Copenhagen 0
Denmark

The **Vejviser i statistikken (Guide to Statistics)** is published every three or four years and the latest issue appeared in 1988. An annual list of publications, **Danmarks Statistiks publikationer** (Publications issued by Danmarks Statistik) is available in Danish and English and general details of the main titles are given in English at the back of the statistical yearbook, **Statistisk Arbog**. In January each year, the work programme is published, including details of any planned new statistics, and this is available free from DS. On-line and disc versions of the main economic and industrial statistical series are produced in:

On-line services

DSTB

A databank of economic, industry and trade statistics available from DS or the host system, **UNI-C**. The database has figures from 1950 onwards and is updated daily.

Other on-line services include **ABBA** for labour market statistics and **KSDB** for social statistics.

GENERAL STATISTICAL TITLES

Compilations

The annual compilation of statistics is **Statistisk Arbog** with Danish and some international statistics. There are subject indexes, table headings and a contents page in Danish and English. Updated information for many of the series in the yearbook is included in the monthly **Statistisk manedsoversigt** and, again, there are English table headings and a contents page. **Statistisk tiarsoversigt** is an annual compilation with statistical tables covering the last 10 years.

Nyt fra Danmarks Statistik is a rapid release service giving summary results of the main monthly, quarterly and annual surveys with more detailed results appearing later in other publications. The service is primarily intended for the news media and there are approximately 360 issues per year.

More detailed results, covering a range of subjects, are published in two series of titles known as **Statistiske efterretninger** (Statistical News) and **Statistikservice** (Statistics Service). Various titles, covering different subject areas, are published in each series and subscriptions can be taken out for the whole series or specific subject areas.

Statistiske efterretninger is divided into 13 subject groups each with their own set of publications and the titles on manufacturing and industry are described in more detail in the 'General Industrial Statistics' section:

Agriculture
Manufacturing industry & energy
Construction industry
Transport & tourism
General economic statistics & internal trade (including retailing & VAT statistics)
External trade
Money & credit market

National accounts, public finance & balance of payments
Population & elections
Education & culture
Social security & justice
Labour market
Income, consumption, prices

Statistikservice is a series of publications providing a greater level of detail than the above series and the data usually covers a number of years. There are 10 titles in the series:

Manufacturer's Sales of Commodities (four volumes), quarterly
Industrial Sales & Order Books, monthly
Industrial Employment & Labour Costs, monthly
Labour Market Statistics, quarterly
Earnings and Income Statistics, six issues per year
External Trade by Commodities and Countries, quarterly
Price Statistics, monthly
Retail Prices, quarterly
Social Statistics, 6–10 issues per year
Economic Trends in Selected Countries, twice a month

Economic data

Generel erhvervsstatistik og handel is a regular title in the **Statistike efterretninger** series and specific titles on prices, national accounts, public finance and balance of payments are also part of this series. The statistical yearbook and monthly review of statistics also contain economic data.

A regular survey of consumer opinion on economic and financial conditions is carried out in January, April and October based on telephone interviews with 2,000 people supplemented by some face-to-face interviews. In the other months of the year, excluding July, a sample of 1,800 is surveyed. The results are published in the title, **Income, consumption and prices**, in the **Statistiske efterretninger** series and are also passed onto the EC to appear in **European Economy** (*see* Chapter 2). On-line economic data can be found on the **DSTB** service described earlier.

Danish Bulletin published quarterly by the **Den Danske Bank** has articles, graphs and tables on economic trends and is published in English. Economic data is also published by the **Danmarks Nationalbank** although its quarterly title, **Monetary Review**, mainly covers money and banking and is included in the section on '**Financial Services**' on page 68. The national industrial organisation, **Industriradet** publishes the **Nordic Economic Outlook** twice a year.

Demographic and social statistics

Denmark has a Central Population Register (**CPR**) and movements and changes in the population are entered into this register on a regular basis. From this register, **DS**'s population statistics register is kept up-to-date and provides figures for **Befolkning og valg** in the **Statistiske efterretninger** series. This title has data on the population size, births, deaths, internal and external migration, population projections and national and local elections. An annual publication is **Befolkningens bevoegelser**.

A population census is undertaken every 10 years and the results are published in a series of reports under the general title, **Folke- og boligtaellingen**. All the reports from the 1981 census have been published and the results from the 1991 census should be published in the early 1990s.

Sector data

General industrial statistics

Danish statistics on economic and sector activity are based on a Danish version of the **ISIC**. The Danish version is known as **Danmarks Statistiks Occupational Classification (DSE)** and corresponds to **ISIC** except that as well as the 2-, 3- and 4-digit breakdown of the major divisions, a 5-digit breakdown has been added creating a further Danish, or joint Nordic, sub-grouping as shown in Table 5.1.

1 Agriculture, forestry, fishing
2 Mining & quarrying
3 Manufacturing
4 Electricity, gas, water
5 Construction
6 Wholesale & retail trade, restaurants, hotels
7 Transport, storage, communications
8 Finance & banking, insurance, real estate & business services
9 Community, social & personal services

Table 5.1 Denmark – Classification of economic activities

Statistics on industrial structure and activity are based on the **DSE** classification but data on the production of individual commodities and products is based on the **HS** overseas trade classification. This means that, unlike most other European countries, production statistics and trade statistics are harmonised and can be compared relatively easily.

DS also carries out regular business opinion surveys and the results are published in the **Statistiske efterretninger** series, the monthly bulletin of statistics, and are passed onto the EC for inclusion in **European Economy** (*see* Chapter 2). The opinion survey for manufacturing known as the **Tendency**

Varestatistik for industrien – Salg af egne produkter

Varenr cn	Varebeskrivelse (Kun varenr hvor omsætningen er større end O kr er medtaget)	Mængde-enhed	2.kvt. 1991 Mængde	1000 kr	1.2.kvt. 1991 Mængde	1000 kr
8503 0099 00	Dele (ej umagnetiske akselringe), til elektriske motorer, generatorer og rote-rende omformere, ej af støbejern og-stål	tons	...	742	...	16 657
8504 1091 00	Induktionsspoler, også med tilkoblet kondensator, til udladningslamper og -rør, undt til civile fly	stk	5 010	161	12 984	425
8504 2100 01	Transformatorer med væskeisolation, effekt max 25 kVA	stk	35	199	83	402
8504 2100 03	Transformatorer med væskeisolation, effekt 0 25 max 350 kVA	stk	280	15 635	557	28 734
8504 3131 00	Spændingstransformatorer til måleinstrumenter,max 1 kVA,undt til civile fly	stk	1 508	138	2 667	260
8504 3139 00	Tørtransformatorer til måleinstrumenter, max 1 kVA, undt til civile fly og spændingstransformatorer	stk	...	5 980	...	12 742
8504 3190 00	Tørtransformatorer, max 1 kVA, undt til måleinstrumenter og til civile fly	1000 stk	1 332	52 983	2 622	104 740
8504 3229 00	Tørtransformatorer til måleinstrumenter, o 1 max 16 kVA, undt spændings-transformatorer og til civile fly	stk	...	989	...	2 348
8504 3290 00	Tørtransformatorer, o 1 max 16 kVA, undt til måleinstrumenter og til civile fly.	stk	57 692	11 752	113 976	24 324
8504 4050 10	Tørensrettere og -ensretterapparater baseret på germanium og silicium, undt til civile fly	stk	7 868	16 353	15 742	31 615
8504 4050 90	Ensrettere med polykrystallinsk halvleder, undt tørensrettere og -ensretterapparater	stk	1 833	41 428	3 408	75 351
8504 4093 00	Statiske omformere, akkumulatorladere	stk	...	4 792	...	9 455
8504 4094 00	Statiske ensrettere,undt med polykrystallinsk halvleder, ej til civile fly	stk	1	12	7	55
8504 4096 00	Statiske omformere, max 7,5 kVA,ej (til civile fly,ensrettere og -ensretterapparater, til svejsning, akkumulatorladere)	stk	...	53 025	...	97 965
8504 4097 00	Statiske omformere,o 7,5 kVA, ej (til civile fly, ensrettere og -ensretterapparter, til svejsning, akkumulatorladere)	stk	...	33 813	...	70 937
8504 5090 00	Induktionsspoler, undt til civile fly	stk	...	1 863	...	4 426
8504 9011 00	Ferritkerner, til transformatorer og induktionsspoler	tons	...	1 060	...	2 373
8504 9019 00	Dele til transformatorer og induktionsspoler, ej ferritkerner	tons	658	6 978	1 424	16 102
8504 9090 00	Dele til satiske omformere	tons	...	...	...	...
85051100 00	Permanente magneter og emner til fremstilling af permanente magneter ved magnetisering, af metal	stk	88 900	601	176 170	1 191
8505 9010 00	Elektromagneter	stk	...	...	...	...

Kode	Varebeskrivelse	Enhed					
8505 9090 00	Dele til elektromagneter, permanente magneter og emner dertil, elektromagnetiske koblinger, -bremser, - bæremagneter o l	tons	..	..	..	..	30 198
8506 1110 00	Mangandioxidelementer og -batterier, alkaliske, volumen max 300 kubikcm	1000 stk	0	172	16 082	0	284
8506 1190 00	Mangandioxidelementer og -batterier, undt alkaliske, volumen max 300 kubikcm	1000 stk	32	1 362	..	62	4 462
8506 1910 00	Lithiumelementer og-batterier, volumen max 300 kubikcm	1000 stk	..	5	..	..	28
8506 9000 00	Dele til primærelementer og - batterier	tons					
8507 1099 00	Blyakkumulatorer til start af stempelmotorer, o 5 kg, undt til civile fly	stk	33 217	10 752	66 562	..	22 743
8507 3099 00	Nikkel-cadmiumakkumulatorer, ikke- gastætte, undt til civile fly	stk	821	641	2 629	..	1 179
8507 9099 10	Akkumulatorkasser til elektriske akkumulatorer, undt til civile fly	stk	335 011	10 386	658 534	..	19 821
8507 9099 90	Dele til eletriske akkumulatoree, undt akkumulatorplader, -kasser samt dele til civile	1000 stk	1 590	890	3 235	..	2 197
8508 1099 00	Håndboremaskiner, med indbygget elektromotor, som fungerer med ydre energikilde, und elektropneumatiske	stk	2	6	4	..	13
8509 1010 00	Støvsugere til husholdningsbrug, med indbygget elektromotor, min 110 volt	stk	43 964	39 661	83 470	..	74 733
8509 9010 00	Dele til støvsugere, bonemaskiner med indbygget elektomotor, til husholdningsbrug	tons	..	53 702	..	..	93 812
8511 4090 00	Startmotorer, også med generatorfunktion, til brug i forbrændingsmotorer, undt i civile fly	stk	56 908	18 792	115 106	..	38 111
8512 1099 00	Forlygter, baglygter, batterilygter o a lys- og visuelt udstyr til cykler, undt dynamoer og sæt med dynamo og forlygte	stk	362 703	5 780	609 900	..	9 739
8512 2000 00	Forlygter, baglygter o a lys- og visuelt signaludstyr, undt til cykler	stk	..	2 435	..	..	4 174
8512 9000 00	Dele til elektrisk lys- og singaludstyr til cykler og motorkøretøjer	tons	20	1 584	31	..	2 491
8513 1000 00	Lommelygter. håndlygter o l transportable elektriske lygter med egen strømkilde, undt til cykler og motorkøretøjer	stk	..	667	..	..	1 499
8514 1091 00	Industriovne, med elektrisk modstandsopvarmning, af vægt max 50 kg	stk	..	116	..	..	205
8514 1099 10	Industriovne med elektrisk modstandsopvarmning til keramisk-, metallurgisk- og glasindustri, o 50 kg	stk	..	1 207	..	..	2 496
8514 1099 90	Industriovne med elektrisk modstandsopvarmning, undt bageri-, biscuits-, metallurgi-, keramik-, og glasovne, o 50kg	stk	9	1 625	22	..	3 110
8514 2010 00	Induktionsovne til industri	stk	63	299	73	..	363
8514 3090 90	Industriovne, ej til metallurgi, keramik, glas, ej induktions-, dielektriske- og stråleovnesamt modstandsopvermede ovne	stk	1	990	3	..	3 625

Table 5.2 Denmark production statistics for electrical equipment

Survey for Manufacturing Industries is quarterly and is based on returns from 700 major manufacturing companies, representing approximately 60 per cent of total employment and covering approximately 1,100 establishments. The quarterly **Construction Industry Tendency Survey** is based on returns from 650 establishments representing more than one-third of total employment in the construction sector.

Denmark maintains a Central Register of Enterprises and Establishments, known as **Erhvervsregister**, which is regularly updated. The register contains information on all businesses and public sector agencies and information on specific organisations on the register can be supplied on request. Special packages can also provide information as printed lists, index cards, mailing labels or on disc or tape. Further information on the register and the **DSE** classification can be obtained from the central statistical office.

PUBLICATIONS PRODUCED BY NATIONAL ORGANISATIONS

General industry and trade

Industristatistik

An annual publication with details of Denmark's industrial structure based on the annual Census of Manufacturing Industries and one or two other sources. Data includes the total number of establishments in divisions 2 and 3 of **DSE** plus detailed statistics on employment, sales, wage and salary costs, prices, value added, investment and energy consumption. Some tables provide information down to the 5-digit level of **DSE**.

Summary statistics cover the latest three years with more detailed data for the latest year available. The 1989 issue for example, published in October 1990, has summary data for 1987–9, with detailed data for 1989.

Industri og energi

Part of the **Statistiske efterretninger** series, the title appears approximately 22 times a year with various tables on employment and labour costs, sales and order books, accounts, tendency surveys, energy balance sheet, energy supplies and manufacturers' energy consumption.

Manedlig ordre- og omsoetningsstatistik for industri

Monthly statistics of industrial sales and order books with indices for 30 industry groups. Part of the **Statistikservice** series.

Manedlig beskaeftigelses- og lonstatistik for industri

Monthly statistics of industrial employment and labour costs based on a survey of 2,000 establishments, and published in the **Statistikservice** series.

Varestatistik for industri

Quarterly data on the production of specific commodities and products is included in four publications with the general title, **Varestatistik for industri**. The titles are published in the **Statistikservice** series and the individual titles are:

Series A   **Animalske og vegetabilske produkter, samt andre naerings- og nydelsesmidler** (Animal & vegetable products)

Series B   **Mineralske og kemiske produkter, trae og papir samt varer deraf** (Minerals & chemical products)

Series C   **Tekstilvarer, fodtoj, sportsartikler** (Textiles, footwear, sports articles)

Series D   **Metaller, metalvarer, maskiner, apparater og instrumenter, samt transportmidler** (Metals, metalworking, machinery, apparatus & instrumentation)

Each publication has details of the production of individual products, by value and volume, and the product headings are based on the **HS** classification and broken down into 10-digit headings. However, not every product heading included in the **HS** classification is included in these publications. The example from **Series D** covering electrical appliances in Table 5.2 gives some idea of the level of detail. Heading 8509 1010 00 relates to vacuum cleaners with a voltage of 110 volts or more and corresponds to the **HS** code. Only one other heading in the 8509 group is included although there are actually another 11 headings in this group in the **HS** classification.

Each issue contains cumulative data for the year and the statistics are published approximately five months after the period to which they relate. Problems of confidentiality and the lack of response means that, as with most other countries, there are gaps in the figures for specific product headings.

Regnskabsstatistik for industrien

An annual publication with financial statistics on industrial enterprises in Denmark. Unlike the other surveys noted above, the figures are based on a survey of companies with 20 or more employees.

Udenrigshandelen fordelt pa varer og lande

This quarterly publication is part of the **Statistikservice** series and covers Denmark's external trade (including Greenland and the Faroe Islands), by commodities and countries. Detailed product statistics are arranged according to the **HS** and **CN** classifications, with 9 digits, and the figures are cumulative so that each quarterly issue has data for that quarter and the total for the year to date.

Danmarks vareindforsel og- udforsel

General trends in Denmark's trade (including Greenland and the Faroe Islands), by **SITC** sections and **HS** chapters, are shown in this annual publication.

Udenrigshandel

Short-term trends in external trade published as part of the **Statistiske Efterretninger** series.

Construction

Bygge- og anloegsvirksomhed

Comprises a series of monthly, quarterly and annual publications covering units, output, current work and employment in the construction sector. A census of the construction sector has been carried out in 1984 and 1988 and surveys of the sector are based on the establishments identified in these censuses. For example, quarterly data on construction employment comes from a survey of a sample of 3,600 establishments based on the census files.

Building construction statistics come from the **BBR**, the Register of Buildings and Dwellings. This is a register of building projects started but not yet completed and the building statistics are based on monthly updates from this register.

Food and drink

Danske Slagterier Statistics

Annual statistics from **Danske Slagterier**, the Federation of Danish Pig Producers and Slaughterhouses, published in English. Statistics on Danish and international meat markets and meat products.

Dybfrostradet

Annual market data for frozen foods in Denmark with statistics on specific products and the retailing and catering sectors. Published by **Dybfrostinstituttet (DFR)** and an English language version is available.

Tal fra Bryggeriforeningen 199–

Basic statistics on brewing and alcoholic drinks, published in a pocket-book, from the trade association **Bryggeriforeningen**.

Chemicals and chemical products

Arsberetning

The **Oliebranchens Faellesrepraesentation (OFR)** publishes an annual report with statistics on petroleum and petroleum products plus a regular pamphlet, **Petroleum Industry's Key Figures**.

Tal og data 199–, Medicin og Sundhedsvaesen

Commentary and statistics on medicines and health care in Denmark with some comparative international data. English translations of headings and the commentary are included. This annual report is published by **Foreningen af danske Medicinfabrikker (MEFA)**, the Association of the Danish Pharmaceutical Industry. Subjects covered include production, markets, trade, prices, consumption, advertising, investment, employment, profits, R&D and health care.

Textiles and clothing

Danish Textile and Clothing Industry Survey
Prognosis

The first title is an English language survey of trends in the textiles and clothing sectors with figures for the last three years. The second title is published twice a year in Danish and considers the trends and the outlook for the industry. Both are published by **Textil- og Beklaedningsindustrien**, the Federation of Danish Textile and Clothing Industries, which also publishes an annual report.

Electronics

Elektronikstatistik

Annual statistics relating to electronic equipment production and external trade from **Elektronikfabrikantforeningen**.

Regular statistics are also produced by the domestic electrical appliances trade association, **FEHA**.

Retailing and distribution

An official retail census was last carried out in 1985 but more up-to-date figures on sales and employment are based on VAT registrations. These registrations can also provide details of the number of outlets as each outlet is treated separately for VAT purposes.

Supermarkeder

The organisation, **Per Press**, publishes annual statistics on supermarkets in Denmark with data on their numbers, type, sales, turnover, location and product areas. There is also an annual report on discount stores, **Discountbutikker**, and other reports on retailing.

Financial services

Penge- og kapitalmarked

Part of the **Statistiske efterretninger** series, it is published approximately 18–20 times a year and has data on money and credit. Included are sections on banks, mortgages, bond issues, insurance and pension funds.

Danmarks Nationalbank Monetary Review

A quarterly report with text and statistics on the money, financial and banking sectors in Denmark. The report is available in English.

Facts about Danish Bankers Association

The above is an annual English language pocket-book with brief statistics on banking. More detailed statistics are available from **Danske Pengeinstitutters Forening**, the Danish Bankers Association.

Arsberetning

An annual report from **Realkreditradet**, the Council of Danish Mortgage Credit Institutions. Statistics on mortgages are included and there is an English synopsis of the report.

Transportation

Samfoerdsel og turisme

Part of the **Statistiske efterretninger** series, this publication covers transport and tourism with data on vehicle registrations, vehicle stock, private car sales, goods transport by road and sea, holidays, travel, sales of package tours, nights spent at hotels, camp sites, travellers' currency, etc.

Vejtransporten i Tal og Tekst
Statistik over registrering af nye Automobiler i Denmark

Two regular publications from the **Automobil Importorernes Sammenslutning**. The first is an annual containing detailed current and historical statistics on motor vehicles in Denmark plus information on related areas such as traffic, accidents and road expenditure. The second title is published monthly with details of new registrations of vehicles by make, model broken down by local area. A pocket-book of basic data, **Bilismen i Danmark**, is also published annually.

Skibsfartsberetning

An annual report from **Danmarks Rederiforening** covering the shipping fleet, tonnage, freight and fuel prices. Various statistical tables accompany a commentary on the sector. An English language booklet, **Danish Shipping in 199–**, is also published at regular intervals with basic data.

Public sector

Statistik

The Electricity Supply in Denmark

Two titles from **Danske Elvaerkers Forening**. The first is a general compilation of statistics on the electricity supply sector and an English summary and translations of table headings is available. The second title provides basic data, in English, on the sector.

Advertising statistics

Advertising expenditure statistics, by product and media type, are available through various services from two main sources, **Brogger & Nygart/IM** and **AGB Gallup**.

6 FINLAND

Business statistics

INTRODUCTION

The **Central Statistical Office of Finland** or **Statistikcentralen (CSO)** is an independent government agency set up under the Central Statistical Office Act of 1970. The **CSO** is responsible to the Ministry of Finance but, as an independent body, the **CSO** decides on the publication of its results and on the contents of its publications. The **CSO** compiles 65 per cent of official statistics and the rest are produced by other government departments and agencies although the results are still usually published by the **CSO**.

Important departments producing statistics include the **Board of Customs (Tullihallitus), Ministry of Trade and Industry (Kauppa- ja Teollisuusministerio)** and the **Ministry of Finance (Valtiovarainministerio)**. A Statistics Council monitors the extent to which the **CSO** satisfies the needs of society for information and it can initiate changes.

The **CSO** is based in Helsinki at:

Central Statistical Office
CSO
PO Box 504
SF-00101
Helsinki
Finland

Virtually all official publications have English translations of contents and table headings plus a brief description of the publication. A publications catalogue, **Government Statistics**, is published annually. Trade association data complements the official statistics and, as with the central government information, many of the titles have English translations of headings and contents.

GENERAL STATISTICAL TITLES

Compilations

The statistical yearbook, **Suomen tilastollinen vuosikir ja**, has general statistics on Finland plus an international section. An alphabetical subject index and the contents page has English and Finnish headings and all tables have English headings. English translations are also given in **Tilastokatsauksia, neljannesvuosijulkaisu**, a quarterly bulletin of statistics with monthly and quarterly series for the key subject areas. A monthly supplement to this publication is **Tilastokatsauksia, kuukausikatsaus**. This is a four-page pamphlet updating the most important figures. **Finland in Figures** is an annual English language pocket-book with basic data.

Regular data on important subject areas is published through a series of **Tilastoteidotukset**, or statistical reports. There are 14 separate series of these reports and each series covers an important subject area. The number of reports published per year varies from one subject to another. Subject areas which will be described in more detail in later sections of this chapter include **Teollisuus** (industry), **Yritykset** (enterprises), **Kauppa** (trade) and **Rahoitus** (financial statistics). Other subject areas covered are population, housing, living conditions, energy, prices, public economy, agriculture and forestry, wages, income and consumption, labour market.

Economic data

The annual **Economic Survey** is an English language publication translated from the appendix to the Government's budget proposals.

The **Union Bank of Finland** publishes **Unitas Economic Quarterly Review** with articles on economic trends and a statistical appendix. An English language version is available.

Demographic and social statistics

Vaestolaskenat, asunto- ja elinkeinotutkimus is a series of reports from the population and housing census while various reports on population are published in the statistical report series **Vaesto**.

Sector data

General industrial statistics

Annual statistics on industrial activity and production and monthly indices are produced, based on the **Toimialaluokitus Naringsgrensindelningen** or the

Standard Industrial Classification (SIC). Detailed figures on the output of specific commodities are also published, based on the international HS classification.

Up until the late 1980s, the national **SIC** classification closely followed the international **ISIC** classification but the latest revision of the **SIC** in 1988 has reduced the links with **ISIC**. The **SIC** has 19 main classes and each of these is given a letter code. These are listed in Table 6.1. There are 68 2-digit classes and, within each of these, further 3-digit and 4-digit breakdowns. For example:

D	Manufacturing
26	Electrical products & instruments
263	Electrical machinery & equipment & domestic appliance manufacturing
2633	Domestic appliance manufacturing

A	Agriculture, fishing & trapping
B	Forestry & logging
C	Mining & quarrying
D	Manufacturing
E	Energy & water supply
F	Construction
G	Wholesale & retail trades
H	Hotels & restaurants
I	Transport
J	Communications
K	Finance & insurance
L	Real estate, cleaning & rental services
M	Technical & business services
N	Public administration & defence
O	Education & research
P	Health & social welfare services
R	Recreation & cultural services
S	Organisations & religious activities
T	Other services

Table 6.1 **Main classes of the Finnish SIC**

The 2-digit breakdown in the manufacturing sector is shown in Table 6.2.

11	Food, drink & tobacco
12	Textiles
13	Wearing apparel, leather goods & footwear
14	Wood & wood products
15	Pulp, paper & paper products
16	Publishing & printing
17	Furniture manufacturers
18	Chemicals & chemical products
19	Petroleum, coal products & nuclear fuel
21	Rubber & plastics products
22	Glass, glazing & stone products
23	Basic metals

Table 6.2 **Class D – Manufacturing**

24	Fabricated metal products
25	Machinery & equipment
26	Electrical products & instruments
27	Transport equipment
29	Other manufacturing

Table 6.2 Class D – Manufacturing (*cont.*)

In the annual industrial inquiry, all units with five employees or more are surveyed and, in selected sectors such as publishing, electricity, lighting and power, all units are surveyed. The survey claims to cover approximately 99 per cent of gross output and 97 per cent of manufacturing employment.

Detailed commodity import and export data is based mainly on the **HS** classification although data based on the **SITC** classification is also published.

PUBLICATIONS PRODUCED BY NATIONAL ORGANISATIONS

General industry and trade

Teollisuuden vuosikirja

This yearbook of industrial statistics is published annually in two volumes. Volume 1 includes data on industrial structure and activity with information on mining, quarrying, manufacturing, energy and water supply. Summary data is followed by statistics by branch of industry and by provinces and municipalities. Statistical tables cover the number of establishments, turnover, personnel, hours, salaries, social costs, acquisition costs of inputs, acquisition of fixed capital, value of stocks, energy consumption and production and the shipments of commodities down to the 4-digit level of the SIC. The results of the 1988 industrial inquiry were published in August 1990.

Volume 2 has details of shipments of individual commodities, by value and volume, according to the **HS** classification. The section relating to domestic appliances is shown in Table 6.3.

Teollisuustuotannon volyymi – indeksi

A monthly pamphlet with indices of industrial production. Part of the **Tilastotiedotukset** statistical reports series.

Ulkomaankauppa (Foreign Trade)

There are annual and monthly publications with the same general title. The annual publication has three volumes. Volume 1 has detailed commodity imports and exports arranged by the HS classification and broken down by major trading partners. Volume 2 covers various specific topics including

TUOTTEIDEN TOIMITUKSET V. 1988 nimike/position 84.18
LEVERANSER AV PRODUKTER ÅR 1988
SHIPMENTS OF GOODS PRODUCED 1988

Nimike Position Heading	Tavaralaji Varuslag Description of goods	Mittayksikkö Måttenhet Unit	Määrä Mängd Quantity	Arvo Värde Value 1000 mk
84.18 0000	Jääkaapit, pakastimet ja muut jäähdytys- tai jäädytyslaitteet ja -laitteistot, sähköllä toimivat ja muut; lämpöpumput, muut kuin nimik-keen 84.15 ilmastointilaitteet – Kylskåp, fry-sar och annan kyl-eller trysutrustning, elektriska och andra; värme pumpar, andra äan luftkonditioneringsapparater e nligt position 84.15			
	jääkaappi-pakastin-yhdistelmät, joissa on enrilliset ovet – kombinerade kyl- och frys-skåp med separata dörrar			
1010	-jääkaappi-pakastin-yhdistelmät, joissa on erilliset koneistot (kompressorit) jääkaa-pille ja pakastimelle – kombinerade kyl- och frysskåp med separata kompressorer för kyl-skåp och frtsskåp	kpl-st	49620	100757
1090	-muut – andra	kpl-st		24500
	taloustyyppiset jääkaapit – kylskåp av hus-hållstyp			
	-kompressorijääkaapit – kompressionskylskåp			
2110	--vetoisuus enintään 200 1 – med en rymd av högst 200 1	kpl-st	55830	57000
2190	--muut – andra	kpl-st	34649	73473
2200	-absorptiojääkaapit, sähköllä toimivat – ab-sorptionskylskåp, elektriska	kpl-st		14087
2900	-muut – andra	kpl-st		
	säiliöpakastimet, vetoisuus enintään 800 1 - frysboxar med en rymd av högst 800 1			
3010	-vetoisuus yli 300 1 – med en rymd av mer än 300 1	kpl-st		
3090	-muut – andra	kpl-st		
	kaappipakastimet, vetoisuus enintään 900 1 - frysskåp med enrymd av högst 900 1			
4010	-vetoisuus yli 200 1 – med en rymd av mer än 200 1	kpl-st	12246	31964
4090	-muut – andra	kpl-st	15966	17982
5000	tiskit, kaapit, altaat, laskot ja niiden kal-taiset kylmä- tai pakastekalusteet – diskar, skåp, montrar och liknande frys- eller kylut-rustning	kpl-st	37571	266127
	muut jäähdytys- tai jäädytyslaitteet ja -laitteistot; lämpöpumput – annan kyl- eller frysutrustning; värmepumpar			
6100	-kompressorityyppiset yksiköt, joiden lauhdut-timet ovat lämmönvaihtimia – enheter av kom-pressionstyp, vilkas kondensatorer är värme-växlare	kpl-st	6792	54467
6900	-muut – andra	kpl-st	12149	13648
	osat -delar			
9100	-huonekalut, jotka ovat tarkoitetut jäähdytys- tai jäädytyslaitteita varten – möbler konst-ruerade för kyl- eller frysutrustning	kpl- st		13665
9900	-muut – andra	kpl-st		44754
	YHT.-SUMMA			**712424**

Table 6.3 Finnish production statistics – extracts of entries for electrical equipment

special trade, transportation, traffic, taxes and trade concentration. Volume 3 covers annual imports and exports, by country, broken down by **SITC** chapters.

A monthly publication on external trade has imports and exports, by **HS** groups and sub-headings, imports and exports, by **SITC** sections and divisions and imports and exports, by country, regions and industries. Another monthly, **Ulkomaankauppa, Kuukausikatsaus** has brief details of general trends in external trade.

Construction

Talonrakennustilasto
An annual volume of construction statistics.

Asuntotuotanto
An annual volume concentrating on the construction of dwellings.

Construction statistics are also published by the building association, **Rakennusmestarien Keskusliitto ry**.

Food and drink

Facts about the Finnish Food Industry
An English language pamphlet from the food and drink federation, **Elintaruiketeollis uusliitto (ETL)**. The federation also publishes an annual report with statistics.

Alkoholitilastollinen vuosikirja
The alcohol statistical yearbook from the Finnish State Alcohol Co, **Oy Alko Ab**. There are English translations and the tables include data on production, consumption, sales, imports, exports, employment and the detrimental effects of alcohol. Historical figures are included.

Chemicals and chemical products

Statistical Yearbook
Published annually, with English translations, by the chemical industries association, **Kemian Keskusliitto (KKL)**.

Annual Report
An annual report, with an English summary, from the **Finnish Petroleum Federation**. A statistical section has data on the petroleum economy, prices, taxation, vehicle traffic and petrol stations.

Textiles and clothing

Tekstilindustrins arsbok
A statistical yearbook from the association of Finnish textile industries, **Tekstiiliteolisuusliitto**. An English commentary is included.

Electrical and mechanical engineering

Finnish Metal and Engineering Industry
Published annually, in English and Finnish, by **FIMET**, the Federation of Finnish Metal, Engineering and Electrotechnical Industries. Detailed statistics, usually for the latest three or five years, provide information on production, foreign trade, industrial structure, employment, investment, prices and R&D. There are also some international comparisons. Based on a combination of official statistics and the federation's own data.

Services – general

The employers' federation for the services industries, **Liiketyonantajain Keskusliitto (LTK)** produces various statistics. The association encompasses hotels and catering, shops, banks and other financial services.

Retailing and distribution

Tukku- ja vahittaiskaupan yritystilasto
An annual report on enterprises in the wholesaling and retailing sectors which is part of the **Tilastotiedotukset** statistical report series.

Wholesale and Retail Trade in Finland
An occasional English language review from the central organisation for the wholesale and retail trade, **Kaupan Keskusualiokunta (KAUKEVA)**. More detailed statistics are available in Finnish.

Financial services

Pankit
A monthly report in the **Tilastotiedotukset** statistical report series with data on banking, including the Bank of Finland, commercial banks, savings banks, foreign owned banks, mortgage banks, etc.

Finnish Banking System
A regular report, in English, from **Suomen Pankkiyhdistys**, the commercial banking organisation. The organisation also publishes an annual report.

Osuuspankkijarjeston Taloudellinen Katsass

A quarterly economic survey, with English summaries, of the co-operative banking sector in Finland. Published by **Osuuspankkien Keskusliitto (OKL)**.

Finnish Insurance Review

A quarterly publication, with English translations, from the **Suomen Vakuutusyhtioiden Keskusliitto**. Other general reports are also published.

Leisure and tourism

Matkailun kehityu: matkailualan tilastojulkaisu

Annual tourist statistics from the Finnish Tourist Board. The Board also publishes a monthly review.

Transportation

Liikenteen yritystilasto

Annual data on enterprises in the transport and communications sectors published as part of the **Tilastotiedotukset** statistical report series.

Rekisteriin merkityt uudet ajoneuvot 199–

Two reports with monthly and annual registrations of new motor vehicles published in the **Tilastotiedotukset** statistical report series.

Auto ja tie

Commentary and statistics, with English translations, on roads, traffic and vehicle registrations plus related data on accidents, road construction, taxes and fuels. Some comparative international data is also given. Published by **Suomen Tieyhdistys**, the Finnish Road Federation.

Suomen Satamaliiton Tilastot

Statistics on ports, arrivals, traffic, passengers, cargo, etc. published annually by **Suomen Satamaliitoo**.

Autoilijan Kalenteri

Annual statistics from the **Suomen Kuorma-Autoliitto (KAL)** covering road haulage, road transport, vehicles and roads.

7 FRANCE
Business statistics

INTRODUCTION

A considerable amount of resources are devoted to government statistical activities in France and the result is one of the best national statistical services in Europe. Virtually all the statistics are only published in French and the data produced is relatively up-to-date and accurate. Unlike the official statistics in most other European countries, there is a strong emphasis on data analysis and intepretation and the visual presentation of the data. A number of publications have commentaries accompanying and interpreting the statistics and tables are often presented in graph or chart form as well as the standard statistical tables with columns of data.

The headquarters of the official statistical office are based in Paris but every French region also has its own statistical information point. These official statistics are supported by a range of other statistics from trade associations, journals, market research agencies, chambers of commerce and local development agencies. There is also co-operation between official and non-official producers with the annual industrial statistics based on a combination of official and trade association data.

The main publisher of statistics is the national statistical office, **Institut National de la Statistique et des Etudes Economiques**, usually referred to as **INSEE**, based in Paris:

INSEE
18 boulevard Adolphe Pinard
F-75675 Paris Cedex 14
France

An annual publications catalogue with prices, **Catalogue INSEE**, is available from the above office. **INSEE** also has a library of national and international statistics open to the general public. Most of the official publications and services come from **INSEE** but there are exceptions including industry statistics, trade statistics, construction data and transport statistics.

Since 1986, industry statistics have been the responsibility of **Le Service des Statistiques industrielles** or **SESSI** and **SESSI's** offices in Paris house another good collection of official and non-official statistics which is open to the public. From June 1991, import and export data has been published by the new **Ministere de l'Industrie et du Commerce Exterieur**. Construction statistics are the responsibility of the **Sous-direction des Actions Statistiques (SAS)** while transport data is covered by the **Observatoire Economique et Statistique des Transports (OEST)** and both of these units are in the **Ministere de l'Equipement, du Logement, des Transports et de la Mer**:

SESSI
85 boulevard du Montparnasse
F-75270 Paris Cedex 06
France

Ministere de l'Industrie et du Commerce Exterieur
161 chemin de Lestang
F-31057 Toulouse Cedex
France

SAS
Ministere de l'Equipement, du Logement, des Transports et de la Mer
29–31 quai Voltaire
F-75344 Paris
France

OEST
55–57 rue Brillat Savarin
F-75013 Paris
France

France also has a network of official statistical offices in each of its 22 regions, reflecting the administrative importance of these regions and the increasing emphasis on the decentralisation of economic activity away from the powerful Paris centre. These regional 'economic observatories', as they are known, collect and publish economic data on their specific areas and provide an access point to the range of **INSEE** publications and other services. Brief details of these regional offices are given in Table 7.1 and full addresses are included in the organisation index. **INSEE** branches are also located overseas in the French territories of Antilles-Guyane, Guadeloupe, Guyane, Martinique and Reunion.

National statistical agencies:

INSEE
SESSI

Key departments:

Ministere de l'Industrie et du Commerce Exterieur Ministere de l'Equipement du
Logement, des Transports et de la Mer (SAS and OEST)

Regional economic observatories:

Region	Town
Alsace	Strasbourg
Aquitaine	Bordeaux
Auvergne	Chamalieres
Bourgogne	Dijon
Brittany	Rennes
Centre	Orleans
Champagne-Ardenne	Reims
Corsica	Ajaccio
Franche-Comte	Besancon
Languedoc-Roussillon	Montpellier
Limousin	Limoges
Lorraine	Nancy
Midi-Pyrenees	Toulouse
Nord-Pas-de-Calais	Lille
Basse Normandie	Caen
Haute-Normandie	Rouen
Ile-de-France	Paris
Pays de la Loire	Nantes
Picardie	Amiens
Poitou-Charentes	Poitiers
Provence-Alpes-Cote d'Azur	Marseille
Rhone-Alpes	Lyon

Table 7.1 France – The organisation of official statistics.

On-line services

In addition to hard copy publications, **INSEE** offers an on-line service and can
provide disc copies or tapes of most of the major statistical series. The **INSEE**
on-line databases are available on the host system GSI-ECO through one
subscription and the databases are :

Banque de Donnees Macroeconomique (BDM)

Comprising 700,000 economic time series on France and other countries. Some
data from 1945 onwards.

Batiment

Statistics on housing construction and construction costs. Data from 1959 onwards.

CJIND

Monthly data on specific industrial products plus forecasts.

CJTRES

Earnings performance figures for 4,000 industrial companies plus aggregated data for 90 industrial sectors. The file begins in 1967 and is updated twice a year.

CONSO

Comprising 6,800 annual time series on the household consumption of specific goods and services. Data from 1959 onwards.

INDUS/IPI

Statistics on industrial sectors updated monthly. Data from 1975 onwards. IPI is a database of industrial production indices.

Prix 295

Consumer price indices for 295 goods and services updated monthly. Data from 1949 onwards.

Systeme Informatique pour la Conjoncture (SIC)

Comprising 7,000 monthly, quarterly and annual time series on specific economic indicators. Data from 1960 onwards. Updated monthly.

Tendances de la Conjoncture, Cahier 1
Tendances de la Conjoncture, Cahier 2

File 1 has 600 monthly and quarterly time series on economic trends from 1973 onwards. File 2 concentrates on quarterly national accounts data from 1973 onwards.

GENERAL STATISTICAL TITLES

Compilations

The basic starting point for French statistics is the **Annuaire statistique de la France**, an annual compilation of the main social, economic and demographic indicators. A list of the main statistical titles is also included at the back of the annual volume. Some of the statistics in this annual compilation are updated in the monthly, **Bulletin mensuel de statistique. La France et ses regions** is an annual compilation of regional data.

Brief details of and commentary on the key statistical surveys and topics are included in **INSEE premiere**, a series of four-page pamphlets published approximately 60 times per year. The basic results of key statistical surveys are published relatively quickly in individual pamphlets and the series acts as a good monitor of new surveys. **INSEE premiere** often publishes general results before the detailed results of a survey appear at a later date. For example, the preliminary results of the 1990 population census appeared in an **INSEE premiere** issue in June 1990 and basic results of the household consumption survey for 1991 were published in a May 1991 issue.

Informations rapides is a series of 300 pamphlets per year presenting the most up-to-date data on particular subjects. **INSEE Resultats** are a series of reports, appearing at regular intervals throughout the year, publishing the detailed results of **INSEE** surveys. The reports are published in five subject themes – economy, the productive system, demography and society, consumption and way of life, employment and income – and subscriptions are available for individual themes or for the complete set of reports.

Economic data

Tableaux de l'economie francaise includes an annual commentary and statistics on French economic trends, presented in an easily understandable form.

Regular economic statistics and analysis are covered by **Tendances de la conjoncture**, published quarterly in two volumes with monthly supplements and notes. Volume 1 has monthly data on 600 series for the latest 10 years and Volume 2 has quarterly data, in tables and graphs, on 600 series for the last 20 years. An on-line version is also available and this, along with other **INSEE** economic databases, is briefly described in the introductory section.

Economie et statistique, published 11 times a year, gives a regular analysis of current economic and social trends and **Note de conjoncture**, published five times a year, reviews economic trends and prospects. **La conjoncture in France**, published twice a year, is an English language version with summary data from the above publication.

The **Groupe d'Analyse Macroeconomique Applique (GAMA)** produces an on-line database of historical economic data and five-year forecasts. The database, **PROTEE**, is updated monthly and is available from **GAMA** along with **Household Consumption Nap 600,** a database covering the consumption of 200 products.

Bulletin trimestriel, Statistiques trimestriel and Statistiques mensuelles are three publications from the **Banque de France**. The first is a quarterly bulletin with commentary and statistics on economic trends and the financial sector, the second is a quarterly statistical bulletin on the same sectors while the third title gives monthly data.

The **Chambre de Commerce et d'Industrie de Paris** also has a series of regular reports on economic and business trends including the monthlies **La**

Lettre Mensuelle de Conjoncture and Les Indicateurs du Centre d'Observation Economique.

Demographic and social statistics

Recensement de la population 1990 is the latest population census with the results being published in various volumes from the end of 1990 onwards. General social statistics are published annually in **Donnees sociales**.

Sector data

General industrial statistics

Official statistics on industrial activity and products are based on the French classification of activities known as the **NAP** classification. **NAP** is the 'official nomenclature of activities and products' and it classifies industry, utilities, mining, commerce and services. General sections of **NAP** are given a 2-digit number code and specific sectors are allocated 4-digit codes within these sections. For example, **NAP** section 30 covers household machinery and equipment and, within this section, 4-digit categories are:

3001   Refrigerators, clothes washing machines and dishwashers
3002   Cookers, water heaters and non-electric heaters
3003   Other household equipment

NAP sections 04 to 54 cover industrial activity, mining and utilities and these provide the framework for the industrial statistics published by **SESSI**. These sections are listed in Table 7.2. Unfortunately, the **NAP** headings are not yet comparable with the headings used in the **NACE** classification of industry developed by the EC.

NAP code	Sector
04	Solid fuels, minerals & coke products
05	Petroleum & natural gas
06	Electricity
07	Gas
08	Water & heating
09	Iron ores
10	Iron & steel
11	Primary products of steel
12	Non-ferrous minerals
13	Non-ferrous metals & semi-products
14	Miscellaneous minerals
15	Construction materials & ceramics
16	Glass
17	Basic chemicals
18	Chemical products

Table 7.2 NAP classification – Industrial activities

19	Pharmaceuticals
20	Foundries
21	Metal working
22	Agricultural machinery
23	Machine tools
24	Industrial equipment
25	Handling equipment, mining equipment, civil engineering equipment, etc.
27	Office machinery & data processing equipment
28	Electrical machinery
29	Electronic machinery
30	Household machinery & equipment
31	Motor vehicles & other transport equipment (for terrestial vehicles)
32	Shipbuilding
33	Aircraft & equipment
34	Precision instruments & machinery
35	Meat
36	Dairy products
37	Tinned & canned foods
39	Grain & cereals
40	Miscellaneous food products
41	Soft drinks & alcoholic drinks
42	Tobacco
43	Artificial & synthetic fibres & textiles
44	Textiles
45	Leather & articles of leather
46	Footwear
47	Clothing
48	Mechanical working of wood
49	Furniture
50	Paper & board
51	Publishing, printing products, etc
52	Tyres & other rubber products
53	Working of micellaneous materials
54	Miscellaneous industries

Table 7.2 NAP classification – Industrial activities (*cont.*)

Information on specific products is based on the **Nodep** classification, 'detailed official nomenclature of products'. **Nodep** is a 6-digit classification derived from **NAP** covering approximately 10,000 headings. For example, the **Nodep** heading 300101 covers domestic refrigerators and is a detailed product heading within the 4-digit **NAP** code 3001 noted above. **Nodep** is also linked to the third classification, **NAPCE**, 'Nomenclature d'Activities et de Produits pour le Commerce Exterieur', which is used as the basis for import and export data.

A series of annual, monthly and quarterly publications from **SESSI** provide data on industrial structure and characteristics and the production, deliveries, invoiced value and imports and exports of specific products. The information in most of these publications is based on a combination of figures from **SESSI** surveys and data supplied by 70 trade associations and specialised industry bodies. Approximately 40 per cent of industrial activities are covered by official surveys but the majority are covered by non-official surveys and a list of the associations supplying data for official publications is given in Table 7.3.

France is unique in Europe in operating this dual system of statistical collection for its official industrial statistics and further details of the associations involved are given in the **Annuaire de statistique industrielle**, one of the general sources listed below. Major trade association publishers of statistics in their own right are described in the individual sector sections in this chapter.

One advantage resulting from this dual approach is that official and non-official industry statistics are usually comparable as they use the same classification scheme, product headings and units of measurement. A disadvantage stems from the fact that some trade associations are not as up-to-date or as comprehensive in their collecting procedures as others and this creates gaps in the published tables.

Association d'etudes et de statistiques pour l'industrie textile (ESITEX)
Association des constructeurs de composants et d'equipements laitiers (ACCEL)
Association francaise des industries de la robinetterie (AFIR)
Bureau de statistiques du commerce des produits siderurgiques
Bureau intersyndical des constructeurs et reparateurs de materiel ferroviaire
Chambre francaise de l'horlogerie et des microtechniques
Chambre syndicale de la siderurgie francaise
Chambre syndicale des fabricants de tubes d'acier (CSFTA)
Chambre syndicale des mines de fer de France
Chambre syndicale nationale de la mecanique de haute precision
Comite central de la laine et des fibres associees
Comite de l'importation charbonniere (CIC)
Comite national du chauffage urbain (CNCU)
Confederation des industries ceramiques de France
Confederation des producteurs de papiers, cartons et celluloses (COPACEL)
Confederation generale des filateurs et tisseurs de lin Conseil national du cuir
Federation de l'ennoblissement textile
Federation francaise de l'imprimerie et des industries graphiques (FFIG)
Federation des chambres syndicales des minerais et des metaux non ferreux (FMMNF)
Federation des fabricants de tuiles et de briques de France
Federation des industries electriques et electroniques (FIEE)
Federation des industries nautiques
Federation francaise de la bijouterie, joaillerie, orfevrerie, du cadeau, des diamants, pierres et perles et activites qui s'y rattachent (FFBJOC)
Federation francaise de la brosserie
Federation francaise de l'industrie de la maille et de la bonneterie
Federation francaise des industries du sport et des loisirs (FIFAS)
Federation francaise du cartonnage
Federation nationale de l'industrie des engrais (FNIE)
Federation nationale des dentelles, tulles, broderies, guipures et passementeries
Federation nationale des industries du jouet
Federation nationale des transformateurs de papier (FNTP)
Gaz de France (GDF)

Table 7.3 Associations supplying data for official publications

Groupement des industries diverses du textile (GID)
Groupement des industries francaises de l'optique (GIFO)
MECASTAT
Service interprofessionel de l'equipement lourd (SIEL)
Service intersyndical d'enquetes professionnelles et de statistiques de l'automobile, du cycle et du motocycle (SIEPAC)
Service intersyndical de statistique d'equipements mecaniques (SISTEM)
Syndicat de la machine-outil, de l'assemblage et de la productique associee (SYMAP)
Syndicat de la mesure, du controle et de la regulation automatique (SYMECORA)
Syndicat des constructeurs de compresseurs
Syndicat des constructeurs de machines pour l'alimentation (SYMA)
Syndicat des constructeurs de materiels pour le genie chimique (SYMAGEC)
Syndicat des constructeurs de materiels pour mines et travaux souterrains (SMMS)
Syndicat des constructeurs de moteurs a combustion interne
Syndicat des constructeurs de pompes (SCP)
Syndicat des constructeurs de turbines hydrauliques, conduites forcees et vannes
Syndicat des constructeurs francais de materiel pour le caoutchouc et les matieres plastiques (SYMACAP)
Syndicat des fabricants d'appareils de production d'eau chaude par le gaz (SAPEC)
Syndicat des fabricants d'engrenages et constructeurs d'organes de transmission (SYNECOT)
Syndicat du pesage et du comptage
Syndicat francais des textiles artificiels et synthetiques
Syndicat general de la filterie francaise
Syndicat general des fabricants de ficelles, cordages, filets, sacs et tissus a usage industriel (FILCORSAC)
Syndicat general des fabricants d'outillage mecanique
Syndicat general des fondeurs de France et industries connexes (SGFFIC)
Syndicat general des constructeurs de tracteurs et machines agricoles (SYGMA)
Syndicat national de la chaudronnerie, de la tolere et de la tuyauterie industrielle (SNCT)
Syndicat national de l'edition
Syndicat national de l'equipement des grandes cuisines (SYNEG)
Syndicat national des chaines mecaniques (SNCM)
Syndicat national des constructeurs de materiel de chauffage central (CMC)
Syndicat national des entreprises du froid, d'equipement de cuisines professionnelles et du conditionnement de l'air (SNEFCCA)
Syndicat national des fabricants de ciments et de chaux
Syndicat national des fabricants de materiels de soudage
Syndicat national des industries d'equipements (MTPS)
Syndicat national des industries et commerces de la recuperation des ferrailles
Union des constructeurs de materiel textile de France
Union des fabricants francais d'equipements pour boulangerie-patisserie, biscuiterie, biscotterie, glacerie- chocolotarie (UFFEB)
Union des syndicats de la premiere transformation de l'acier (USTRA)
Union intersyndicale des constructeurs de materiel aeraulique, thermique et frigorifique (UNICLIMA)
Union intersyndicale pour les statistiques de la manutention
Union nationale des industries de carrieres et materiaux de construction (UNICEM)
Union nationale des industries de machines pour chaussures, tanneries et maroquinerie (UMCTM)
Union nationale des industries de transmissions oleohydrauliques et pneumatiques (UNITOP)

Table 7.3 Associations supplying data for official publications (*cont.*)

Where official statisticians are collecting industrial data, the information is usually obtained from questionnaires sent to enterprises and establishments. Questionnaires are sent to relevant organisations, the details of which are held on a regularly updated database which is also available to outside users. **SIRENE** is a database of organisations, including companies, professional bodies and local authorities and it is available from **INSEE** on fiche, magnetic tape, on-line or through the French telecommunications network, Minitel. **INSEE** on-line databases covering industrial sectors are listed in the introductory section to this chapter on page 80.

PUBLICATIONS PRODUCED BY NATIONAL ORGANISATIONS

General industry and trade

La situation de l'industrie

Every year, various government statistical departments co-operate in the **Enquete annuelle d'enterprise (EAE)**. Individual surveys cover industry, agriculture, transport, construction, internal trade and services and the results of the industry survey are published in **Le situation de l'industrie**.

The published results provide structural and performance data for industry as a whole and for 250 specific sectors (down to the 4-digit level of **NAP**) with statistics on the number of enterprises, employment, turnover, production, exports, salaries, value added, and investment. Additional information covers selected performance ratios, investment by type of investment, levels of concentration and diversification in the sector, the principal manufacturing regions and the names of the top companies.

The survey is based on questionnaires sent to all enterprises employing 10 or more people although the level of information requested varies: enterprises employing 100 or more are sent a detailed questionnaire, those employing between 20 and 99 are asked to complete a simplified questionnaire and those employing 10 to 19 only have to respond to two basic questions on numbers employed and turnover.

The survey claims to cover more than 80 per cent of all manufacturing turnover although the usefulness of the results varies from sector to sector. In sectors with a large number of small companies, such as furniture and certain clothing sectors, only the minimum amount of data is obtained from a large percentage of companies in the sector because these companies employ fewer than 20 people. Where enterprises fail to respond, a manual estimate is included in the results for enterprises which are considered to be of strategic importance to a particular sector and an automatic estimate is made for other enterprises. In

NAP 30. ÉQUIPMENT MÉNAGER

A. VIII. FACTURATIONS, IMPORTATIONS ET EXPORTATIONS EN 1988
Nomenclature détaillée de produits (NODEP)

Unité: million de francs

Numéro de poste	Libellé	Facturations	1988 Importations	1988 Exportations
	Produits			
300101	Réfrigérateurs domestiques	⎱ 966	1.822	159
300102	Congélateurs-conservateurs domestiques	⎰	761	99
300103	Machines à laver le linge domestiques	⎱ 3.151	2.002	898
300104	Lave-vaisselle domestiques	⎰	909	131
300201	Cuisinières, fours et tables de cuisson domestiques à gaz	...	389	236
300202	Chauffe-eau, chauffe-bain et appareils de chauffage domestiques non électriques.	...	468	591
300203	Chaudières de type mural	...	55	970
300301	Cuisinières, fours et tables de cuisson domestiques électriques	3.226	1.640	1.148
300302	Chauffe-eau et chauffe-bain électriques	739	273	112
300303	Radiateurs électriques	917	375	170
300304	Fers à repasser et machines à repasser domestiques	682	261	396
300305	Appareils électriques domestiques d'hygiène et de soins esthétiques	71	519	63
300306	Aspirateurs de poussière et cireuses domestiques	1.193	899	693
300307	Hottes aspirantes et ventilateurs domestiques	176	346	69
300308	Appareils électromécaniques domestiques pout la cuisine	1.458	509	1.176
300309	Appareils de cuisson électriques domestiques divers	1.725	486	347
300310	Petits appareils électriques électrothermiques divers	744	247	629
300311	Machines à coudre et à tricoter domestiques	⎱ 127	315	88
300312	Appareils professionnels pour la coiffure et l'hygiène	⎰	71	34

Table 7.4 French production statistics – entries for household equipment

1989, the total survey results covered 37,318 enterprises and over a third of these – 12,842 – employed fewer than 20 people. Detailed information was available for 4,832 large companies and modified information for the remaining 17,674 organisations.

The results of the survey are published in three sets of publications. The final data for the survey is collected at the end of the calendar year and, just six months later around June or July, the first results are published in **La situation de l'industrie 199–: Premiers resultats par secteur d'enterprise**. Brief details of enterprise numbers, turnover, employment, exports and selected ratios are given for total industry and specific sectors. In November, a second publication, **La situation de l'industrie 199–: Resultats semi-definitifs**, gives more detailed information on 40 key sectors. The final detailed results for 250 sectors are usually published just over a year after the survey takes place in a four volume publication, **La situation de l'industrie 199–: resultats definitifs** and the example page in Table 7.4 is taken from this publication.

Annuaire de statistique industrielle

This annual publication provides a general review of industrial activity and performance plus trends in key product areas with individual chapters covering each 2-digit category of **NAP**. Most of the industrial structure and performance data comes from the **EAE** described above while the product data is usually supplied by the relevant trade association. In each chapter, a general section provides data on the number of enterprises, total employment and employment by size of enterprise, investment, total imports and exports, turnover, value added and various ratios. There are also product tables in each chapter with figures on deliveries, imports and exports of key products. Table 7.4 is an example of the type of product data available from the chapter on household equipment. Other tables provide information on energy consumption, involvement of overseas companies and the principal export markets. A list of the largest enterprises, in terms of employment, is included in each chapter.

Inevitably, because of the need to collect and analyse data from various sources, the publication is not particularly up-to-date with the most recent figures referring to two years earlier and, in some cases, three years earlier. The volume published in 1990, for example, has figures up to 1988 or, in some cases, up to 1987. Basic information on the structure of each industry sector is given for the latest six years and product data covers the latest seven years. Other tables usually only cover the latest year available.

Les chiffres cles de l'industrie

An annual publication with summary data on French industrial trends in tables and graphs. Based largely on extracts from the two publications noted above.

Bulletin mensuel de statistique industrielle
A monthly statistical bulletin with basic data on the production, invoiced value and deliveries of 700 products.

Resultats mensuels des enquetes de branche
Resultats trimestriels des enquetes de branche
A series of monthly and quarterly publications, with specific titles on selected sectors, provide relatively up-to-date information on key sectors and products. Each title includes data on areas such as product deliveries, invoiced value, exports and stocks. The monthly publications present the information in index form for a selection of products while quarterly titles provide actual figures on trends in the sector. A subscription to a quarterly title also includes a volume with annual data. The various titles available are:

Monthly series
Glass industry
Basic chemicals
Chemical products
Pharmaceuticals industry
Working of metals
Mechanical working of wood
Furniture
Rubber industry

Quarterly series
Glass industry
Basic chemicals
Chemical products
Working of metals
Manufacture of medical & surgical equipment
Clothing industry
Mechanical working of wood
Furniture industry
Manufacture of stationery products
Rubber industry
Plastic materials & products
Laboratory, photographic and cinematographic industry

Statistiques du commerce exterieur
Statistics on the imports and exports of specific products, based on customs forms filled out by individual exporters and importers, are published monthly, quarterly and annually. The annual publication, **Statistiques du commerce exterieur**, appears in four volumes in the spring after the year to which it relates and gives import and export totals, for specific products, arranged by the HS classification, by principal countries of origin and destination. **Resultats**

trimestriels gives similar data on a quarterly basis and monthly trade figures are also available on fiche or computer print-out from the **Ministere de l'Industrie et du Commerce Exterieur**.

Construction

The building and civil engineering sectors are covered by section 55 of **NAP** and the **Ministere de l'Equipement, du Logement, des Transports et de la Mer** carries out an annual survey of the building industry as part of the EAE. Information is collected on the number of enterprises, employment, working hours, salaries, output, investment, sites and the type of work undertaken, although some of this information is only collected from the larger organisations in the industry.

Annually, the survey aims to cover all enterprises with 20 or more employees but carries out sample surveys for enterprises employing between 6 and 19 people. In addition, every few years, a sample of enterprises employing between 1 and 5 people is also included in the survey. Detailed questionnaires are sent to organisations with 50 or more employees but only simplified questionnaires are sent to the remaining organisations. The importance of small firms in the sector, and the need to collect adequate data on these companies, is reflected in the number of organisations surveyed in 1986 when the smaller companies were included. In this year, 16,200 enterprises employing 6 or more people were covered but a sizeable number of companies employing fewer than 6 people, 9,500 in total, were also included.

Statistiques et Etudes Generales

Results from the annual survey appear in this volume published by the ministry noted above but the detailed results take some time to appear. For example, the results from the 1983 survey were published in 1986 and the 1986 results appeared in July 1988.

Statistiques de la Construction

Monthly figures on construction trends, including data on new buildings started and completed, also published by the above ministry.

Annuaire

A yearbook, with some statistics from the building confederation, **Groupement National des Entrepreneurs Constructeurs Immobiliers de la Federation Nationale du Batiment (GNECI-FNB)**. The federation also publishes a quarterly journal, **Echo du GNECI**.

Statistics relating to likely future trends in the industry, based on an opinion survey of construction companies, are published by the **Federation Nationale du Batiment**.

Food and drink

Les industries agricoles et alimentaires en 19– –

Published by **INSEE**, this is an annual publication on the food and agricultural sectors. Indices and actual figures provide indicators of trends by sector with data, in most tables, over a six-year period. The full results are usually published in the summer of the year after the survey but preliminary results are published in an **INSEE Premiere** title in the spring.

Various trade associations cover specific food and drink sectors but the association for the sector as a whole, **Association Nationale des Industries Agro-Alimentaires** makes few statistics available publicly. A useful source of general statistics on the food industry and market, however, is:

Les Chiffres Cles L'Industrie Alimentaire

Published by the private company, **Agra Alimentation**. This publication has only been established for a few years with the 3rd edition published in 1991. Using statistics collected from various official and non-official sources, it includes tables, with historical runs of data, on industry structure, production in specific sectors and of specific products, trade, consumption and prices.

Important publishers in specific areas include:

Rapport Economique

An annual report from the **Confederation Francaise de la Conserve (CFC)** with statistics on tinned and canned foods.

Rapport Statistique

Published by the **Federation des Industries et Commerces Utilisateurs des Basses Temperatures (FICUR), Rapport Statistique** is an annual statistical review of the frozen foods sector, with information on specific products, based on a combination of data from members' returns and official statistics. Data for the last two years is usually included.

Boissons de France

A monthly journal from the **Federation Nationale des Boissons**, the trade association for the drinks industry. A regular statistical section covers specific drinks and there are special features on particular products.

L'Economie Laitiere Principales Donnees

An annual statistical review from the **Federation Nationale de l'Industries Laitiere**. A review of the milk and dairy products sectors based on a compilation of data from official and non-official sources.

Annuaire de la Meuniere Francaise

An annual report on flour milling and bakeries from the **Association Nationale de la Meunierie Francaise**.

France's importance as a wine producing nation also means that there are numerous national and regional associations linked to this activity:

Cahier de Statistiques

The **Federation des Exportateurs de Vins et Spiriteux de France (FEVS)** publishes annual statistics on the wine and spirits trade in **Cahier de Statistiques** and more regular statistics are available to member companies.

The Bureau National Interprofessionel du Cognac

Has a series of annual and monthly titles on the growing, harvesting, sales and market trends for cognac liqueurs and wines and all the individual wine growing regions also have regional bodies producing statistics on their areas. Examples include the **Conseil Interprofessional des Vins d'Anjou et de Saumur, Comite Interprofessional des Vins des Cote-du-Rhone** and the **Federation des Syndicats des Grands Vins de Bordeaux**.

Chemicals and chemical products

Rapport Annuel: Exercice
Bulletin Trimestriel de Conjoncture

The above publications are produced by the trade association for the chemicals sector, **Union des Industries Chimiques**. The **Rapport Annuel** has commentary and statistics on the main sectors with data on structure, production, products, investment, employment and earnings. Some data is collected by the association itself but most is reproduced from government statistics. The **Bulletin Trimestriel de Conjoncture** is a quarterly title covering general economic trends in the chemical industry.

Annuaire

Includes annual statistics on specific chemical products from the **Chambre Syndicale Nationale du Commerce Chimique.**

L'Industrie Francaise du Petrole

An annual publication from the **Union des Chambres Syndicales de l'Industrie du Petrole (UCSIP).** Commentary and statistics on the petroleum industry with sections on France and international trends. Graphs, maps and tables cover production, reserves, consumption, trade, prices, etc.

Petrole 199–
Bulletin Mensuel
Le Marche Petrolier Francais en 199–

Three regular titles from the **Comite Professionel du Petrole**. The first has detailed statistics over the last four or five years for petroleum in France and worldwide. The second title has key monthly data on the French oil industry.

The third has annual data for the French oil market with tables for specific regions and local areas.

Enquete Annuelle d'Activite

From the **Federation Francaise de l'Industrie des Produits de Parfumerie, de Beaute et de Toilette,** an annual statistical survey with structural data and sales and market information for specific cosmetic, toiletries and perfume product areas.

Annuaire

Annual statistics on the pharmaceuticals sector from the trade association, **Syndicat National de l'Industrie Pharmaceutique (SNIP).**

Textiles and clothing

Fascicules Statistiques

An annual publication from the **Syndicat General de l'Industrie Cotonniere Francaise (SGICF)** with data on the production, consumption, sales, imports, exports and prices of cotton and textiles.

Industrie Lainiere Francais

The generic title for a series of individual reports on specific areas, such as production, labour, investment, prices, in the woollen sector published by the **Comite Centrale de la Laine et des Fibres Associees.**

Annuaire

Statistics on cotton products published annually by the **Federation Nationale des Fabricants-Transformateurs de l'Industrie Cotonniere.**

Chiffre-cles de l'Habillement

A regularly updated report on the French clothing sector from the **Union des Industries de l'Habillement (UIH),** the association of French clothing manufacturers.

Les Industries Francaises de Cuir en 199–

The **Conseil National du Cuir** publishes an annual review of the leather industry, with sections on footwear and gloves. Monthly **Monographies Statistiques** have index figures showing production and turnover trends.

Statistiques Production et Commerce Exterieur

The **Federation Nationale des Dentelles Tulles Broderies Guipures et Passementeries** publishes an annual statistical review with production, trade and turnover data for laces, silks and embroidery. All the data comes from a survey of members.

Engineering

Annuaire de la Mecanique

An annual statistical yearbook of the mechanical engineering sector from the **Federation des Industries Mecaniques et Transformatrices de Metaux (FIMTM)**. The association also publishes 20 issues a year of **Les Industries Mecaniques** with updated statistics.

Bulletin Statistique
la siderurgie francaise en 19– –

The **Chambre Syndicale de la Siderurgie Francaise (CSSF)** is responsible for regular iron and steel data through its main title, **Bulletin Statistique**, published monthly. An annual compilation is **la siderurgie francaise en 19– –** with figures for France and some international data. The organisation also publishes international production and external trade statistics.

Annuaire du Syndicat General des Fondeurs de France et Industries Connexes

An annual review of the foundry industry with some statistics. Published by the **Syndicat General des Fondeurs de France et Industries Connexes** which also publishes a monthly review with a statistical insert.

Le Fer Blanc en France et dans le Monde

Annual statistics on tin-plate and sheet metal from the **Chambre Syndicale des Producteurs de Fer-Blanc et de Fer-Noir.**

Reportoire Machines – Outils Francaises

An annual report on machine tools and other equipment from the **Syndicat de la Machine – Outil de l'Assemblage et de la Productique Associee (SYMAP).**

La Construction Navale

An annual volume from the **Chambre Syndicale des Constructeurs de Navires** with statistics on French and world shipbuilding and fleets. The French data comes from the association's own survey while the international data is based on Lloyd's Register of Shipping. A commentary accompanies the statistics which, in many tables, cover a number of years. Monthly data on shipbuilding activity is also collected.

Annuaire du GIFAS

An annual report on the aerospace industry, with statistics on output and sales, from the **Groupement des Industries Francaises Aeronautiques et Spatiales (GIFAS).**

Electronics

Rapport Annuel

The main source of data on the electronics industry and its products is the **Federation des Industries Electriques et Electroniques (FIEE).** Its annual report has detailed information on industry structure, turnover, production, trade, employment and earnings with comparative figures for earlier years. Both industrial and consumer products are covered and the annual is published relatively soon after the year to which the figures relate. A regular newsletter from the association has updated figures and sections of the newsletter are occasionally published in English.

Annuaire Statistique

Figures on the deliveries and sales of specific domestic electrical appliances are published annually by the **Groupement des Industries Francaises des Appareils d'Equipement Menager (GIFAM).** More up-to-date statistics on deliveries and sales are available to member companies.

Rapport d'Activite

Annual data on the electronics sector with general industry figures and figures on specific product areas. Published by the **Groupement des Industries Electriques (GIEL).**

Statistiques 199–

Annual data on the wholesale trade in electrical goods arranged into nine product areas. Included are figures on sales, purchases, supplies, stocks and profits. The report comes from the **Federation Nationale des Syndicats de Grossistes Distributeurs en Materiel Electrique et Electronique.**

Services – general

Service activities form part of the **NAP** classification and the major chapters are 56, 66, 67, 73, 74, 77, 78,79, 80, 81 and 86 to 90. Some service sectors are included in the annual **EAE** and approximately 65,000 companies are sampled. All companies employing 20 or more people are included for most sectors while a sample of companies employing fewer than 20 is taken. Statistics are published in a series of titles with the general heading, **Enquete annuelle d'enterprises dans les services.** The results of the **EAE** are published in a series of titles with the general heading noted above, although only certain service sectors are covered in detail in specific reports. These include advertising, cinematographic activities, travel agencies, financial institutions and insurance companies. Other sectors are covered in general reports on the service sectors.

Retailing and distribution

Retailing and wholesaling activities are included in the **NAP** classification as chapters 57 to 65, plus sections 38.40 and 38.50 of chapter 38 detailing bakers and cake shops respectively:

NAP 57-59	Wholesaling sectors
NAP 60	Trading intermediaries, including central buying groups
NAP 61-64	Retailing sectors
NAP 65	Motor vehicle traders and repairers

A detailed **Census of Distribution** was last undertaken in 1967 but more regular information has been available from annual surveys of retailing and wholesaling which were developed in the 1970s and 1980s. Successive surveys have increased their coverage and detail with the latest generation of annual surveys beginning in 1984.

All enterprises with 20 or more employees are surveyed using a detailed questionnaire but only a sample of enterprises below this point are covered and these are only sent a simplified questionnaire. In total, the annual survey covers approximately 44,000 organisations but inevitably, given the number of small traders in retailing and wholesaling, many retailers are excluded from the survey. The inquiry obtains information on number of establishments, retailing turnover, margins, value added, stocks, employment and investment and the results are published by **INSEE** in the year following the survey in **Collections de l'INSEE, serie E, Enquete annuelle d'entreprise dans le commerce – Principaux resultats**.

Les Comptes du Commerce en 19– –

An annual review of the retail trade from **INSEE** usually published in the August after the year to which it relates, while monthly indices of retail turnover by sector are published in the **Information Rapides** series as Series D.

Important sources of non-official data concentrate on the large retailing concerns and include the regular surveys of supermarkets and hypermarkets undertaken by **L'Institut francais du Libre-Service** and published in its journal, **Libre-Service Actualites (LSA)** and the annual census of retailing published by the journal, **Points de vente.** Summary data from both surveys is included in **INSEE's Annuaire statistique de la France.**

Atlas LSA des Hypers and Supers

This lists the number of hypermarkets and supermarkets in January of each year with details of the total selling area, turnover, performance, persons employed, number of checkouts and number of parking spaces. Figures are also given for local areas and some general data on specific companies is included. An update of the survey is carried out in July of each year and the results are published quickly in the **LSA** weekly journal, usually in August. **LSA** also carries out regular surveys of department stores, popular stores, shopping centres and superettes.

Panorama Points de Vente

An annual survey of large shops including hypermarkets, supermarkets, department stores, hardware and DIY stores, garden centres and shopping centres. The survey contains similar information to the **LSA** survey above but also includes detailed data on store developments by company.

Financial services

As in other countries, the financial services sector remains fragmented and there are few organisations publishing data on the sector as a whole. The main source of information is the **Banque de France** with a series of publications:

Statistiques mensuelles de la Banque de France
Bulletin trimestriel de la Banque de France
La Monnaie

There are monthly and quarterly statistics on financial trends and the banking sector and more detailed annual statistics on money, banking and credit. The Bank produces an annual report and the statistics are also available via its own on-line service.

Regular insurance statistics are published by the Federation **Francaise des Societes d'Assurances (FFSA).**

Leisure and tourism

Annuaire statistique du tourisme

Detailed statistics from **INSEE** covering number of hotels, capacity, occupancy, sports and tourism expenditure, sports and tourism equipment, employment and regional data.

Transportation

L'Observatoire economique et statistique des Transports (OEST) was established in 1985 and is part of the Ministere de l'Equipement, du Logement, des Transports et de la Mer. Transport statistics based on the **NAP** classifications 6801, 69 (except 6923 and 6926), 70,71,72 and 74 (except 7409 and 7410) come from this department.

Annuaire des transports

This yearbook is a compilation of the main transport statistics.

Memento de Statistiques des Transports

A regular publication with updated figures on the main transport series such as traffic (collected weekly), transport equipment, employment, infrastructure, enterprises, accidents and overseas statistics.

Le Fichier central des Automobiles

A file of passenger and commercial vehicle data, published annually including registration statistics in total and by geographical area, make, model, fuel type, etc.

More detailed information comes from the **EAE** which annually surveys approximately 14,000 enterprises in the transport sector. The samples used to collect the data vary from sector to sector. For enterprises involved in road passenger transport, river and sea transport, all enterprises with over 5 employees are sampled. Only companies with over 10 employees are sampled in the road haulage sector but all companies in air transportation are covered. Rail travel is excluded from the survey although other figures are published by **SNCF** (*see* page 100).

Information collected includes the number and size of enterprises, turnover, investment, purchases, employment and vehicle stock. Summary results are published in the year following the survey in the **Memento de statistiques des transports** and detailed results are available in a series of six microfiches, **Notes d'information**, with each fiche covering a particular transport sector.

A number of associations publish regular statistics on transport sectors including:

Statistiques et Ratios

An annual publication with data, by regions and towns, on public transport trends including mode of transport, total trips and trips per inhabitant, mileage, fuels used, taxes and frequency of trips. Published by the **Union des Transports Publics (UTP).**

Statistiques Automobiles
Notes de Conjoncture

Publications from the **Chambre Syndicale des Constructeurs d'Automobiles (CSCA). Statistiques Automobiles** is an annual compilation of vehicle data and the monthly **Notes de Conjoncture** includes registrations of new cars by make, model and region. Similar figures for motor cycles are published by the **Chambre Syndicale Nationale du Motocycle.**

Resultats de l'Exploitation des Ports Maritimes: Statistiques

Direction des Ports et de la Navigation Maritimes publishes the above yearbook. It includes traffic data for French ports by country of origin and passenger, cargo and shipping trends. A monthly bulletin provides provisional data updating these annual figures.

SNCF, the national railways organisation, publishes an annual review of operations, **La SNCF en** – – – –, including statistics on traffic, investment, turnover and stock.

Advertising statistics

Annuaire Statistique

Monthly, quarterly and annual expenditure data for specific brands and products comes from **Secodip-Pige**, an independent expenditure monitoring service.

8 GERMANY

Business statistics

INTRODUCTION

Germany has a constitutional federal democracy and this is reflected in the structure of official statistics with a central federal statistical office known as the **Statistisches Bundesamt** and statistical offices in most of the individual Lander or states. Three city states – Hamburg, Berlin and Bremen – also have statistical offices and, in Bonn, an Advisory Service of the Statistical Information Service advises individuals and organisations about using official statistics. In the former West Germany, there were eleven Landers and each one had its own statistical office. With the reunification of Germany, another five Landers have been created in the former East Germany.

It is taking time for German statistics to reflect reunification and it is likely to be well into 1992 before most of the main statistical series cover the new united Germany.

The central office co-ordinates official statistical activity and publishes most of the official titles but the collection and processing of statistics is essentially decentralised with the majority of work carried out by the statistical offices in the Lander. In some instances, such as with population census data and agricultural statistics, the collection and processing of statistics is undertaken at a lower level than the Lander and many large cities and towns have their own statistical offices. This dual level of responsibility, which sometimes has a third level, can be confusing to the user.

The **Statistisches Bundesamt** is an independent federal authority within the Department of the Federal Ministry of the Interior. It employs approximately 2,700 people and has an annual budget of DM 187 million (1987). It is split into eight divisions with Division IV responsible for statistics on production industries, building activity and the environment. Other relevant divisions are V covering food and agriculture and trade and transport and Division VI for prices, wages and foreign trade.

The authority's main offices are in Wiesbaden with a branch office in Berlin and a subsidiary office in Dusseldorf. The Dusseldorf office concentrates on iron and steel statistics while, in Berlin, the major areas of interest are income and expenditure data, aviation statistics, statistical reports on foreign countries and, before unification, data on East Germany. The addresses of the central offices are given below and Table 8.1 gives brief details of the Lander statistical offices (full addresses are given in the organisation index):

Statistisches Bundesamt

Gustav – Stresemann – Ring 11

W-6200 Wiesbaden 1

Germany

Statistisches Bundesamt

Zweigstelle Berlin (Branch office – Berlin)

Kurfurstenstrasse 87

W-1000 Berlin 30

Germany

Statistisches Bundesamt

Aussenstelle Dusseldorf – Eisen – und Stahlstatistik (Subsidiary office –
    Dusseldorf, Iron & Steel Statistics)

Huttenstrasse 5A

W-4000 Dusseldorf 1

Germany

Central federal statistical office:

Statistisches Bundesamt – Wiesbaden
Other offices in Berlin, Dusseldorf

Lander statistical offices:

Lander	Location
Schlesweg-Holstein	Kiel
Lower Saxon Land	Hannover
North Rhine-Westphalia	Dusseldorf
Hessian	Wiesbaden
Rhineland-Palatinate	Bad Ems
Baden-Wuerttemberg	Stuttgart
Bavaria	Munich
Saar	Saarbrucken
Mecklenburg-Western Pomerania	Schwerin

Table 8.1 Germany – The organisation of official statistics

Saxony-Anhalt	Halle/Saale
Bradenberg	Potsdam
Thuringen	Erfurt
Saxony	Dresden

City state statistical offices:

Berlin
Bremen
Hamburg

Table 8.1 Germany – The organisation of official statistics (*cont.*)

An advisory committee advises the **Statistisches Bundesamt** on its activities and most official statistics are based on legislation.

Most national statistical publications are produced by the **Statistisches Bundesamt** although some statistics come from other government departments and agencies – notably the Federal Ministry of Economics, Federal Institute for Employment, Federal Ministry of Transport and the Federal Ministry of Food, Agriculture & Forestry. The offices in the individual Lander areas also publish many statistics on their area and lists of the subject areas covered by both national and Lander publications are given in the following section.

A list of statistical publications, **Verzeichnis der Veroffentlichungen** is published annually and, every few years, **Das Arbeitsgebiet der Bundesstatistik** (an English language version is **Survey of German Federal Statistics**), describes the work of the federal statistics offices and lists the key surveys and publications. The latest issue was published in 1989. New publications are also announced in the weekly **Statistischer Wochendienst** and the monthly **Wirtschaft und Statistik** described in the sections to follow. The actual publications are available from the publisher:

Verlag Metzler – Poeschel
Herman Leins GmbH & Co KG
Holzwiesenstrasse 2
PO Box 1152
W-7408 Kusterdingen
Germany

Some figures on selected areas are also issued via 'Bildschirmtext', or interactive videotext, and the files issued in this way include a compendium of German figures, monthly business figures and the world in figures.

The **DRI Europe** on-line service (*see* Chapter 2) and databases from the **WEFA Group** contain statistical series from the **Statistiches Bundesamt** and on-line services are also offering data from other organisations including the **Deutsche Bundesbank, IfO, Dresdner Bank** and **Deutsches Institut fur Wirtschaftsforschung**. These are described in later sections of this chapter.

GENERAL STATISTICAL TITLES

Compilations

Key statistics on a range of subjects are included in **Statistiches Jahrbuch fur die Bundesrepublik Deutschland** (Statistical Yearbook for the Federal Republic of Germany) which also includes an international section and, before unification, an appendix on the German Democratic Republic. Up-to-date statistics on economic and social subjects are found in the monthly **Wirtschaft und Statistik** (Economics & Statistics) which contains new items and articles on recent surveys, articles on methodology plus a regular statistical section.

The monthly **Konjunktur Aktuell** has a brief commentary and monthly statistics for the last three years on selected topics including production, external trade, retailing and wholesaling, prices and labour. The quickest information on new statistics comes from the weekly **Statistischer Wochendienst** (Information on Statistics).

The economic research institute, **Ifo – Institut fur Wirtschaftsforschung** publishes **Spiegel der Wirtschaft** annually with historical data over the last 10 and 20 years on economic and social trends presented in tables and graphs. Forecasts are also included.

General statistics on the individual Lander areas can be found in the annual **Bevolkerungsstruktur und Wirtschaftskraft der Bundeslander.** (Population Structure and Economic Resources of the Federal Lander).

More detailed statistical publications are divided into 19 subject series or **Fachserie** and, within each series, there are often further subdivisions with groups of statistical titles on particular topic areas. The detailed topic areas in **Fachserie 2, 4, 5, 6, 7** and **8** will be described in the sections to follow but the 19 general series are:

1   Population & employment
    (Bevolkerung und Erwerbstatigkeit
2   Enterprises & local units
    (Unternehmen und Arbeitsstatten)
3   Agriculture, forestry & fisheries
    (Land- und Forstwirtschaft, Fischerei)
4   Production industries
    (Produzierendes Gewerbe)
5   Building activity & dwellings
    (Bautatigkeit und Wohnungen)
6   Commerce, hotel & restaurant industry, tourism
    (Handel, Gastgewerbe, Reiseverkehr)
7   Foreign trade
    (Aussenhandel)

8   Transport & communications
    (Verkehr)
9   Money & credit
    (Geld und Kredit)
10 Justice
    (Rechtspflege)
11 Education & culture
    (Bildung und Kultur)
12 Public health
    (Gesundheitswesen)
13 Social security schemes
    (Sozialleistungen)
14 Finance & taxes
    (Finanzen und Steuern)
15 Family budget surveys
    (Wirtschaftsrechnungen)
16 Wages & salaries
    (Lohne und Gehalter)
17 Prices
    (Preise)
18 National accounts
    (Volkswirtschaftliche Gesamtrechnungen)
19 Environmental protection
    (Umweltschutz)

Publications available in the individual Lander areas are also split into subject categories arranged by 17 letter codes:

A   Population & employment
B   Education, justice, elections
C   Agriculture, forestry, fisheries
D   Enterprises & local units
E   Production industries
F   Building activity, dwellings
G   Commerce, hotels & retailing
H   Transport
J   Money & credit
K   Social security schemes
L   Finance & taxes
M   Price & price indices
N   Wages & salaries
O   Consumption
P   National accounts
Q   Environmental protection
Z   Summary reports

Economic data

Economic Situation in the Federal Republic of Germany is a monthly English language publication with tables and commentary on economic trends. It is published by the Federal Ministry of Economics. Other economic titles are published by the **Deutsche Bundesbank** including the **Monthly Report of the Deutsche Bundesbank** and the **Annual Report of the Deutsche Bundesbank**, both available in English.

The monthly **Statistiche Beihefte zu den Monatsberichten der Deutschen Bundesbank 4: Saisonbereinigte Wirtschaftszahlen** contains seasonally adjusted monthly and quarterly economic indicators and notes and descriptions of the tables are available in an English supplement. This latter title is one of five supplements to the **Monthly Report of the Deutsche Bundesbank**, with the same generic name, but the other four titles have detailed statistics on money and financial services and these are described later in this chapter. The bank's statistics can be purchased on CD-Rom and disc and 13,000 series from 1948, and updated monthly, are available on-line via **DRI** and **IP Sharp**.

The **Deutsche Bank Bulletin** is a monthly pamphlet with basic economic data and an economic commentary. The **Dresdner Bank** has an on-line service, supplied through **High Technology Verlag GmbH**, offering an analysis of economic data and trends in 24 industrial sectors. The service is also accessible via **Data-Star** and **Dialog**.

Germany has a number of economic research institutes publishing economic data and forecasts and these include **Ifo – Institut fur Wirtschaftsforschung** and the **Deutsches Institut fur Wirtschaftsforschung (DIW)**. The former publishes the fortnightly **Ifo Schnell-dienst** and the quarterly **Ifo Digest** which is available in English. The latter has a weekly bulletin, **Wochenbericht**, with commentary and statistics usually on a specific economic sector. Both **IFO** and **DIW** offer data in machine readable format and on-line access to their databases is available from **DRI Europe** (both) and **IP Sharp** (IFO).

Both **IFO** and **DIW** are part of a larger association which is made up of five economic research institutes. This association, **Arbeitsgemeinschaft Deutscher Wirtschaftswissenschaftlicher Forschungsinstitute**, publishes a biannual report on economic trends, **Die Lage der Weltwirtschaft und der Westdeutschen Wirtschaft.**

Bundesverband der Deutschen Industrie (BDI), the Confederation of German Industry, publishes the monthly **BDI Informationen und Meinungen.**

Demographic and social statistics

In theory, the population census is carried out approximately every 10 years but, after the 1970 census, the 1981 census never took place because of objections made under the constitutional law. A census finally took place on 25 May 1987 and the first results were published in November 1988. The results of the 1970 census were published in 26 separate volumes. Every year in April, a microcensus of the population is carried out based on a 1 per cent sample and the main results are published in **Haushalte und Familien,** (Households & families), part of the Fachserie 1 series which has four separate series in it:

Gebiet und Bevolkerung (Area & population) – a series of quarterly and annual reports

Auslander (Aliens)

Haushalte und Familien (Households & families)

Erwerbstatigkeit (Employment)

Sector data

General industrial statistics

Sector statistics are based on the **Industrial Classification of Economic Activities 1979** which includes 10 divisions. Divisions 0 to 10 cover private enterprises, 8 is private non-profit institutions and private households and 9 is central and local government and social insurance. The classification deviates considerably from the European **NACE** classification although the 1979 revision of the German classification did improve compatability with **NACE** in certain areas. Derived from the above classification is the **Industrial Classification of Economic Activities: Version for Statistics of Production Industries or SYPRO.**

Detailed production statistics covering specific products and commodities are based on another scheme known as the **Classification of Goods for Production Statistics 1982 edition**, or **GP** for short. This covers industrial production plus agriculture, forestry, fishing, energy and water supply, mining, prefabricated construction. While, for the first time in 1978, a commodity classification scheme for goods traded in retailing and wholesaling and related sectors was introduced known as the **Commodity Classification for Domestic Trade Statistics or WB.** The detailed breakdown in this classification largely follows Division 4 of the **Industrial Classification of Economic Activities**.

Commodity import and export statistics are arranged according to the **Commodity Classification for Foreign Trade Statistics (WA)** which is based on the EC's **Combined Nomenclature (CN)**.

The last detailed census of production, **Zensus im Produzierenden Gewerbe**, took place in 1979 and the results were published in seven volumes. A census of non-agricultural local units (**Arbeitsstattenzahlung**), including those in services, the non-profit sector and local authorities, is usually carried out jointly with the population census. The results of the census of 1970 were

MELDE-NR	ERZEUGNIS	EINHEIT	MENGE			WERT IN 1000 DM			ANZAHL DER BETR.
			1990 1. VJ	1990 4. VJ	1991 1. VJ	1990 1. VJ	1990 4. VJ	1991 1. VJ	1991 1. VJ
	ELEKTROMOTORISCHE WIRTSCHAFTS-GERAETE GEWERBLICHE								
3637 12	ELEKTROBOHRERMASCHINEN	ST	8 171	9 788	8 655	10 070	11 879	11 214	7
3637 14	ELEKTRISCHE HAARSCHNEIDE-MASCHINEN	ST	81 943	129 289	99 347	3 919	6 124	4 786	4
3637 17	ELEKTRISCHE HAENDETROCKNER	ST	19 112	15 100	17 068	3 053	2 539	2 710	3
3637 19	SONSTIGE GEWERBLICHE ELEKTRONMOTORISCHE WIRTSCHAFTSGERAETE FUER DEN HAUSHALT	ST	56 796	68 650	57 028	7 684	6 790	8 297	10
	ELEKTROMOTORISCHE KUECHEN-GERAETE								
3637 31	KAFFEEMUEHLEN (AUCH GEWUERZMUEHLEN)	ST	48 972	60 779	55 803	2 013	2 546	2 168	5
3637 34	MIXGERAETE (AUCH HANDRUEHRGERAETE)	ST	338 943	257 134	235 801	40 122	23 607	22 538	5
3637 35	ELEKTRO-ENTSAFTER	ST	83 080	113 303	125 987	5 758	8 040	9 119	4
3637 37	RUNDSCHNEIDEMASCHINEN (OHNE GROSS-KUECHENMASCHINEN)	ST	162 093	268 643	238 086	15 451	24 665	20 426	6
3637 38	ZUSATZGERAETE	ST	199 764	198 866	168 666	3 938	3 787	3 220	6
3637 39	SONSTIGE ELEKTROMOTORISCHE KUECHENGE-RAETE	ST	187 283	388 004	322 432	12 008	30 527	21 669	9
3637 40	GESCHIRRSPUELMASCHINEN FUER DEN HAUSHALT	ST	690 720	675 697	730 735	471 846	456 293	505 344	5
	ELEKTROMOTORISCHE GERAETE ZUR HAUT- U. HAARBEHANDLUNG								
3637 51	RASIERAPPARATE (AUCH BATTERIEBETRIEBEN)	ST	2 204 156	2 310 678	2 170 304	158 787	175 605	169 619	3
3637 56	LUFTDUSCHEN U. HAARTROCKNER	ST	440 503	341 639	294 523	9 332	8 537	7 470	8
3637 58	HEIMTROCKENHAUBEN	ST	13 369	17 682	14 597	1 246	1 127	1 263	4
3637 59	SONSTIGE GERAETE ZUR HAUT- U. HAARBEHANDLUNG	ST	78 439	117 530	80 128	15 379	29 513	16 315	10
3637 60	ELEKTROMOTORISCHE GERAETE FUER DIE MUNDHYGIENE	ST	485 169	436 999	370 843	30 559	26 475	23 647	5
	ELEKTRISCHE STAUBSAUGER								
3637 82	KLOPF-/BUERSTSTAUBSAUGER ANDERE STAUBSAUGER	ST	39 423	34 816	33 350	11 849	9 739	11 288	3
3637 83	HANDSTAUBSAUGER	ST	587 808	648 735	728 580	76 961	75 292	85 931	7
3637 86	BODENSTAUBSAUGER ANDERE ELEKTROMOTORISCHE WIRT. SCHAFTSGERAETE	ST	800 550	806 984	866 224	152 220	154 986	168 630	9
3637 91	DUNSTABZUGSHAUBEN	ST	236 645	187 916	222 582	48 298	39 945	45 047	9
3637 94	LUFTBEFEUCHTER, ORTSBEWEGLICH	ST	19 409	21 372	17 546	5 842	5 943	4 800	4
3637 99	SONSTIGE WIRTSCHAFTSGERAETE FUER DEN HAUSHALT	ST	297 688	239 108	270 732	46 188	35 173	37 680	10
3637 06	ZUBEHOER, EINZEL- U. ERSATZTEILE FUER GEWERBLICHE GERAETE	T	23	21	28	1 592	1 693	1 792	5

Meldenr.	Bezeichnung	Einheit							20
3637 07	FUER HAUSHALTSGERAETE	T	1 757	1 555	1 786	64 664	56 395	63 609	20
3637	INSGESAMT		.	.	.	1 198 779	1 197 310	1 248 582	
	ELEKTRISCHE HAUSHALTSKUEHLMOEBEL MIT ELEKTRISCH ANGETRIEBENEM KOMPRESSOR HAUSHALTSKUEHLSCHRAENKE								
3638 12	TISCHKUEHLSCHRAENKE	ST	150 089	173 105	183 183	61 396	72 663	77 266	4
3638 13	EINBAUKUEHLSCHRAENKE	ST	414 074	328 704	390 002	214 507	172 901	204 950	4
3638 16	SONSTIGE HAUSHALTSKUEHL-SCHRAENKE 1)	ST	.A	.A	366 639	.A	.A	170 641	3
3638 23	KOMBINIERTE KUEHL- U. GEFRIERSCHRAENKE 2) HAUSHALTSGEFRIERSCHRAENKE U.-TRUHEN BIS 250 LTR	ST							2
3638 32	EINBAUGERAETE	ST	66 587	50 555	65 978	32 584	25 046	33 658	4
3638 33	STANDGERAETE 3)	ST	.A	.A	162 705	.A	.A	104 815	3
3638 34	EINBAU- U. STANDGERAETE UEBER 250 LTR 4)	ST							2
3638 50	KAELTEMITTELVERDICHTER, -VER-DICHTERSAETZE BIS 0,4 KW	ST	1 467 836	1 355 607	1 410 673	115 575	105 878	109 552	5
3638 09	ZUBEHOER, EINZEL- U. ERSATZTEILE	T	4 782	1 585	2 857	21 643	14 778	17 021	7
3638	INSGESAMT		.	.	.	669 603	624 638	717 903	.
	ELEKTRISCHE HAUSHALTSWASCHMASCHINEN U.-GERAETE WASCHMASCHINEN MIT EINEM FUELL-GEWICHT BIS G KG TROCKENWAESCHE								
3639 11	BOTTICH- U. TROMMELWASCH- MASCHINEN 5)	ST							2
	VOLLAUTOMATEN MIT U. OHNE TROCKENGANG								
3639 31	FRONTBESCHICKT (FRONTLADER)	ST	613 960	553 487	684 547	597 363	557 083	691 319	5
3639 35	MANTELBESCHICKT (TOPLADER) 6)	ST	130 530	122 270	141 365	113 499	110 991	130 296	4
3639 50	WAESCHESCHLEUDERN MIT EINEM FUELLGEWICHT BIS 6 KG TROCKENWAESCHE	ST	70 248	93 040	99 104	8 566	11 655	12 434	3
3639 61	MIT KONDENSATION	ST	108 472	144 244	137 646	100 675	128 146	125 384	5
3639 65	MIT ABLUFT	ST	144 101	136 749	125 119	94 117	91 970	84 082	6
3639 80	BUEGELMASCHINEN FUER DEN HAUSHALT	ST	11 926	15 423	14 992	13 479	16 413	16 096	3
3639 90	SONSTIGE HAUSCHALTSGERAETE FUER WAESCHE U. BEKLEIDUNG	ST	–	–	–	–	–	–	–
3639 09	ZUBEHOER, EINZEL- U. ERSATZTEILE	T	2 697	2 423	2 738	37 657	32 102	37 151	15
3639	INSGESAMT		.	.	.	965 356	948 360	1 096 722	.

1) IN MELDENUMMER 3638 23 ENTHALTEN. -2) ENTHAELT AUCH DIE MELDENUMMER 3638 16. - 3) IN MELDENUMMER 3638 34 ENTHALTEN.
4) ENTHAELT AUCH DIE MELDENUMMER 3638 33. - 5) IN MELDENUMMER 3639 35 ENTHALTEN. - 6) ENTHAELT AUCH DIE MELDENUMMER 3639 11.

Table 8.2 German production statistics – extracts of entries, including washing machines.

published in nine main volumes and two special issues and the results of the latest census in 1987 are now starting to appear. This provides details of the number of units, legal entity, economic activity, number of employees, by age and sex, wages and salaries, etc. Regional breakdowns are also included.

More up-to-date statistics on industry and products are published in various titles in **Fachserie 2** (Series 2), **Unternehmen und Arbeitsstatten** (Enterprises & local units) and **Fachserie 4** (Series 4), **Produzierendes Gewerbe** (Production industries).

A regular monthly survey of local units in mining and manufacturing is based on a sample of enterprises employing 20 or more people. Monthly production surveys are also based on surveys of enterprises employing 20 or more people while quarterly production surveys include enterprises with fewer than 20 employees. The quarterly production survey claims to cover 98 per cent of the estimated value of the total production of all units.

PUBLICATIONS PRODUCED BY NATIONAL ORGANISATIONS

General industry and trade

Fachserie 2 – Unternehmen und Arbeitsstatten

A series of publications on enterprises and local units broken down into four groups of titles:

2.1 Kostenstruktur in ausgewahlten Wirtschaftszweigen (Cost structure in selected branches of economic activity)
2.2 Kapitalgesellschaften (Incorporated enterprises)
2.3 Abschlusse der Offentlichen Versorgungs- und Verkehrsunter nehmen (Balance sheets of public utility and transport enterprises)
2.4 Zahlungsschwierigkeiten (Insolvencies)

In the 2.1 group, there are 13 separate quarterly titles on specific sectors each including data on receipts, turnover, stocks, net value of production, gross proceeds and costs.

Fachserie 4 – Produzierendes Gewerbe

The Production Industries series 4 is split into eight groups of titles:

4.2 Indizes fur das Produzierende Gewerbe (Indices for production industries)
4.3 Produktion im Produzierenden (Output of production industries)
4.4 Bergbau und Verarbeitendes Gewerbe (mining & manufacturing)
4.5 Baugewerbe (Building industry)
4.6 Energie- und Wasserversorgung (Power & water supply)
4.7 Handwerk (Handicrafts)
4.8 Fach statistiken (Specialised statistics)

Titles in the groups 4.2, 4.3, 4.4 and 4.5 are described below:

4.2.1 Indizes der Produktion und der Arbeitsproduktivat (Indices of production and labour productivity)

4.2.2 Produktion ausgewahlter Erzeugnisse im Produzierenden

Indices of production and of labour productivity are published monthly along with production data for a selection of commodities (approximately 1,000 products).

4.3.1 Produktion im Produzierenden Gewerbe Produktion im Produzierenden Gewerbe des In- und Auslandes

This title has quarterly and annual issues with production data for approximately 6,000 products, based on the **GP** classification. Quantity and value figures are usually given for individual products and, in the quarterly series, the statistics cover the latest quarter and cumulative figures for the year. The annual volume has production information for the latest three years. An extract showing part of the data on domestic appliances is included as Table 8.2.

4.3.2 Struktur der Produktion im Produzierenden Gewerbe

An annual publication with structural data on the production industries.

4.4 Bergbau und Verarbeitendes Gewerbe (Mining and manufacturing industries)

A series of 16 regular titles on the structure of mining and manufacturing sectors plus employment and turnover. Selected major titles include:

4.4.11 Beschaftigung, Umsatz und Energieversorgung der Unternehmen und Betriebe im Bergbau und im Verarbeitenden Gewerbe (Employment, turnover & energy supply of enterprises & local units in mining and manufacturing)

A monthly and annual series of reports.

Betriebe, Beschaftigte und Umsatz im Bergbau und im Verarbeitenden Gewerbe nach Beschaftigtengrossenklassen (Local units, persons engaged & turnover in mining and manufacturing by size classes of persons engaged)

An annual publication.

Beschaftigung und Umsatz der Betriebe im Bergbau und im Verarbeitenden Gewerbe nach Bundeslandern (Employment & turnover of local units in mining & manufacturing by Lander)

An annual publication.

4.5 Baugewerbe

Production data for the building industry is published in three titles here but official data on building activity and housing stock is contained in the **Fachserie 5** series described later in the 'Construction section' on page 112.

Fachserie 7 – Aussenhandel

Eight groups of titles in series 7 provide information on foreign trade in general and the imports and exports of specific products. The major titles are:

7.1 Zusammenfassende Ubersichten fur den Aussenhandel (Summary survey of foreign trade)

A monthly publication with general details of trends in Germany's foreign trade.

7.2 Aussenhandel nach Waren und Landern [Spezialhandel] (Foreign trade by commodities & countries [Special trade])

A monthly publication with details of the imports and exports of specific products, by country, with data for the latest month, in quantities and values, and cumulative data for the year. The statistics are based on the European **CN** classification.

7.3 Aussenhandel nach Landern und Warengruppen [Spezialhandel]
(Foreign trade by countries & commodity groups [Special trade])

Published twice a year with detailed statistics for individual trading partners.

7.8 Aussenhandel nach dem Internationalen Warenverzeichnis fur den Aussenhandel (SITC) und Landern [Spezialhandel] (Foreign trade according to the SITC & by countries) [Special trade]

An annual publication showing the imports and exports of products according to the **SITC**.

Construction

An official census of buildings is undertaken at regular intervals with the latest in May 1987 to coincide with the population census. The census includes data on the age of buildings, structure, type, number of rooms, heating, rents, etc.

Every four to six years, a sample survey of households is carried out and the latest survey took place in 1990. Statistics on construction activity and output comes from the **Fachserie 5** series:

Fachserie 5 – Bautatigkeit und Wohnungen

The two major groups of titles in this official series are:

5.1 Bautatigkeit (Building activity)

Published monthly and annually with data on building permits and completions and annual data on work under construction.

5.3 Bestand an Wohnungen (Housing stock)

Published annually.

Baustatistisches Jahrbuch

Trade association data on the building industry comes from the **Hauptverband der Deutschen Bauindustrie** which publishes the above yearbook. This includes data on new buildings, orders, completions, work under way, etc.

Food and drink

Statistisches Jahrbuch uber Ernahrung, Landwirtschaft und Forsten
(Statistical Yearbook of Food, Agriculture, Forestry)
This annual publication is produced by the Federal Ministry of Food, Agriculture and Forestry.

Jahresbericht 199–

An annual yearbook with statistics from the **Bundesvereinigung der Deutschen Ernahrungsindustrie**, the trade association for the food industry. A series of graphs provide basic data on the sector and a list of trade associations in specific food sectors is given at the end of the publication.

ZMP Reports

ZMP is a private publisher of annual reports on foodstuffs and the food industry. Each report has detailed statistics for a number of years and commentary on production, markets, trade, prices with data for Germany and a section on other European countries. Report titles include:

Vieh und Fleisch – data on livestock & meat

Milch und Milcherzeugnisse – data on milk & milk products

Gemuse – data on vegetables

Kartoffein – data on potatoes

Obst – data on fruit

Geschaftsbericht

An annual statistical yearbook, with commentary, on the meat industry and market from the **Bundesverband der Deutschen Fleischwarenindustrie**. Tables on industry structure, turnover, production, employment, salaries, etc. are largely based on official statistics or figures from **ZMP** (see entry above).

Susswarentaschenbuch

An annual pocket-book with detailed figures on the confectionery industry and markets from the **Bundesverband der Deutschen Sussenwarenindustrie**.

Die Spirituoenindustrie
Statistiche Informationen

Publications from the **Bundesverband der Deutschen Spirituosen Industrie** covering spirits and liqueurs. The first is an annual compilation and commentary on the sector and the second title comprises approximately 50 issues per year each providing data on a specific area within the industry.

Chemicals and chemical products

Chemiewirtschaft in Zahlen

Annual statistics on the German chemical industry from the **Verband der Chemischen Industrie (VCI)**. Most of the statistical series cover a number of years and include data on production, sales, imports, exports, consumption.

Jahresbericht
Erdgas und Erdol in Zahl

The first title is a yearbook from the **Wirtschaftsverband Erdol und Erdgasgetwinnung** with current and historical data on the petroleum and gas industry. The second title provides annual summary statistics on the sector and it is produced in a pocket-book format.

Textiles and clothing

Jahrbuch der Textilindustrie 199–

Detailed statistics on the German and international textiles industries published annually by the **Gesamttextil, Gesamtverband der Textilindustriein der Bundesrepublik Deutschland**. The publication is largely based on official statistics.

textil-fakten

A loose-leaf annual statistical review of the textiles and clothing sectors from **Deutscher Fachverlag GmbH**. Detailed statistics, for a number of years, look at production, external trade, industrial structure and specific markets.

Statisticher Jahresbericht

Annual statistics on the hosiery and knitwear industries and markets with information on specific product areas. The annual is published by the **Gesamtverband der Deutschen Maschen-Industrie**.

Jahresbericht

The **Verband der Deutschen Heimtextilien Industrie** publishes an annual statistical yearbook on household textiles and fabrics. The statistics largely cover production and external trade and are based on official statistics.

Schuhe 199–

Annual statistics on footwear production, exports, imports, consumption and prices from the **Hauptverband der Deutschen Schuhindustrie**. Most of the figures come from official sources.

Electrical and mechanical engineering

Statistiches Handbuch fur den Maschinenbau

Annual statistics in a pocket-book from the engineering association, **Verband Deutscher Maschinen- und Anlagenbau (VDMA)**. There are statistics on production and external trade for specific machinery and data on industry structure, turnover, prices, costs, etc. Some international data is also included. Mainly based on official statistics.

Jahresbericht

Annual statistics on the steel industry based on a combination of sources and published by the **Bundesverband Deutscher Stahlhandel**. Monthly statistics on German and EC steel industries are also produced.

Statistiches Jahrbuch der Stahlindustrie

Current and historical statistics on the German steel industry from the **Wirtschaftsvereinigung Stahlindustrie**.

Mitglieder-und Produktions-Verzeichnis

Quarterly statistics for non-ferrous metal smelters and foundries published by the **Fachvereinigung Metallhutten und Umschmelzwerke (FMU)**. Based on data from member companies.

Deutscher Schiffbau

The **Verband fur Schiffbau und Meerestechnik** produces an annual report on shipbuilding and shipping with a commentary followed by statistics on production, orders, deliveries, turnover, etc. The report contains English translations of table headings.

Other statistics are occasionally published by the metalworking and mechanical engineering association, **Fachverband Metallwaren- und Verwandte Industrien**.

Electronics

BVB Statistik

Production, trade and market data published twice a year by the **Bundesverband Vertriebsunternehmen Buro, Informations- und Kommunikationstechnik (BVB)**. This association covers office machinery, including electronic equipment.

Produktionsbericht fur die Elektrotechnik- und Elektronikindustrie
Die Elektrotechnische Industrie
The first title is a quarterly statistical report from the consumer electronics trade association, **Zentralverband Elektrotechnik- und Elektronikindustrie (ZVEI)**. Statistics on consumer electronics products including TVs, radio, VCRs, compact discs, etc. and based on members' returns. The second title, from the same organisation, provides a compilation of annual statistics for the sector.

Retailing and distribution

Handels- und Gaststattenzahlung (Census of Distribution)
A census of distribution has been carried out at irregular intervals up to the mid-1980s with the latest census in 1985 and a previous census in 1979. They are now scheduled to take place every 10 years.

Fachserie 6 – Handel, Gastgewerbe, Reiseverkehr (Commerce, hotel & restaurant industry, tourism)
There are seven groups of titles in this series and the two main groups relating to retailing and distribution are:

6.1 Groshandel (Wholesaling)
Covers five titles (two relating to statistical methodology).

6.3 Einzelhandel (Retailing)
Covers four titles (one relating to statistical methodology). The titles include the results of the regular sample surveys of wholesaling and retailing which are carried out at monthly and annual intervals. These surveys collect information on turnover, employees, stocks, investments, materials received and wages and salaries. Most of the remaining groups of titles relate to leisure and tourism and these are described on page 118.

Arbeitsbericht
The major association for the retailing sector is the **Hauptgemeinschaft des Deutschen Einzelhandels (HDE)** which publishes the above yearbook. It consists largely of commentary on retailing trends but there are statistics on enterprise numbers, turnover, employment and retail sales performance. There are also regional associations publishing data on specific local areas.

Geschaftsbericht
An annual report with statistics from the association for medium-sized and large general retailing firms, **Bundesarbeitsgemeinschaft der Mittel- und Grossbetriebe des Einzelhandels**.

SB in Zahlen

Basic statistics on self-service retailing, stores and sales published annually by the **Institut fur Selbstbedienung und Warenwirtschaft (ISB)**. The association also publishes a monthly journal, **Dynamik im Handel**, which often contains statistics and a report on the structure of the self-service sector.

Financial services

Fachserie 9 – Geld und Kredit (Money & credit)
There is just one monthly title in this series, **Aktienmarkte** (Share markets).

Monthly Report of the Deutsche Bundesbank

In addition to general economic data, the monthly report has sections on banking, the Deutsche Bundesbank and other financial services. Copies are available in English.

Statistiche Beihefte zu den Monatsberichten der Deutschen Bundesbank 1: Bankenstatistik nach Bankengruppen

Statistiche Beihefte zu den Monatsberichten der Deutschen Bundesbank 2: Wertpapier – statistik

Statistiche Beihefte zu den Monatsberichten der Deutschen Bundesbank 3: Zahlungsbilanz – statistik

Statistiche Beihefte zu den Monatsberichten der Deutschen Bundesbank 5: Die Wahrungen der Welt

The Deutsche Bundesbank publishes four monthly publications providing detailed statistics on money, banking and financial trends. Title 1 includes detailed banking statistics by category of bank and has monthly and quarterly series for a number of years. Title 2 covers securities and Title 3 has a detailed breakdown of the balance of payments. Title 5 looks at currencies of the world. English language versions of the notes and descriptions of the tables are available and the data is also housed on an on-line service.

A fourth monthly title with the same generic name has statistics on German economic trends and this is listed in the earlier section headed 'Economic Data' on page 106.

Die Deutsche Versicherungswirtschaft Jahrbuch

A yearbook of insurance statistics with data for Germany and international comparisons. A large part of the yearbook, published by the **Gesamtverband der Deutschen Versicherungswirtschaft (GDV)**, comprises commentary and most of the tables have statistical series over a number of years.

Jahrbuch

An annual report containing general statistics about life insurance from the **Verband der Lebensversicherungs Unternehmen**. The statistics are largely based on returns from members.

Bericht uber das Geschaftsjahr
Privates Bausparwesen 199–

The first publication is an annual report looking at the housing market and housing finance. Most of the statistical data is collected by the publisher, the **Verband der Privaten Bausparkassen**, and the statistics cover areas such as housing investment, mortgages and loans, savings, etc. by house type, area and type of loan. The second publication is an annual review, with statistics, of the activities of private savings and building credit banks.

Leisure and tourism

The hotel and restaurant sector is covered by the **Census of Distribution** (*see* section headed 'Retailing and Distribution' on page 116) but more up-to-date figures come from the **Fachserie 6** series.

Fachserie 6 – Handel, Gastgewerbe, Reiseverkehr (Commerce, hotel & restaurant industry, tourism)

Two groups of titles in this official series concentrate on the leisure and tourism sectors:

Fachserie 6.4 Gastgewerbe (Hotel & restaurant industry)

Comprises four titles (one relating to statistical methodology).

Fachserie 6.7 Reiserverkehr (Tourism)

Comprises four separate titles published monthly and annually.

Tourismus in Zahlen

A regular compilation of basic tourism statistics from the central statistical office.

The **Deutsche Zentrale fur Tourismus** also publishes an annual, **Jahresbericht**, but this is mainly commentary and news items on tourism with just a few statistics. The **Deutscher Reiseburo-Verband** also has occasional reports on travel trends such as **Fakten und Zahlen zum deutschen Reisemarkt**, a general survey of travel trends of Germans.

Transportation

Fachserie 8 – Serkehr (Transport & communications)

Another series from **Statistiches Bundesamt** with seven groups of regular titles covering:

8.1 Guterverkehr der Verkehrszwerge (Goods transport by branches of transport) – quarterly and annual

8.2 Eisenbahnverkehr (Rail transport) – monthly and annual

8.3 Strassenpersonenverkehr (Road transport) – quarterly and annual

8.4 Binnenschiffahrt (Inland water transport) – monthly and annual

8.5 Seeschiffahrt (Merchant shipping) – monthly and annual

8.6 Luftverkehr (Air transport) – monthly and annual

8.7 Verkehrsunfalle (Transport and traffic) – monthly and annual

Verkehr in Zahlen

'Transport in Figures' is a compendium of transport statistics published annually by the Federal Ministry of Transport. Individual titles are also published on transport sectors such as road, waterways and shipping. The Ministry also offers **Allgemeiner Statistischer Dienst** (General Statistical Service) with regular data on transport sectors.

Statistische Mitteilungen

A regular statistical information bulletin from the Federal Office for Motor Traffic which also produces specific titles on registrations and the vehicle stock and carries out an annual census (1st July) of motor vehicles and trailers.

Monatsbericht

A monthly report from the Federal Office of Civil Aeronautics.

Tatsachen und Zahlen aus der Kraftverkehrswirtschaft

An annual statistical compilation on the motor vehicles sector from the **Verband der Automobilindustrie**. Statistics cover production, shipments, registrations, trade, licences, traffic, roads, fuels, vehicle parc, etc. and many tables have detailed data by make, model and geographical area.

VOV Statistik

The public transport organisation, **Verband Offentlicher Verkehrsbetriebe (VOV)**, publishes annual statistics on the different public transport sectors. Most of the data is collected by **VOV**. Summary data, in pocket-book format, is published annually as **VOV Aktuell**.

Verkehrsleistungen der Deutschen Verkehrsflughafen

An annual report from the **Arbeitsgemeinschaft Deutscher Verkehrsflughafen (ADV)**, the trade association involved with air traffic and airports. Part 1 is a commentary and Part 2 has graphs and tables on traffic, passengers, freight and mail at German airports. The report is based on a combination of official statistics and data from individual airports. Basic monthly statistics are also produced.

Jahresbericht

Daten der Deutschen Seeschiffahrt

Jahresbericht is a yearbook from the **Verband Deutscher Reeder** with statistics on German shipping. Most of the data is collected by the trade association. The second publication concentrates on shipping traffic and journeys into and out of Germany.

BDE Faltblatt

Annual statistics on the German private railway system published by the **Bundesverband Deutscher Eisenbahnen (BDE)**.

Public sector

Statistik fur das Jahr 199–

Schnellstatistik

Annual statistics for the electricity supply sector in Germany from the **Verenigung Deutscher Elektrizitatswerke (VDEW)**. The association also publishes a fortnightly bulletin and annual data on energy balances.

BGW Gasstatistik

The **Bundesverband der Deutschen Gas und Wasserwirtschaft (BGW)** publishes annual statistics on gas supply and demand. There is also an annual statistical yearbook on water supply.

Advertising statistics

Nielsen Werbeforschung S&P produces regular statistics for advertising expenditure, by brands, media, sector, etc.

9 GREECE
Business statistics

INTRODUCTION

Official statistical activity is the responsibility of the **National Statistical Service of Greece** but, although this national office has a range of titles, many of these take a considerable time to be published. The office is based in Athens at:

National Statistical Service of Greece
14–16 Lycourgou Street
GR-10166 Athens
Greece

Publications can be obtained from this address and most of these will have, at least, English translations of contents and headings. Some are actually published in English. Others are also available in French. Of all the EC countries, Greek statistics take the longest to be processed and published and few major censuses and surveys are carried out on a regular basis. Gaps in official statistics can sometimes be filled by data from the banks and a few trade associations such as those in the shipping sector.

GENERAL STATISTICAL TITLES

Compilations

The **Statistical Yearbook of Greece**, published in English and Greek, is the major source of the range of official statistics while more up-to-date statistics for many of the series can be found in the **Monthly Statistical Bulletin**, also in English and Greek.

Economic data

Economic data can be found in the above compilations plus the **Bank of Greece** has a monthly **Statistical Bulletin**, published in English, with sections on general economic and financial trends.

The **Greek Economy in Figures** appears anually from **Elektra Press Publications**. Brief commentary and statistics for a number of years cover economic and social trends and English translations are included.

Demographic and social statistics

Population censuses are conducted every 10 years with the latest in 1981 and 1991 and there are general volumes of results plus volumes on specific topics based on a 10 per cent sample. The census reports are published under the general title, **Population de la Grece au recensement du ....**

An annual title is **Mouvement naturel de la population de la Grece**.

Sector data

General industrial statistics

Industrial and handicraft censuses took place in 1969, 1978 and 1984 but the national statistical service carries out an annual industrial survey and an annual survey of mines, quarries and salterns. There is also an annual survey of electricity and gas.

The industrial survey is split into 'large scale industry' involving establishments with 10 or more employees, and 'small scale industry' for establishments with fewer than 10 employees. There is also a monthly survey of manufacturing production based on returns from approximately 1,800 factories selected according to their size and the results are used to produce an index of production.

The surveys are based on the **Statistical Classification of Economic Activities 1980** which has been adapted from the international **ISIC** classification. Section 1 of the classification covers mining and quarrying and Sections 2 and 3 relate to manufacturing activities. The 2-digit codes in Sections 2 and 3 are listed below:

20   Food
21   Beverages
22   Tobacco
23   Textiles
24   Footwear, wearing apparel & made up textile goods
25   Wood & cork
26   Furniture & fixtures
27   Paper & paper products

28   Printing, publishing & other allied industries
29   Leather, fur & leather & fur products
30   Rubber & plastic products
31   Chemical industries
32   Petroleum & coal products
33   Non-metallic mineral products
34   Basic metal industries
35   Metal products, excluding machinery & transport equipment
36   Machinery & appliances, except electrical ones & transport equipment
37   Electrical machinery, apparatus, appliances & supplies
38   Transport equipment
39   Miscellaneous sectors

PUBLICATIONS PRODUCED BY NATIONAL ORGANISATIONS

General industry and trade

Annual Industrial Survey

Published in Greek and English with statistics on industrial structure and activity. Detailed results by sector. A second report, **Annual Statistical Survey on Mines**, contains similiar information for this sector.

Industrial activity and production statistics are also published in some detail in the **Statistical Yearbook of Greece**, which includes production data for selected commodities produced by manufacturing units of five persons or more, and in the **Monthly Statistical Bulletin** which includes the monthly index of manufacturing production down to the 4-digit level of the economic classification.

Bulletin de statistique du commerce exterieur

Quarterly import and export statistics published in French and Greek.

Construction

Building Activity Surveys

A monthly survey covers private building activity and a quarterly survey looks at public sector building.

Textiles and clothing

Elliniki Plektiki

Published six times a year by the **Federation Hellenique de la Maille** with statistics on the knitting industry and market.

Retailing and distribution

A **Wholesale and Retail Trade Census** was undertaken in 1969, 1978 and 1984 to coincide with the industrial censuses in the same years. The surveys include motor dealers and filling stations as well as traditional outlets. The results of the 1984 census started to be published in the late 1980s and 1990. A new census of wholesaling and retailing took place in 1988 but the results are unlikely to be published for some time. More up-to-date statistics on sales come from a monthly index of retail sales value produced by the Ministry of Finance.

Financial services

The **Statistical Bulletin** from the **Bank of Greece** noted in the 'Economic Data' section on page 122 has figures on money and banking and some statistics on the insurance sector are published by the **Enosis Asfalistikon Etairion**.

Leisure and tourism

Tourist Statistics

Annual data on tourist trends, hotel capacity and the development of hotel establishments. Available in English.

Transportation

Transport and Communication Statistics

A general annual compilation of transport and communications data, available in English.

Shipping Statistics

Annual shipping statistics covering passengers, goods and freight.

Advertising statistics

Nielsen Hellas Ltd offers various media research services including the monthly **Nielsen Monitor** which collects advertising expenditure data from all the print media, TV, radio and outdoor advertising.

10 IRELAND

Business statistics

INTRODUCTION

Ireland's **Central Statistics Office (CSO)** is the main source of official statistics although a number of other government departments publish statistics in specialist areas. A list of the major departments is given in Table 10.1. Other statistics come from some trade associations, the Central Bank of Ireland, the Confederation of Irish Industry and the Irish Tourist Board.

The **CSO** is not governed by any particular legislation and, although it is attached to the Prime Minister's office, in practice it is independent in its professional activities. Its headquarters and a branch office are based in Dublin and the branch office deals mainly with inquiries on demographic topics, industry, labour, building and construction and the **CSO Databank**.

Publications themselves can be obtained from the two **Government Publications Sales Offices**, also in Dublin. One office is for personal callers and the other deals with postal orders:

Central Statistics Office
CSO
St. Stephen's Green House
Earlsfort Terrace
Dublin 2
Ireland

CSO Branch Office
Ardee Road
Rathmines
Dublin 6
Ireland

Government Publications Sales Office (personal callers)

Sun Alliance House

Molesworth Street

Dublin 2

Ireland

Government Publications Sales Office (postal orders)

Bishop Street

Dublin 8

Ireland

Central Statistics Office

Individual departments:
Department of Agriculture and Food
Department of Industry and Commerce
Department of Energy
Department of the Environment
Department of Labour
Department of Finance

Table 10.1 Main official departments/agencies publishing statistics

The **CSO Guide to Publications and Information Services** is published annually and includes descriptions of the publications, an alphabetical subject index and contact points for specific statistical series.

EOLAS is the **CSO**'s statistical databank with data on economic trends, agriculture, industry, building, transport and distribution, external trade, prices, the labour market and population and vital statistics. The databank is managed using the SAS software package and it is stored in the Central Computing Service (CCS) computer. It is accessible, in batch or interactive mode, to users of the CSS and selected portions of **EOLAS** are also available on eight separate discs with each disc covering one of the subject areas noted above. The **CSO** can also provide special services and analyses, for a fee, tailored to the needs of individual users.

The **CSO Library** in the headquarters in Dublin is open to the public from Monday to Friday.

GENERAL STATISTICAL TITLES

Compilations

The **Statistical Abstract** is the annual compilation of statistics from the **CSO** and other government departments. Most tables have an historical series of figures and an appendix provides basic data on Northern Ireland. The quarterly **Statistical Bulletin** provides detailed results of all the regular short-term **CSO** inquiries and occasional articles giving the results of annual inquiries.

The first basic results of statistical inquiries appear in a series of **Statistical Releases**. There are monthly, quarterly, annual and biannual **Statistical Releases** and 38 releases on specific topics. Individual titles are mentioned in the relevant subject sections but the general subject areas covered are:

Agriculture	7 releases
Distribution	3 releases
Industry	10 releases
Labour	6 releases
Prices	4 releases
Tourism	1 release
Trade	1 release
Transport	4 releases
National income	1 release

A further set of monthly **Economic Series** publications reproduce the principal results of surveys and provide five years' retrospective details for 143 series grouped into the following nine categories: prices; industry; building; agriculture; external trade; distribution and transport; finance; labour; vital statistics.

Detailed results of surveys subsequently appear in the quarterly **Statistical Bulletin** and basic details are included in the **Statistical Abstract**.

Economic data

Apart from the **Statistical Release** and the **Economic Release** services noted above, a major source of economic data is the **Central Bank of Ireland Quarterly Bulletin**. This has articles on economic issues and a detailed statistical appendix covering economic trends, finance, trade and the banking sector. The bank also publishes a monthly **Statistical Supplement** and a periodic **Folder of Irish Economic Statistics**.

Articles on the domestic economy, by sector, plus a statistical appendix are also included in the **Economic and Social Research Institute's Quarterly Economic Commentary**. The **Confederation of Irish Industry** publishes **Quarterly Review, Economic Trends** with commentary and statistics on the economic situation plus summary results from a monthly survey of business expectations. For futher details of the latter, see the entry headed 'Monthly Industrial Survey, Business Forecast'.

Demographic and social statistics

A census of population is carried out every five years with recent ones taken in 1981, 1986 and 1991. Various volumes covering general data, specific topics and local areas are published and more detailed data is also available on computer print-outs and magnetic tapes. There is a **Quarterly Report on Vital Statistics** and an **Annual Report on Vital Statistics** plus survey results in the **Statistical Bulletin** and **Economic Series**.

Sector data

General industrial statistics

The annual **Census of Industrial Establishments** is a long-standing inquiry, started in 1926, which provides information on the structure and production activity of the industrial sector. The latest series of censuses began in 1979 and these cover all establishments with three or more persons and include those in the manufacturing, mining, quarrying, turf production, electricity, gas and water sectors. In addition, an annual **Census of Industrial Enterprises** was started in 1975 covering those enterprises with 20 or more employees. This supplementary inquiry is undertaken in compliance with EC directives and focuses on the trading dimensions such as turnover, purchases, taxes, etc. of firms.

Both inquiries are based on the **NACE** classification of economic activities and approximately 5,000 establishments are sampled in the former census and 1,700 in the latter census. There are also monthly production and turnover inquiries sampling firms with 20 or more employees. These are used to produce industrial production indices and industrial turnover indices and no actual production figures are published. Monthly production estimates for selected products are available on request from the **CSO**.

An annual **Census of Building and Construction** surveys private construction companies with 20 or more persons. The 1988 survey sampled 234 firms. Up to 1987, some results were also obtained from companies employing between 5 and 19 people but this coverage was discontinued from 1988 onwards.

External trade statistics are based on the SITC classification and are published monthly although more detailed analysis is available on magnetic tape, microfiche or computer print-out.

PUBLICATIONS PRODUCED BY NATIONAL ORGANISATIONS

General industry and trade

Regular statistics on the industrial sector are published in a series of **Statistical Releases**, with further figures in the **Economic Series** and the **Statistical Bulletin**. Details of the main titles are given in the separate entries listed below but the full list of **Statistical Releases** is as follows:

Census of Production Results	annual
Industrial Employment	quarterly
Industrial Earnings & Hours Worked	quarterly
Industrial Employment, Earnings & Hours Worked –	
Supplementary NACE Groups	quarterly
Industrial Production Index	monthly
Industrial Turnover Index	monthly
Census of Building & Construction	annual
Average Earnings & Hours Worked in Building	
& Construction	quarterly
Index of Employment in Building & Construction	monthly
Planning Permissions	quarterly

Census of Industrial Production Statistical Releases
Census of Production Annual Report

The **Statistical Release** provides the overall results of the census but there is a minimum two-year time lag in the publication of these initial results. More detailed results are published later in the **Annual Report** and an article, with statistics, is also published in the quarterly **Statistical Bulletin**. The 1988 annual report was published in May 1991. There is summary data on Irish industry and breakdowns by sector, at the 3-digit level of the **NACE** classification. Details include the number of establishments, gross output, input, wages and salaries, employment, stocks and capital assets.

The results of the annual **Census of Industrial Enterprises** are also included in the above series of annual reports. This has data on turnover, gross value added, labour costs, purchases, other costs, employment and taxes; but, as only 1,700 enterprises are covered, there is limited scope for analysis because of confidentiality constraints.

Industrial Production Index

A monthly index monitoring trends in the volume of production of establishments. The results are published in a **Statistical Release**, an **Economic Series** and each issue of the **Statistical Bulletin**. Seasonally adjusted and unadjusted indices are published for 49 **NACE** industrial sectors and groupings.

Industrial Turnover Index

A monthly series measuring the change in the level of sales of industrial products and seasonally adjusted and unadjusted indices are published for the same **NACE** headings as the production indices except that the electricity, gas and water sector is not included. Published as a **Statistical Release**, an **Economic Series** and in each issue of the **Statistical Bulletin**.

External Trade – Provisional Figures Statistical Release

Two releases are issued each month with the first giving provisional value figures for aggregate imports and exports and the second containing provisional details of the value of imports and exports by SITC sections and divisions. A country breakdown is also included in the second release.

Monthly Industrial Survey, Business Forecast

The **Confederation of Irish Industry** and the **Economic and Social Research Institute** carry out a monthly survey of a representative sample of Irish companies and the same sample is used each month. The survey asks business people about their expectations for the coming months and covers production, home sales, exports, employment, order book, stocks, capacity utilisation, production ensured and production constraints and selling prices. General data is followed by data for specific sectors.

Trade Statistics of Ireland

A monthly detailed analysis of external trade with data for specific commodities, arranged by **SITC** sections and divisions. Under each commodity heading, the details of the main trading partners are given and each issue has data for the latest month and the cumulative year-to-date.

Construction

Census of Building and Construction Statistical Releases
Statistical Bulletin

The annual **Statistical Release** has initial grossed national results for firms with 20 or more employees. More detailed results are published later in the **Statistical Bulletin**. The 1988 census results were reported in the spring 1990 issue of the **Statistical Bulletin**. The results are arranged by five **NACE** groups and statistics are provided on the number of establishments, employment, labour costs, turnover, purchases, stocks and stock changes, capital assets and a series of derived variables calculated from the above data.

Planning Permission

A quarterly **Statistical Release** showing the number and floor area of planning permissions granted in each county, county borough and planning region. The data is classified by four types of development and eight functional categories. Other results appear in an **Economic Series** report and in each issue of the **Statistical Bulletin**.

There are also other **Statistical Releases** on building costs, employment, average earnings and hours worked, house completions, new house and home improvement grants approved and the number of new loans approved. Regular house building data is published by the Department of the Environment.

Services

The last Census of Distribution was undertaken in 1977 but, in 1988, there was a **Census of Services** (including personal and business services as well as retailing and wholesaling). A total of 80,000 postal questionnaires were sent out with approximately 50 per cent to distribution outlets and 26,936 retail outlets replied (85 per cent of the retail sample) and 3,653 wholesalers (95 per cent of the wholesale sample).

Census of Services 1988

The first results were published in a **Statistical Release** and in the December 1990 issue of the **Statistical Bulletin**. The detailed results were being published in 1991. The census covers personal and business services, excluding the financial sector and the public sector, as well as retailing and wholesaling. Results have been published by specific sectors and include data on the number of establishments, turnover, purchases, VAT, stocks, employment, wages and salaries and selling space.

Electronics

The **Information and Computing Services Association (ISCA)** publishes a regular newsletter which occasionally contains statistics on the computer market.

Retailing and distribution

A detailed census of the sector has been undertaken as part of the **Census of Services 1988** (*see* previous entry).

Retail Sales Index Statistical Release

A monthly series measuring the changes in both the value and volume levels of retail sales covering 14 types of retail businesses. Results are also reproduced in an **Economic Series** publication and in each issue of the **Statistical Bulletin**.

Items Retained for Home Consumption

A monthly **Economic Series** publication with data on the retailing of beer, potable spirits, manufactured tobacco and cigarettes.

Financial services

The **Central Bank of Ireland** publications mentioned in the 'Economic Data' section on page 127 include statistics on banking and financial services. Other titles are:

Registrar of Building Societies Annual Report

Annual statistics on the building society sector with data on structure and activity.

Hire Purchase and Credit Sales

An annual **Statistical Release** with details of the number and value of new hire purchase and credit sale agreements entered into with finance companies and trading concerns, classified by the type of goods. The results are also published in the **Statistical Bulletin**.

Leisure and tourism

Tourism and Travel

Annual and quarterly **Statistical Releases** giving the number, average length of stay and expenditure of visitors to Ireland and of Irish visitors abroad. Estimates are obtained from continuous sample surveys of passengers at airports, seaports and cross-border routes. The results are also published in the **Statistical Bulletin**.

Board Failte Eireann Surveys

Annual surveys from the **Irish Tourist Board** cover international travellers, home holidays and hotels.

Transportation

Annual Vehicle Census

Detailed data on the number and type of vehicles in Ireland, published by the Department of the Environment.

Vehicles Registered and Licensed for the First Time
Motor Registrations – Provisional Results

The first title consists of an annual and monthly analysis with details of vehicles registered and licensed in each county and county borough by taxation class, make and size. The second title gives provisional results for the number of vehicles registered and licensed for the first time by taxation class. Both series are published as a monthly **Statistical Release** (the first series also appears annually) plus a monthly **Economic Series** report and statistics in each issue of the **Statistical Bulletin**.

Statistics of Port Traffic

An annual inquiry giving information for each harbour authority on the number of arrivals, tonnage, type of traffic, etc. Published as an annual **Statistical Release** plus a **Statistical Bulletin** article.

Passenger Movement by Sea

Details of outward and inward passenger movements are compiled each month and published as an **Economic Series** title. Also in each issue of the **Statistical Bulletin**.

Air Traffic Statistics

A monthly **Economic Series** title on outward and inward passenger, freight and mail movement through Dublin, Cork and Shannon airports. Figures are reproduced in the **Statistical Bulletin**.

Other statistics are published annually on road freight transport.

Advertising statistics

Business of Advertising Agencies

Annual details of the gross amount charged by advertising agencies to clients for advertising space, production work and other work such as research and promotions. Data is also available on the number of people employed and wages and salaries. The results are based on responses from a mailing to all known agencies and they are published as an annual **Statistical Release** with detailed figures in the **Statistical Bulletin**. The 1989 survey, for example, was reported in the September 1991 bulletin.

Advertising expenditure statistics are published by **Advertising Statistics Ireland**.

11 ITALY
Business statistics

INTRODUCTION

Of all the major EC countries, Italian statistics are probably the weakest with only limited data available on business and industrial sectors and significant time lags between the dates of surveys and the dates of the publication of the results. Virtually everything is published in Italian although one or two publications have English indexes and one official publication, **Italian Statistical Abstract**, is actually published in English.

The Central Institute of Statistics was set up by Act of Parliament in 1926 and further legislation in 1988 reorganised the Institute when it became the National Institute of Statistics (Istituto nazionale di statistica) or **ISTAT**. **ISTAT** is the central statistical agency and, although its budget is approved by the Cabinet Office, it is legally and administratively autonomous and controls the statistical activities carried out by central government departments and various autonomous agencies.

Istituto nazionale di statistica
ISTAT
Via Cesare Balbo 16
I-00100 Rome
Italy

The **Catalogo 199–** is an annual catalogue of **ISTAT**'s publications.

On-line services

Economic statistics, price information and trade data are available on-line direct from **ISTAT** in three databases:

Indicatori Statistici

A database of 15,000 monthly, quarterly and annual economic time series with data from 1959 onwards.

Prezzi

A statistical database covering 350,000 consumer prices from 1947 onwards. The database is updated monthly.

Commercio con L'Estero

Detailed product import and export statistics and aggregated trade data.

The organisation **CERVED** also offers a range of on-line statistics including aggregate data on sectors such as the number of companies, companies by region, companies by employment size and general economic and demographic statistics.

GENERAL STATISTICAL TITLES

Compilations

The annual **Annuario statistico italiano** (Italian Statistical Yearbook is a compilation of all the major official series including sections on population, agriculture, industry, transport, internal and external trade, insurance and financial markets, prices, employment, consumption, national accounts, economic indicators and international statistics. Most tables contain at least five years' data and various tables have regional breakdowns. The **Compendio statistico italiano** (Compendium of Italian Statistics) is an annual handbook with summary data, in tables, graphs and charts, from the Italian statistical yearbook. The **Italian Statistical Abstract** is a condensed version of the Italian statistical yearbook, published in English.

Monthly updates of the most important statistics contained in the statistical yearbook are found in the **Bollettino mensile di statistica** and the key statistics on areas such as population, production, trade, prices and salaries are published quickly in the monthly **Indicatori mensile** before they appear in the more traditional publications noted above.

A series of four-page pamphlets with the general title, **Notiziari Istat**, are published monthly with specific titles on important areas of economic and social life. There are four series of titles covered by **Notiziari Istat** and, within each series, there are individual titles on specific topics:

Series 1   **Statistiche demografiche e sociali** (Demographic and social statistics)

Series 2   **Statistiche dell'attivita produttiva** (Productive activity)

Series 3   **Statistiche del lavoro, delle retribuzioni e dei prezzi** (Labour market, wages and salaries, prices)

Series 4   **Argomenti vari** (Miscellaneous topics)

Within **Series 2**, for example, there are eight individual titles covering:

21   Agriculture, forestry, hunting & fishing (three titles)
22   Industrial production
23   Industrial turnover and orders
25   External trade
26   Travel and tourism
27   Internal trade sales

Economic data

Apart from the monthly and annual compilations noted above, economic data is also covered by **Indicatori trimestrali** (Quarterly Indicators), published quarterly. The annual **I Conti degli Italiani** presents the key economic indicators in graphs and tables. The on-line service, **Indicatori Statistici**, noted in the introductory section also covers economic data.

A number of regular publications from the **Istituto Nazionale per lo Studio della Congiuntura** also look at economic trends. The bi-annual **Rapporto Semestrale** provides a commentary with a statistical appendix on Italian economic trends plus a forecast up to 18 months ahead. Summary data from this publication is also available in an English language version, **Bi-annual Report on the Italian Economic Situation**. Other publications from the Institute include the monthly **Congiuntura Italiana: Rassegna Mensile**, with text and statistics, and the annual **Quaderni Analitici** with data and an analysis of economic and business trends. The Institute also produces an on-line service, **ISCO**, which is available outside Italy from **DRI**.

Quarterly economic data is included in the **Bolletino Statistico** from the **Banca d'Italia** and there are also bulletin supplements on specific topics. The bank also publishes a monthly **Economic Bulletin** in English, with a statistical appendix, and the quarterly, **Review of Economic Conditions in Italy**, with extensive articles and book reviews in English.

Demographic and social statistics

A population census is currently taking place every 10 years with the latest censuses in 1981 and 1991. Various volumes have been published with the results from the 1981 census under the general title, **12esimo censimento generale della popolazione** and similar reports from the 1991 census will appear in the 1990s.

The annual **Statistiche Demografiche** (Demographic Statistics), usually published in two volumes, has statistics covering population changes due to migration and births and deaths.

Sector data

General industrial statistics

The **ISTAT Classification of Economic Activites**, last updated in 1981, provides the basis for Italian industrial statistics and headings are based on the EC **NACE** classification. The Statistical Yearbook gives details of the most important sectors covered by the major classes of the classification and these are listed below (all corresponding to **NACE** headings):

13	Oil, natural gas extraction
16	Electricity, gas, steam
22	Metal industries
24	Non-metallic minerals manufactures
25	Chemicals
32	Mechanical engineering
34	Electrical and electronic machinery
35	Motor vehicles and parts
41	Basic food industries
43	Textiles
46	Wood and wooden furniture

There is no detailed classification for specific products although some monthly and annual production figures are published.

Annual industrial inquiries are based on records of enterprises held on a computerised file known as **SIRIO** and this covers all enterprises with 10 or more employees, including enterprises in commerce, transport and services. The last detailed industrial census was in 1981 and this provided the basic data for the above records but they are updated regularly using other sources. Most of the results from the annual industrial inquiry are based on results from companies with 20 or more employees.

External trade statistics are based on the **CN** trade classification.

PUBLICATIONS PRODUCED BY NATIONAL ORGANISATIONS

General industry and trade

Statistiche industriali

An annual publication with limited data on industrial structure but a large amount of data, in index form, on industrial production and turnover. There are also figures showing the actual production, in value and volume, for approximately 3,000 products. The table covering domestic electrical appliances is included as Table 11.1. There is some delay in publishing the

Produzione di apparecchi elettrodomestici (a)

PRODOTTI	1983	1984	1985	1986	1987
	NUMERO				
Condizionatori d'aria portatili o da finestra	117.862	153.585	131.205	124.384	129.576
Frigoriferi domestici (b)	3.900.268	3.575.513	3.357.251	3.589.671	3.767.006
Congelatori domestici (c)	1.670.886	1.526.318	1.303.971	1.498.744	1.433.283
Fino a 250 litri	*924.937*	*830.795*	*753.486*	*837.803*	*761.508*
Da 250 a 600 litri	*745.949*	*695.523*	*550.485*	*660.941*	*671.775*
Lavabiancheria	3.306.533	3.392.872	3.691.981	3.991.200	4.140.481
Lavastoviglie	432.898	448.139	427.332	536.276	614.597
Aspirapolvere	388.137	364.760	332.807	282.872	290.938
Lucidatrici, battitappeto	178.694	177.805	155.307	142.629	146.965
Frullatori, sbattitori app. per tritare	762.366	541.651	547.528	483.398	344.569
Cappe aspiranti	333.639	359.147	354.764	353.913	352.571
Ventilatori	1.328.386	1.510.588	1.238.798	923.090	1.050.148
Termoventilatori	227.853	339.848	519.842	379.716	429.729
Asciugacapelli	871.313	750.636	825.498	543.467	491.963
Cucine elettriche	670.045	541.647	505.891	518.828	560.906
Cucine a gas	1.052.531	1.204.088	983.977	886.466	853.301
Piani di cottura ad incasso	441.304	530.422	547.553	599.664	679.384
Scaldabagni elettrici	1.989.477	1.980.357	1.726.762	1.647.583	1.955.939
Scaldabagni a gas	126.319	98.111	96.344	96.038	107.496
Stufe e radiatori elettrici	61.463	60.676	60.432	54.772	33.285
Termconvettori	155.153	120.119	103.905	106.247	171.222
Ferri da stiro	1.264.100	1.111.372	1.014.487	1.201.765	1.197.275
	VALORE IN MILIONI DI LIRE (d)				
Condizionatori d'aria portatili o da finestra	62.864	93.199	102.822	122.514	159.258
Frigoriferi domestici (b)	796.710	783.771	809.883	941.068	1.031.759
Congelatori domestici (c)	354.026	362.942	332.991	400.558	401.484
Fino a 250 litri	*176.245*	*179.280*	*173.799*	*185.083*	*175.284*
Da 250 a 600 litri	*177.781*	*183.662*	*159.192*	*215.475*	*226.200*
Lavabiancheria	871.596	958.456	1.011.012	1.260.171	1.385.363
Lavastoviglie	125.274	124.139	133.054	168.016	194.666
Aspirapolvere	19.847	31.273	24.862	22.505	21.951
Lucidatrici, battitappeto	11.123	19.936	18.269	18.946	22.479
Frullatori, sbattitori, app. per tritare	24.754	21.178	19.497	18.624	14.932
Cappe aspiranti	14.688	15.361	17.403	18.161	18.067
Ventilatori	28.603	32.716	30.590	30.906	36.661
Termoventilatori	5.268	5.703	11.591	9.705	7.253
Asciugacapelli	9.334	9.560	9.609	7.434	12.682
Cucine elettriche	135.327	119.124	125.815	138.840	152.871
Cucine a gas	182.370	216.653	197.649	207.396	206.934
Piani di cottura ad incasso	39.856	53.640	51.644	59.772	79.009
Scaldabagni elettrici	115.951	143.353	107.616	113.519	136.251
Scaldabagni a gas	20.691	14.386	15.463	14.660	17.084
Stufe e radiatori elettrici	1.086	955	1.111	1.012	736
Termconvettori	5.622	4.787	4.455	6.864	10.571
Ferri da stiro	26.384	32.037	24.149	33.119	35.629

(a) Dati raccolti dall'ISTAT con l'indagine mensile della produzione industriale. I dati riguardano le sole ditte con 20 addetti e più, escluse quelle di assemblaggio di parti staccate. - (b) Sono compresi i frigoriferi con il reparto di congelamento.-(c) Sono escluse le vetrine di conservazione ed i conservatori di gelato. - (d) I valori sono espressi al prezzo di vendita su base di listino franco stabilimento (esclusa IVA).

Table 11.1 Italian production statistics – section on household electrical equipment

results with the 1990 edition covering 1986 and 1987. There are also regular production statistics in the **Notiziari Istat** series noted above.

Statistica del Commercio con l'Estero

Annual and quarterly external trade statistics with data on specific products, broken down by the **CN** classification, and trading partners.

Comercio con l'Estero

An on-line database from **ISTAT** with three files on Italian imports and exports. One file has monthly time series, a second file has detailed product data for the last three years and a third file has aggregated data from 1974.

GIANO

The on-line host system **GIANO** has databases produced by the research organisation **Confindustria**. **Statistiche Economiche** has 12,000 monthly, quarterly and annual time series on Italian industrial production and plant utilisation. The database is updated annually. **Statistiche del Commercio Estero dell'Italia** contains monthly product import and export statistics from 1978 onwards.

Construction

Monthly statistics on building authorisations are collected by **ISTAT** and appear in the monthly compilation noted in the earlier section and other publications are:

L'Industria delle Costruzioni
Bolletino di Statistica

The **Associazione Nazionale Costruttori Edili (ANCE)** publish various statistics on the construction sector based on a combination of official data and data based on its own surveys. **L'Industria delle Costruzioni** appears monthly and annually with data on new work, investment, employment, finance and prices. The quarterly, **Bolletino di Statistica**, has a commentary on construction industry trends plus statistics on residential and non-residential building by type of buildings and local areas. The association publishes other statistics on building materials and public works.

Food and drink

Relazione Annuale
Il Mondo del Latte

An annual report and a monthly review, both with statistics on the milk market, from **Associazione Italiana Lattiero Casearia**.

Chemicals and chemical products

Compendio Statistico

The trade association, **Associazione Nazionale dell'Industria Chimica (ASCHIMICI)** publishes annual statistics on the chemicals industry including data on production, imports, exports, prices, etc.

Rapporto Sullo Stato dell'Industria Chimica in Italia

Graphs and tables in a yearbook on the Italian chemicals sector from the association, **FEDERCHIMICA**. Statistics on industrial structure plus production, investment, external trade, consumption, etc. with data broken down by major sectors. Some international figures are also included. A half-yearly review of the industry based mainly on members' returns, **Resoconto del Panel Congiunturale**, is also published.

Annuario Statistico

Annual statistics on petroleum and energy trends in Italy plus tables on the world situation. The publication comes from the **Unione Petrolifera** which also publishes the monthly **Notizie Statistiche Petrolifere**, with basic data, and the annual **Relazione Annuale**, with an analysis of the industry.

Indicatori Farmaceutica

Annual statistics on the pharmaceutical sector from the association, **Farmindustria**. It also publishes a quarterly bulletin, **Notizario** and an annual report, **Relazione Annuele**.

Textiles and clothing

Industria Cotoniera
Rapporto Sulla Industria Cotoniera Italiana

The **Associazione Cotoniera Italiana** publishes monthly and annual statistics on the cotton and textiles sector. The monthly title, **Industria Cotoniera**, has commentary with statistics on the key indicators while the annual title is mainly commentary but some basic data is included. The association also publishes annual figures on the European cotton industry.

Indicatori congiunturali

Published 9 or 10 times per year by the clothing industry association, **Associazione Italiana Industriali Abbigliamento (AIIA)**. Includes basic statistics on the sector and there are other quarterly and annual publications plus publications on specific areas, e.g. menswear, womenswear, etc.

Rivista Laniera

A quarterly review from the wool trade association, **Associazione dell'Industria Laniera Italiana (LANIERA)**.

L'Industria Calzaturiera Italiana

An annual statistical review of the Italian footwear sector from the **Associazione Nazionale Calzaturifici Italiani (ANCI)**. The report includes data on industrial structure by local area as well as production and trade data for specific products.

Electrical and mechanical engineering

Repertorio delle industrie Siderurgiche Italiane

Published approximately every five years with production, trade, consumption, prices data, etc. over a number of years for the steel sector. Available from the **Associazione Industrie Siderurgiche Italiane (ASSIDER)**.

L'Industria Meccanica

A monthly bulletin from the mechanical engineering association, **Federazione delle Associazioni Nazionali dell'Industria Meccanica Varia ed Affini (ANIMA)**. Many smaller associations in specific sectors are also based in **ANIMA**'s offices and most of these publish statistics.

FEDERMECCANICA, the Italian metal working and mechanical engineering trade association, also publishes selected statistics.

Retailing and distribution

A monthly index of sales through 'large selling units' is compiled and published in the monthly titles listed in the 'Compilations' section on page 135. Statistics on the structure of retailing are collected through a retail licensing system but there are many small shops which are outside this system so collecting comprehensive retail statistics is difficult.

Statistiche del commercio intermo

An annual compilation of retailing statistics from **ISTAT**.

Caratteri Strutturali del Sistema Distributivo in Italia

Published by the **Ministero dell' Industria del Commercio e dell' Artigianato**. An annual review of the structure of the Italian distributive sector which includes a relatively wide definition of distribution covering sales of motors and fuels, repair shops, commercial intermediaries, hire companies which may have retail premises, hotels, inns and service establishments dealing directly with the general public.

The national association of retail cooperatives **Associazione Nazionale Cooperative fra Dettaglianti (ANCD)** works closely with the above ministry in the production of retailing statistics.

Financial services

Banche e Banchieri

A monthly bulletin on banking and credit from the **Associazione Nazionale Aziende Ordinarie di Credito (ASSBANK)**.

Notiziario Statistico sulle Societa Italiane per Azioni

Quarterly and annual statistical volumes relating to the financial markets and equities in Italy.

Annuario Italiano delle Imprese Assicuratrici

Insurance statistics are produced by the **Associazione Nazionale fra le Imprese Assicuratrici** and their yearbook contains various statistics over a five-year period.

Leisure and tourism

Statistiche del turismo

Official statistical yearbook on tourism.

The **Federazione delle Associazioni Italiane Alberghi e Turismo (FAIAT)** collects statistics on tourism trends and publishes a fortnightly bulletin, **Turismo d'Italia**.

Transportation

Automobile in Cifre
Notizario Statistico

Annual and monthly statistical publications from the **Associazione Nazionale fra Industrie Automobilistiche (ANFIA)**. Current and historical figures on motor vehicles are included in the annual compilation with current data on registrations and production in the monthly.

L'Auto Estera in Italia
Bollettino Mensile

The first title is an annual compilation of data on the motor vehicles sector and the second title is a monthly with summary data on home production and imports. Both are published by the **Unione Nazionale Distributori Automotoveicoli (UNRAE)**.

Statistiche della navigazione marittima

Annual official statistics on shipping and sea transport from **ISTAT**.

12 LUXEMBOURG
Business statistics

INTRODUCTION

Statistics and economic studies are the responsibility of the **Service Central de la Statistique et des Etudes Economiques (STATEC)**, set up by Act of Parliament in 1962. **STATEC** is part of the Ministry of Economic Affairs and its budget is considered by the Ministry of Finance and voted by Parliament. **STATEC** works closely with other organisations, including trade and professional associations, in the production of statistics and a **High Council of Statistics** advises on the annual programme of **STATEC**. Its offices are based in Luxembourg at:

> **Service Central de la Statistique et des Etudes Economiques**
> **STATEC**
> 19–21 boulevard Royal
> BP 304
> L-2103 Luxembourg

Publications can be obtained from the above office and a regular list of publications is **Liste des publications du STATEC**.

GENERAL STATISTICAL TITLES

Compilations

Annuaire statistique is the basic annual source for the major Luxembourg statistics. It also includes an international section. It has an alphabetical subject index plus a departmental index and a list of international bodies publishing data. **Bulletin du STATEC** is published approximately eight times a year and has analysis and statistics from the main surveys.

Economic data

A quarterly bulletin, **Bulletin trimestral**, published by the **Institut monetaire Luzembourgeois** provides economic and financial data.

Demographic and social statistics

Population censuses are carried out every 10 years with the most recent ones in 1981 and 1991. The results are published in a series of volumes with the general title, **Recensement de la population et mouvement de la population**. More regular population statistics are included in various issues of the **Bulletin du STATEC**.

Sector data

General industrial statistics

An annual survey of industrial production covers enterprises with an average of 20 or more persons employed and the published results are based on the **NACE** classification. The annual survey includes the construction sector. Monthly industrial production indices are also based on **NACE**.

Monthly external trade statistics are published for the Belgium-Luxembourg Economic Union and these publications are described in the Belgium chapter.

PUBLICATIONS PRODUCED BY NATIONAL ORGANISATIONS

General industry and trade

Annuaire statistique

The annual statistical yearbook has the results of the annual industrial production survey which may be broken down by **NACE** headings at the 1-, 2- and 3-digit levels depending on the sector covered. The statistics cover the number of enterprises, employment, salaries and wages, hours worked, value of production, value added, imports, exports, consumption of materials, industrial services, fixed capital formation, turnover and sales.

Food and drink

Rapport sur le millesimo

An annual report from the **Ministere de l'Agriculture, de la Viticulture et des Eaux et Forets, Marque nationale du vin luxembourgeois**. It includes figures on foods and wines.

Leisure and tourism

Rapport d'activite

Annual report, with statistics, of the national office of tourism.

Transportation

Indicateurs rapides, Serie D: Immatriculations de vehicules automoteurs

Monthly statistics on new registrations of motor vehicles and the sales and imports of vehicles. A second Serie D publication has figures on new registrations by make and model.

Rapport annuel des chemins de fer

Annual report, with statistics, of the Luxembourg railways.

13 NETHERLANDS
Business statistics

INTRODUCTION

Official statistical activity is centralised in the **Central Bureau of Statistics (CBS)**, constituted by a Royal Decree of 1899, and is now part of the Ministry of Economic Affairs. It derives its budget from this Ministry but its statistical activities remain independent.

CBS is based in two locations in the Netherlands, Voorburg and Heerlen, and each of these offices is responsible for particular areas of government statistics. The individual departments in each office are listed in Table 13.1.

Central Bureau of Statistics
CBS
Prinses Beatrixlaan 428
PO Box 959
2270 AZ Voorburg
Netherlands

and

Kloosterweg 1
PO Box 4481
6401 CZ Heerlen
Netherlands

Virtually all of the official publications have English translations of their titles plus translations of the table headings, contents pages and notes.

Departments located at both offices
Manufacturing & construction statistics
Distribution & services statistics
Transport statistics
Financial statistics
Health statistics
Education statistics

Table 13.1 CBS – Departments in Voorburg and Heerlen

Socio-cultural statistics
Justice & security statistics
Co-ordination of economic statistics

Voorburg

Agricultural statistics
Price statistics
National accounts
Environmental statistics
Population statistics
Employment & wages statistics
Social accounts

Heerlen

External trade statistics
Economic censuses
Statistics on stocks of capital goods & balance sheets
Social surveys
Income & consumption statistics

Table 13.1 CBS – Departments in Voorburg and Heerlen (cont.)

Libraries in both offices are open from 9.00 a.m. to 4.00 p.m., Monday to Friday, and telephone inquiries on the major statistical series can also be dealt with.

Official statistics in the Netherlands are particulary good at tracking demographic and social trends but their industrial statistics are less extensive. In certain areas, such as electrical goods, much of the official data is not published to maintain confidentiality for the company that dominates the sector, Philips. Non-official sources can sometimes fill in the detail absent from official sources.

GENERAL STATISTICAL TITLES

Compilations

The annual **Statistisch Jaarboek** provides a basic compilation of Dutch data and an English language version, usually published some months after the Dutch version, is entitled **Statistical Yearbook of the Netherlands**. The English language edition was published annually up to 1988 but then there was a gap and a new series of English language annuals started in 1990. Both versions have an alphabetical subject index.

The monthly **Maandschrift** is a monthly bulletin covering the main series from the **Yearbook** and each issue also announces new official publications.

Economic data

Data is available in the above publications plus the **De Nederlandsche Bank Quarterly Bulletin,** published in English. It includes articles on economic topics and a statistical annex. **Bank Mees & Hope NV** has a monthly pamphlet, **Economic Review,** with commentary and trends on the key economic indicators. This is also published in English.

The national industrial association, **Verbond van Nederlandse Ondernemingen (VNO),** publishes **The Dutch Economy** twice a year in English.

Demographic and social statistics

A population census was undertaken in 1981 and regular population statistics are published in the monthly **Maandstatistiek van de bevolking** which also contains articles on population issues. **Jaarstatistiek van de bevolking** is an annual population title.

There are also regular monthly statistics on socio-economic trends in **Sociaal-economische maandstatistiek.**

Sector data

General industrial statistics

Economic activities in the Netherlands are classified according to the **Standaard Bedrijfsindeling (SBI)** and commodities are broken down by the **Standaard Geoderennomenclatuur (SGN)** which is compatible with the HS trade classification.

Statistics on the structure and production in particular manufacturing, building and public sectors are collected annually and, for some sectors, there are also monthly or quarterly figures on product sales or production. Whether the figures cover sales or production largely depends on the product. In textile and clothing sectors, for example, the statistics usually refer to production while in the engineering, leather and paper sectors, the statistics cover sales.

Generally, all units with 10 or more employees are surveyed but this again can vary in particular sectors. For example, in engineering, enterprises with 50 or more employees are questioned and 20 per cent of enterprises with between 10 and 50 workers are also consulted.

There is also an irregular economic census or **Algemene bedrijfstelling** which surveys all the main sectors of economic activity including manufacturing and services and the results are published in various volumes.

External trade statistics are broken down by both the **HS** and **SITC** classifications.

PUBLICATIONS PRODUCED BY NATIONAL ORGANISATIONS

General industry and trade

Maandstatistiek van de industrie

Translated as the **Monthly Statistical Bulletin of Manufacturing**, this is the most regular source of sector and product information and it includes English translations of the tables and an English contents page. Statistics on key sectors, and selected products within these sectors, are published monthly while some other sectors and products are covered quarterly. Some tables also appear annually. Details of the areas covered by monthly and quarterly data are given below:

Monthly data
General data
Index numbers of industrial production
Mining & quarrying: energy supply
Manufacture of foodstuffs, beverages & tobacco
Textile & clothing industry
Manufacture of leather & bootwear products
Manufacture of wood & wooden products, including furniture; manufacture of
     building materials & earthenware
Manufacture of paper & paper products; printing industry & publishing companies
Chemical industry; manufacture of rubber products; synthetic processing industry
Metal industry; shipbuilding
Building industry

Quarterly data
General statistics of manufacturing industry
Consumption & sales of potato products manufacturing industry
Sales of soups, broth & beef cubes
Consumption & sales of the confectionery industry
Sales of some (meat) snacks & salads
Consumption of feedingstuffs and production of compound feeds
Deliveries of chocolate articles, by assortment

Annual data
General statistics of manufacturing industry
Bleaching, dyeing & printing of textiles
Raw materials of manufacturing yeast & alcohol (methylated spirits & malt wine)
Storage of basic materials containing alcohol with freedom per excise
Production of alcohol (methylated spirits & malt wine)

Produktiestatistieken industrie

The major source of data on a wide range of products is a series of 109 individual annual titles on specific sectors. Each title has general data on the sector, including number of enterprises, employment, stocks, purchases and energy consumption plus either sales or production figures for selected products. Most titles also have statistics on export sales. Whether production or sales figures are included depends on the products being surveyed. For example, Title 23 on clothing has data on the manufacture and sales of products, Title 31.1 on rubber products just has industrial sales and Title 29.7 covering soaps, cleaning preparations, perfumes and cosmetics has industrial sales and export sales. The number of products covered can also vary from sector to sector. In many cases, for reasons of confidentiality, amalgamations of various product headings take place. In engineering, for example, out of 500 products or product groups surveyed, details on only 140 are actually published regularly.

A list of the annual titles is given in Table 13.2.

Food & beverages
20.1	Slaughtering & meat processing
20.2	Dairy industry
20.3	Canning, preserving & processing of fish
20.4	Flour industry
20.5/21.1	Sugar & starch industries
20.6	Margarine & other vegetable oils, fats
20.7	Canning, processing of fruit & vegetables
20.8	Bread, rusks, pastry, biscuits, cakes
20.9	Cocoa, chocolate & sugar confectionery
21.2	Animal feedstuffs
21.31-34.6/8/9/	Miscellaneous sectors
21.35	Baking additives and ingredients
21.37	Potato products
21.391	Snack foods
21.4	Distilleries
21.5	Brewing
21.6	Soft drinks
21.7	Tobacco

Textiles, clothing & wood industries
22.1/2/4	Cotton, wool & textiles
22.3	Knitting & hosiery mills
22.5	Carpets, rugs & mats
22.6/9	Other textiles
22.7	Made up textile goods
23	Clothing
25	Wood products, including furniture

Table 13.2 *Produktie statistieken industrie* – List of annual titles

Leather & mineral products

24.1	Tanning & leather finishing
24.2	Leather products, excluding clothing
24.3	Footwear
32.11	Bricks
32.12	Roofing tiles
32.21	Pottery & china
32.22	Earthenware
32.3	Sand-lime bricks
32.4/7	Cement,lime & other mineral products
32.51	Concrete articles
32.52/54	Asbestos cement articles & building boards with minerals
32.53	Ready mixed concrete
32.6	Building stone & monumental stone
32.8	Glass & glass products

Paper, printing & publishing

26.1	Paper & board
26.2	Paper products
26.31	Corrugated board & cartons
26.32	Folding cartons
27.1	Printing
27.2	Publishing
27.3	Binding

Oil industry

28.1	Petroleum refining
28.2	Petrol & coal products

Chemical industry

29/30	Chemical industry
29.1	Synthetic fertilisers
29.2	Synthetic resins
29.3	Pigments & dyes
29.4/30	Basic industrial chemicals, incl. artificial & synthetic yarns & man-made fibres
29.5	Paints, lacquers, varnishes & printer's inks
29.6	Drugs & medicines
29.7	Soap, cleaning products, perfumes & cosmetics, toilet preparations
29.8	Chemical pesticides
29.9	Miscellaneous chemical products
31.1	Rubber products
31.3	Plastic products

Metals, mechanical & electrical engineering

33	Basic metals
34.0	Metal products
34.1	Forges, stamping & pressing
34.2	Screws, bolts, nuts & technical springs
34.3	Tanks, reservoirs & industrial pipes
34.4	Structural engineering, excl. products of 34.3
34.5	Metal furniture
34.6	Metal packaging
34.7	Non-electrical heating & cooking appliances

Table 13.2 *Produktie statistieken industrie* – List of annual titles (*cont.*)

34.8	Hand tools, cutlery, lock & key sets, builder's furniture, domestic & general purpose hardware
34.91/92	Blacksmith's workshops & repair of agricultural equipment
34.93	Surface treatment of metals
35	Mechanical engineering
35.1	Agricultural machinery & equipment
35.2	Metalworking machinery & interchangeable machine tools
35.3	Machinery for the food, chemicals & allied industries
35.4	Lifting machinery & other mechanical handling equipment, machinery & equipment used by the mining, construction & basic metal industries
35.5	Gears, bearings & other power transmission equipment
35.6	Wood-working machinery, textile machinery, commercial laundry machines, dry cleaning & pressing machines, leather working machines, paper industry and printing trades machinery
35.7	Steam boilers, engines & turbines
35.8/9	Office machinery, excl. EDP equipment & miscellaneous machinery not elsewhere specified
36.1	Insulated wires & cables
36.21	Electric motors
36.22	Switchgear, switchboards & other basic electrical equipment
36.91-95/97/98	Other electrical equipment including accumulators, batteries, light bulbs, measuring and controlling equipment, electro medical instruments & appliances, telecommunications & signalling equipment, radio & tv receiving sets and apparatus, domestic electrical appliances
36.96	Records & pre-recorded magnetic tapes
36.99	Industrial assembly and installation of electrical engineering products
37.1/3/7	Motor vehicles, parts & accessories, aircraft
37.21	Trailers & semi-trailers
37.22	Motor vehicle bodies
37.4	Shipbuilding and repairing
37.6	Bicycles & motor cycles
37.9	Other transport equipment
38.11/12	Medical, surgical, dental, orthopaedic equipment & artificial limbs
38.13	Dental mechanic's workshops
38.2	Measuring, controlling & other precision equipment
38.3/4	Optical & photographic goods, clocks & watches
39.1	Diamond cutting & polishing & manufacture of goldsmith's/silversmith's wares and jewellery
39.2/9	Musical instruments & miscellaneous goods
39.3	Photographic & cinematographic laboratories
Public utilities	
40.1	Electricity
40.2	Gas
40.3	Water works & supply
Building & installation	
51	Construction of residential & non-residential buildings
52	Installation work on construction projects
52.1	Plumbing, gas fittings & sanitary equipment
52.21	Central heating & air conditioning
52.22	Insulation
52.31	Electrical engineering on construction projects

Table 13.2 *Produktie statistieken industrie* – List of annual titles (*cont.*)

Maandstatistiek van de buitenlandse handel

Monthly external trade statistics arranged by the divisions and classes of the **HS** classification plus sections, divisions and groups of the **SITC**. Import and export data for a select list of important commodities is also included. Also external trade data by country.

Jaarstatistiek van de buitenlandse handel

Annual external trade statistics arranged by the **HS** and **SITC** classifications.

Construction

Apart from the official statistics noted above, the building contractors association, **Algemeen Verbond Bouwbedrijf (AVBB)** publishes statistics in its annual report and produces a weekly bulletin.

An opinion survey based on sample returns from building companies is produced by the **Economisch Instituut voor de Bouwnijverheid (EIB)**. Details are available from the CBS.

Food and drink

Jaarverslag

An annual publication from the **Algemene Nederlandse Bond van Binnenlandse Groothandelaren in Groenten en Fruit.** The report has commentary and statistics on fruit and vegetable markets with data on specific commodities and products.

Zuivel in Cijfers

Data on dairy products and milk production and external trade published annually by the **Koninklijke Nederlandse Zuivelbond (KNZ).** Produced in pocket-book format.

BBM Jaarverslag

An annual report comprising a review of the drinks market and a statistical section with data on specific soft drinks and beers. Some comparative international figures are also included. The report is published by **Algemene Nederlandse Bond van Frisdrankenfabrikanten en Groothandelaren in Dranken (BBM)**. The association also publishes a leaflet with basic data, over a 10-ten year period, on the Dutch soft drinks market.

Chemicals and chemical products

Nederlandse Chemische Industrie

Published in various issues throughout the year, the publication has general data on the chemicals industry and mainly gives production and sales figures.

Published by the **Vereniging van de Nederlandse Chemische Industrie (VNCI)**.

Kosmetiek

Published by the **Bond van Detaillisten in de Parfumeriehandel (BODEPA)**. This monthly publication contains general retailing statistics for cosmetics, toiletries and perfumes.

Textiles and clothing

Jaarboek

A clothing and textiles yearbook, with some statistics, from the **Vereniging van Confectie- en Tricotage- Ondernemingen (FENECON)**. Some textile statistics are also available from another association, **MITEX**.

Kerncijfers

Basic annual statistics on the footwear industry and markets published by the **Federatie van Nederlandse Schoenfabrikanten**.

Electrical and mechanical engineering

Jaarboek

The annual report of the metalworking association, **METAALUNIE**, has some statistics and the association also publishes a monthly journal.

Other statistics are produced by the **Vereniging FME**, the association for machinery, metalworking and electrical engineering and the **Vereniging Nederlandse Scheepsbouw Industrie (VNSI)**, the association for shipbuilders.

Electronics

VLEHAN is the trade association for the domestic electrical appliances sector and it produces some estimates of sales and market sizes for specific products.

Retailing and distribution

The last retail census took place in 1985 but retailing activity is closely monitored at a local and national level and regular statistics appear in:

Maandstatistiek van de binnenlandse handel en dienstverlening

Statistics on turnover and stocks in retailing and wholesaling plus data on employment and wages. There are English language table headings and contents pages.

Other organisations work closely with official statisticians to compile retailing statistics and relevant bodies include the **Hoofbedrijfschap Detailhandel** (Central Industrial Board for the Retail Trade) and the research institute **Economisch Institut voor Het Midden- en Kleinbedrijf (EIM)**.

Financial services

Maandstatistiek van het financiewezen

A monthly statistical report from the **CBS** on the financial services sector including tables for banking, the stock exchange, insurance, pension funds, etc.

There is also a series of official reports on specific financial sectors including:

Statistiek van het consumptief krediet

An annual statistical review of consumer credit.

Financiele gegevens over schade-en levensverzekering

Annual statistics on life and non-life insurance.

Statistiek van de hypotheken

Annual statistics on mortgage banks.

Statistiek van de spaargelden

Annual statistics relating to savings.

Other titles cover investment trends, unit trusts, assets of institutional investors and life assurance.

De Nederlandsche Bank Quarterly Bulletin

An English language quarterly with articles and statistics on banking developments.

Jaarboek

An annual report with some statistics from the insurance association, **Nederlandse Vereniging van Makelaars in Assurantien en Assurantie-aduiseurs (NVA)**.

Other financial statistics include regular figures from **Nederlandse Vereniging van Hypotheckbanken** (mortgage banks) and annual and quarterly data from **Nederlandse Vereniging van Participatiemaatschappijen** (investment and venture capital).

Leisure and tourism

Statistiek vreemdelingenverkeer

Annual official statistics bringing together a range of data on tourism and travel trends.

Vakantie onderzoek

An annual survey of holidays and holidaying habits.

Hotels, restaurants, cafe's e.d.

Annual statistics on catering and tourism establishments.

Transportation

Maandstatistiek van verkeer en vervoer

A monthly statistical bulletin for the transport sector.

Statistiek van de motorvoertuigen

An annual statistical compilation for the motor vehicles sector.

Het bezit en gebruik van personenauto's

Annual statistics covering the ownership and use of cars.

Other official statistical publications in the transport sector include:

Statistiek van het personenvervoer

An annual compilation of passenger transport statistics.

Statistiek van de luchtvaart

A yearbook of civil aviation statistics.

Auto in cijfers

Annual statistics on motor vehicles from the **Nederlandse Vereniging de Rijweil- en Automobiel-Industrie (RIA)**. There is an English contents page and English headings for the tables. Statistics relate to vehicle ownership, registrations, production and assembly, external trade, vehicle use, expenditure, energy, roads and traffic. The association also publishes a weekly newsletter with a bi-monthly annex, **RAI Actueel**, which brings together various vehicle statistics from the Netherlands and overseas.

Public sector

Statistisch Jaarboek van de Openbare Gasvoorziening

Annual statistics on the gas supply sector from the industry association, **VEGIN**.

14 NORWAY
Business statistics

INTRODUCTION

Norway has a centralised system of official statistics and the central office is the **Statistisk Sentralbyra** (Central Bureau of Statistics). The Bureau was set up by the Statistical Act of 1907 and it is an independent government agency although its budget comes from the Ministry of Finance and is approved by parliament.

The office is located in Oslo at:

Statistisk Sentralbyra
Skippergata 15
PO Box 8131 Dep
N-0033 Oslo 1
Norway

Publications is an annual pamphlet, in English, which describes the main official titles.

Norway is also a member of the **Nordic Statistical Secretariat** (*see* Chapter 2).

GENERAL STATISTICAL TITLES

Compilations

The annual yearbook, **Statistisk Arbok**, has 558 tables on the main economic, social and demographic trends in Norway. There are English language notes, contents pages and table headings. An alphabetical subject index is included at the back of the yearbook.

The monthly **Statistisk manedshefte** has up-to-date figures for the main official series and this also has English table headings, contents pages and notes. The quick release of statistics comes in the weekly **Statistisk ukehefte** (Weekly Bulletin of Statistics) which is only available in Norwegian.

Economic data

A quarterly publication, **Economic Survey**, is published in English with commentary, analysis and statistics based on the latest quarterly national accounts data.

The **Norges Bank** produces a quarterly **Economic Bulletin** with articles and a statistical annex. The **Norwegian Economic Report** is a regular title from the industrial organisation, **Naeringslivets Houedorganisasja**n.

Demographic and social statistics

Annual population statistics are published in two volumes with the general title, **Befolkningsstatistikk**. Volume 1, **Endringstal for Kommunar**, looks at population changes in Norwegian municipalities and Volume 2, **Folkemengd 1st January**, has data on the population at the beginning of each year.

Sector data

General industrial statistics

Annual statistics on industrial structure and the production of specific commodities are published by the **Statistisk Sentralbyra**. The statistics are based on the Norwegian **Standard Industrial Classification (SIC)** which is a 5-digit classification scheme. The 1-digit code corresponds to 'major divisions' and 2-digits relate to 'divisions' and the mining and manufacturing divisions are listed in Table 14.1. The 3-digit code covers 'major groups', 4-digits correspond to 'groups' and 5-digits to 'sub-groups'. An example of the breakdown is given below:

Major Division 3	Manufacturing
Division 31	Food, beverages & tobacco
Major Group 311–312	Food manufacturing
Group 3112	Dairy products
Sub-group 31123	Ice cream

2	**Oil extraction, mining & quarrying**
21	Coal mining
22	Crude petroleum & natural gas production
23	Metal ore mining
29	Other mining
3	**Manufacturing**
31	Food, beverages & tobacco
32	Textiles, wearing apparel, leather & leather products

Table 14.1 SIC divisions in mining & manufacturing

33	Wood & wood products, incl. furniture
34	Paper & paper products; printing & publishing
35	Chemicals & chemical petroleum, coal, rubber & plastic products
36	Mineral products
37	Basic metals
38	Fabricated metal products, machinery & equipment
39	Other manufacturing industries

Table 14.1 SIC divisions in mining & manufacturing (*cont.*)

The annual industrial inquiry covers establishments in mining, oil extraction, quarrying and manufacturing and all 'large' establishments, i.e., with five or more persons engaged, are sent a detailed questionnaire. Smaller establishments are just asked for total figures on sales and employment. In a few industrial sectors, all the establishments are treated as 'large' and the whole sector is surveyed in detail. These sectors include coal mining, crude petroleum and natural gas production, metal ore mining, oil and gas well machinery and tools, petroleum refining, tobacco products, dairies, condensed and powdered milk and casein, fish oils and fish meal and margarine.

A separate annual inquiry covers the construction sector where all establishments with 10 or more employees are sent a detailed questionnaire. Establishments with between five and nine employees are sent a less detailed questionnaire and other establishments, including those with only one person employed, are just asked for details of total employment and sales.

A central Register of Establishments and Enterprises is maintained and this is based on the Census of Enterprises liable to VAT. Registration is compulsory for all establishments with an annual turnover of NKR 6,000 or more.

Annual external trade statistics are published based on both the **HS** classification and the **SITC** classification and details of the publications are given below.

PUBLICATIONS PRODUCED BY NATIONAL ORGANISATIONS

General industry and trade

Industristatistikk Hefte 1: Naeringstall

Although entitled 'Manufacturing Statistics', the volume also covers mining, quarrying and oil extraction and there are English headings to the tables. There are statistics on the number of establishments, ownership, employment, gross value of production, costs of goods and services consumed, gross fixed capital formation, stocks, wages and salaries, value added and the insurance value of buildings and equipment. Summary figures provide information for the last few years and there are detailed figures for the latest year on specific sectors usually down to the 3-digit level of the **SIC** and, in some cases, down to the 5-digit level. From the 1989 issue onwards, less detail has been published in the annual volume. Several tables which previously had data at the 5-digit level now only go down to the 3-digit level and the figures for individual municipalities are no longer included. More detailed information, however, is available for a fee from the central statistical office.

Industristatistikk Hefte 2: Varetall

Annual statistics on the production, in 'large' establishments, of specific commodities. Production data is given in value and volume and the product headings correspond largely to the **HS** classification of external trade. 8-digit codes are used for each commodity and a sample page is included as Table 14.2. There is an alphabetical index of products covered at the back of each issue.

Regnskapsstatistikk, Industrie og varehandel

Aggregate profit and loss data for various sectors published annually.

Utenrikshandel

An annual publication in two volumes showing product imports and exports, in value and volume terms, by country. The first volume has trade for specific products arranged by the 8-digit codes of the **HS**. The second volume has product trade data arranged by the **SITC** product classification.

Manedsstatistikk over Utenriks-Handelen

Published monthly with general trends in external trade plus imports and exports for the principal commodities in the **HS** classification and the general sections of the **SITC** classification.

Construction

Bygge- og Anleggsstatistikk

Annual construction statistics covering **SIC** Major Division 5 based on a detailed survey of construction establishments with 10 or more employees and a less detailed survey of establishments with less than 10. The survey includes private contractors and central government departments and municipal units. Statistics in the publication cover the number of establishments, persons engaged, value of production, cost of materials, gross fixed capital formation, wages and salaries and industry inputs.

Byggeindustrien

Approximately 15 issues per year with some statistics on construction activity. Published by the building confederation, **Landsforeningen for Bygg og Anlegg (LBA)**.

Produksjon av de enkelte varer i store bedrifter. 1989 Commodities produced in large establishments. 1989

Varenr. 1)	Enhet	Mengde	Verdi 1000 kr	Varenr. 1)	Enhet	Mengde	Verdi 1000 kr
8414.9000		..	27 451	8432.1000)			
8415.1000)				8432.2900)	Stk.	24 300	451 689
8415.8000)		..	123 385	8432.3000)			
8415.9000)				8432.4000)			
8416.9000		:		--			
8417.0000		:	:	8432.8000)			
8418.2200				8432.9000)		..	198 011
8418.5000	Stk.	17 316	91 907	--			
8418.6100		..	110 149	8433.1100)			
8418.6900		..	30 870	8433.2000)			
8418.9100		..	28 714	8433.3000)	Stk.	119 788	392 047
8418.9900		..	137 589	8433.4000)			
8419.2000)				8433.5000)			
8419.3000)		..	63 116	8433.9090		..	73 820
8419.5000		..	21 222	8434.9000		..	5 367
8419.8000		..	53 866	8435.9000		:	:
8419.9000		..	46 557	8436.1000)			
8421.1000)				8436.2000)		..	31 620
8421.3000)		..	105 865	8436.8000)			
8421.9900		..	11 885	8436.9000		..	47 752
8422.1900)				8437.8000		:	:
8422.2000)				8437.9000		:	:
8422.4000)		..	74 655	8438.3000)			
8422.9000)				8438,5000)		..	73 913
8423.8000		:	:	8438.8000)			
8424.1000)				8438.9000		..	8 334
8424.8000)		..	103 069	8439.1000)			
8424.9000)				8439.9000)		..	21 643
8425.1100		..	36 894	8440.1000		:	:
8425.1900		..	44 630	8441.0000		:	:
8425.2000)				8442.4000)			
8425.3000)		..	518 546	8442.5000)		..	593 688
8426.1100		..	119 548	8446.0000		:	:
8426.1200		..	21 333	8448.0000		:	:
8426.1900		..	54 810	8449.0000		:	:
8426.2000)				8451.9000		:	:
8426.3000)				8454.2001		:	:
8426.4000)		..	173 554	8454.2002		:	:
8426.9000)				8454.9000		:	:
8427.2000				8459.0000)		:	:
8428.1001)				8462.0000)		..	33 139
8428.1002)	Stk.	532	289 440	--			
8428.2000		..	96 286	8465.1000)			
8428.3000		..	78 908	8465.9200)			
8428.4000)				8465.9400)			
8428.6000)		..	321 067	8465.9500)		..	11 477
8428.9099)				8465.9600)			
8428.9091	Stk.	54	2 236	8465.9900)			
8428.9099	Se 8428.4000			8465.9100	Stk.	6 244	47 025
8429.5201		:	:	8465.9200)			
8429.5911		:	:	8465.9400)			
8429.5919		:	:	8465.9500)	Se 8465.1000		
8430.1020		:	:	8465.9600)			
8430.2001)				8465.9900)			
8430.2009)		..	39 727	--			
--				8466.1000)			
8430.3100)		:	:	8466.9000)		..	61 242
8430.4100)		..	65 441	8466.3000		..	16 859
8430.5000)				8466.9000	Se 8466.1000		
8430.6900		:	:	8467.8000		:	:
8431.1000)		..	107 021	8468.0000		:	:
8431.2000)				8470.9001		:	:
8431.4300)		..	332 739	8470.9002		:	:
8431.4900)				8471.1000)			
8431.3100		..	65 850	8471.2000)			
8431.3900		..	66 257	8471.9100)			
8431.4100		..	179 746	8471.9200)		..	1 688 719
8431.4300)				8471.9300)			
8431.4900)	Se 8431.2000			8471.9900)			
				8472.0000		:	:
				8473.2900)			
				8473.3000)		..	225 255

Table 14.2 Norwegian production statistics – extracts

Food and drink

Jordbruksstatistikk

This annual mainly contains statistics on the agricultural sector but there are tables covering the production of specific foods.

Alkohol og andre rusmiddel

An annual with statistics on alcohol and pharmaceuticals. Includes data on the production, consumption and prices for alcohol and licences for the sale of alcoholic drinks.

Chemicals and chemical products

Regular chemical industry statistics are available from the trade association, **Norges Kjemiske Industrigruppe (NKI)**.

Oljevirksomhet

An annual compilation of statistics on the production of petroleum and natural gas.

Electrical and mechanical engineering

Branjenytt

An occasional bulletin on the metallurgical industries from the industry association, **Metallurgisk Industris Landsforening (MIL)**.

Some statistics on metalworking and engineering are also included in the annual report of the **Teknologibedriftenes Landsforening**.

Services – general

Tjenesteyting (Services)

This annual publication started in 1979 and, prior to this, there were occasional censuses on the service sector. The current issues of **Tjenesteyting** cover business services and machinery and equipment rental and leasing but previous issues have also included sanitary and related services and laundry and laundry services. These latter two sectors are still covered by the **Weekly Bulletin of Statistics** noted in the 'Compilations' section on page 157.

Detailed questionnaires are sent to all relevant establishments employing three or more people and estimates are made for other establishments. The survey is based on the central Register of Establishments and the published data includes information on sectors down to the 5-digit level of the **SIC**. There are also figures for counties and local areas. The publication contains data on the number of establishments, employment, gross value added of production, goods and services consumed, value added, wages and salaries and gross fixed capital formation.

Retailing and distribution

Varehandelsstatistikk

Annual statistics based on a survey of establishments on the central Register of Establishments. The publication covers divisions 61 (wholesale trade and commisson broking) and 62 (retail trade) of the **SIC** with statistics on the number of establishments, size, employment and sales. The data is broken down by sector and by municipality.

Regnskapsstatistikk

Annual statistics of the financial accounts of enterprises in the retail trade.

Financial services

Bank- og kredittstatistikk aktuelle tall

Approximately 25 issues a year from the central statistical office provide data on the private and public banking system in Norway.

Norges Bank Economic Bulletin

The quarterly bulletin has a statistical annex with figures on banking and insurance.

Insurance in Norway

An English language report, with statistics, from the insurance trade body **Norsk Forsikringsselskapers Forbund**.

Leisure and tourism

Reiselivsstatistikk

Annual travel statistics with data on visitors, accommodation types, expenditure, etc.

Transportation

Samferdselsstatistikk

An annual compilation of statistics covering the transport and communications sectors.

Registrerte kjoretoyer i landets kommuner

Monthly statistics on the registrations of cars by local area.

Arbeidsgiverforeningen for Skip og Offshorefartoyer (ASO)

Collects quarterly statistics on the shipping and offshore sectors.

Advertising statistics

The **Reklamebyra Foreningen** has a statistics and marketing department which collects and supplies some statistics on advertising expenditure in Norway.

15 PORTUGAL
Business statistics

INTRODUCTION

Portugese statistics remain relatively limited although there have been some improvements following Portugal's membership of the EC. Official statistics are centralised and the national statistical office is the **Instituto Nacional de Estatistica (INE)**. The **INE** was set up by legislation in 1973 and it is part of the State Secretariat for Planning. There is also a **National Statistics Board** which is responsible for the guidance and co-ordination of the national statistical system.

INE's offices are based in Lisbon at:

Instituto Nacional de Estatistica
INE
Avenida Antonio Jose de Almeida 5
P-1078 Lisbon
Portugal

Statistical publications are available from:

Imprensa Nacional – Casa da Moeda
Livraria do Estado
Rua Marques de sa da Bandiera 16A
P-1000 Lisbon
Portugal

A catalogue of publications, **Catalogo das Publicacoes do INE** is published regularly.

GENERAL STATISTICAL TITLES

Compilations

The annual statistical yearbook is **Anuario estatistico** with a range of figures from the major official series. There is also an international section and table headings are given in Portugese and French. **Boletim mensal de estatistica** has monthly figures for the main social and economic indicators and, again, the headings are in Portugese and French.

Economic data

Conjuntura Economica is a quarterly review of economic trends and another quarterly is **Informacao economica** from the **Departamento Central de Planeamento** in the **Ministerio do Planeamento e da Administracao do Territorio**. Statistics on Portugese economic trends are presented in graphs and tables. The annual **Estatisticas Monetarias e Financeiras** has data on national financial and monetary trends.

A quarterly, **boletim trimestral**, from the **Banco de Portugal** includes a statistical section on Portugese economic trends with English translations of the table headings.

Demographic and social statistics

Population censuses are held every 10 years with the latest in 1981 and 1991. Reports are published in the series, **Recenseamento da populacao e da habitacao**. Annual statistics on population trends and changes are included in **Estatisticas demograficas**.

Sector data

General industrial statistics

An industrial census, **Recenseamento industrial**, is scheduled for every 10 years but after the 1972 census, the next one did not take place until 1984. The main results are published in **Recenseamento Industrial 1984 – Resultados Definitivos**. This 12-year gap affects the more frequent annual industrial surveys because the census provides the basis for the establishment details used in the samples for the annual surveys.

Annual surveys cover industrial structure and production data for specific products is collected annually and, in some cases, monthly. The surveys are based on a classification of Portugese economic activities known as the **Classificacao das Actividades Economicas Portuguesas por Ramos de Actividade (CAE 1973)**. The classification includes all economic activities and, at a general level, it has 1-digit headings for major divisions such as manufacturing (3), extractive industries (2), electricity, gas and water (4) and construction (5). There are further 2-, 3-, 4-, 5- and 6-digit breakdowns and, at the 3- and 4-digit level, the classification is in line with the international **ISIC** classification.

The annual inquiry covers 140 sectors. All mining establishments, irrespective of size, are surveyed and in most manufacturing sectors, all establishments are covered. There are some manufacturing sectors which are exceptions where only establishments with 10 or more employees are surveyed. For a few industries, the information is treated as confidential and the results are suppressed. Estimates are made for non-respondents and, in total, the annual inquiry claims to cover 85 per cent of Portugese industry. The monthly production inquiry claims to cover approximately 70 per cent of industrial production value.

External trade statistics are based on the European **CN** codes.

PUBLICATIONS PRODUCED BY NATIONAL ORGANISATIONS

General industry and trade

Estatisticas Industriais
A report of the annual industrial inquiry in two volumes. Volume 1 includes the extractive industries, electricity, gas and water and Volume 2 covers the manufacturing sectors. There are summary tables, with data for the last two years, and detailed breakdowns for the latest year in selected tables at the 3- and 6-digit level of the **CAE**. At the 6-digit level, there are statistics on the number of enterprises, persons employed, wages and salaries, hours of work, value of production, consumption and value added. A regional breakdown is also included. The 1987 survey covered 18,000 establishments and the results were published in December 1989.

Indices de producao industrial
Monthly indices of industrial production with tables for specific sectors and products.

Inquerito mensal de conjuntura a industria transformadora
A monthly opinion survey of the manufacturing sector which replaced the previously quarterly inquiry in 1987.

Industria Portuguesa
AIP Informacao

The national industrial federation, **Associacao Industrial Portuguesa (AIP)**, publishes the two monthly bulletins above with news, reviews and some statistics on industrial and business trends.

Estatisticas do Comercio Externo

Annual import and export statistics for specific commodities, broken down by major trading partners, arranged by the 4-digit headings of the European **CN** classification.

Boletim mensal das estatisticas do comercio externo

A monthly bulletin of foreign trade statistics giving trade by major trading partners and imports and exports of products arranged by chapters of the European **CN** classification and divisions of the international **SITC** classification.

Construction

Estatisticas da Construcao e da Habitacao

Annual statistics on construction and housing with detailed regional statistics.

Anuario

An annual report, with some statistics, from the association of civil engineering contractors, **Associacao dos Industriais de Construcao Civil e Obras Publicas do Norte (AICCOPN)**. The association also publishes monthly building price data and the quarterly, **Informacao Economica**.

Electrical and mechanical engineering

Anuario

A yearbook from the **Associacao dos Industrias Metalurgicos e Metalomecanicos do Norte (AIMMN)**, an association for the metallurgical and mechanical engineering sectors. The association also publishes a monthly **Boletim Metal**.

Estatistica maquinas-ferramentas

Annual production and trade figures covering various types of machine tools published by the **Centro de Cooperacao dos Industrias de Maquinas-Ferramentas**.

Electronics

Material Electrico e Electronico Anuario

A review and statistics relating to the electronics and electronic equipment sectors in Portugal. Published by the **Associacao Nacional dos Industriais de Material Electrico e Electronico (ANIMEE)**, which also produces a monthly bulletin.

Retailing and distribution

A detailed census of the distribution and services sector has not been undertaken since 1977 but some regular statistics on the distribution sector are published in:

Inquerito Trimestral de Conjuntura ao Comercio

A quarterly survey of the wholesale and retail trade with summary data, in graphs and tables, and statistics for the main sectors. The publication includes statistics on the volume of sales, orders and prices.

Estatisticas do Comercio Interno

Annual figures for the latest three years on retail outlets and related data. The government department responsible for retail statistics is the **Direccao Geral do Comercio Interno**.

Boletim Informativo

A monthly bulletin from the **Associacao Nacional de Supermercados**, the supermarkets association, and more detailed statistics are also available from this association.

Financial services

Estatisticas Sociedades

Annual statistics on the financial services sector including data on the banks and insurance companies.

The **Associacao Portuguesa de Seguradores (APS)** also publishes quarterly insurance statistics plus regular market reports.

Leisure and tourism

Estatistica do Turismo

Annual statistics on tourists, accommodation, holidays, travel and expenditure on tourism.

Transportation

A census of the transport sector is carried out occasionally with the latest census in 1982. The reports are published in the series entitled, **Recenseamento das Empresas do Sector dos Transportes**.

Estatisticas dos Transportes e Comunicacoes

Annual statistics on the various transport sectors, road, rail, sea, air, plus international trends in transport.

O Comercio e a Industria Automovel em Portugal

Annual statistics on the motor vehicles sector in Portugal published by the **Associacio do Comercio Automovel de Portugal (ACAP)**. Figures for production, assembly, vehicle parc, registrations by make, model, etc. Many of the tables have historical figures and a contents page and summary data is available in English.

16 SPAIN

Business statistics

INTRODUCTION

The provision of statistics in Spain has improved in recent years although there are still information gaps in certain subject areas. Demographic and social statistics are generally good and there is a wide range of data available on Spanish regions. Official statistics on industries and products remain limited and are often out-of-date but, in many sectors, trade associations can offer an alternative source of data.

The central statistical office is the **National Institute of Statistics (INE)**, established under a Statistics Act of 1945, but official statistics are essentially decentralised with many government departments publishing their own statistical titles. The system is also decentralised geographically with local areas producing statistics on their own regions and towns. The main national government departments and agencies involved in statistical publishing are listed in Table 16.1 and these will be described in more detail in the following sections.

Instituto Nacional de Estadistica (INE)
[National statistical office]

Direccion General de Aduanas e Impuestos Especiales
[External trade statistics]

Other major departments:

Ministerio de Economia y Hacienda
Ministerio de Industria y Energia
Ministerio de Transportes, Turismo y Communicacione
Direccion General de Trafico

Table 16.1 Official statistics – Key departments

INE is part of the Ministry of Economic Affairs and its offices are based in Madrid:

Instituto Nacional de Estadistica
INE
Paseo de la Castellana 183
E-28071 Madrid
Spain

The head of the **INE** is the Director General of Statistics appointed by the Council of Ministers on the recommendation of the Minister of Economic Affairs. **Publicaciones en existencia** is an annual list of publications from **INE** and these publications can be obtained from **INE** itself or two other sources:

Libreria Lines-Chiel
Plaza Virgen del Romero 6
E-28027 Madrid
Spain

Distribuciones Oficiales Reunidas SA
C/Plaza 15
E-28043 Madrid
Spain

On-line service

Tempus
An on-line service, **Tempus**, has 80,000 official time series on demographic, socio-economic and business data. The service is produced by **INE** and accessible through the on- line company, **ENTEL SA**.

As well as the on-line service noted above, the country's central statistical office has also been active in developing disc and tape versions of a number of the official series and details are available from **INE**. While the official statistics still have limitations, trade associations in Spain are good at collecting and publishing statistics although UK based users may have difficulty in obtaining a quick response to a request.

GENERAL STATISTICAL TITLES

Compilations

An annual compilation of the main official statistics is **Anuario Estadistico** which also includes an international section and a detailed section of regional statistics. At the beginning of each subject section, there is a list of relevant titles offering more detailed information. More up-to-date information on the key subject areas is found in **Boletin de estadistica** which appears six times a year.

Folletos de divulgacion is a series of leaflets providing preliminary results of surveys and studies in selected subject areas and most of the specific titles cover population, housing and social conditions.

A weekly journal, **Boletin Oficial del Ministerio de Economia y Hacienda**, from the **Ministerio de Economia y Hacienda** contains some statistics along with official announcements and notices.

Economic data

The monthly **Indicadores de coyuntura** includes trends in the major economic indicators while the quarterly **Boletin trimestral de coyuntura** has general studies of the Spanish economy. Both these publications are produced by **INE**. The on-line service, **TEMPUS**, includes some economic data.

The **Banco de Espana** publishes a monthly **Boletin estadistico** with data on economic trends and the annual, **Anexo Estadistico al Informe Anual**.

Demographic and social statistics

Censuses of population are carried out approximately every 10 years, i.e. 1960, 1970, 1981 and the latest one in 1991. The preliminary results from the 1991 Census were published in late summer 1991 and the detailed census volumes will follow.

Regular population data appears in the **Folletos de divulgacion** series noted above in titles such as **Dinamica de la poblacion Espanola, La poblacion espanola y su evolucion and La poblacion de Espana**. The annual **Movimento natural de la poblacion** has three volumes with national, provincial and municipal data on population changes.

Sector data

General industrial statistics

Spain has not had a comprehensive industrial census since 1978 but there is an annual survey of industrial structure, activity and investment. This survey also includes coverage of the production levels of selected products in each sector. All establishments with 20 or more employees are covered in mining, manufacturing and construction plus a sample of establishments with 5 or more employees. Estimates are made for units not covered by the survey and for non-respondents.

The statistics produced by this annual survey are arranged according to the **National Classification of Economic Activities**, with the latest version revised in 1974, and usually abbreviated to **CNAE 74**. CNAE is broken down into major divisions covering industrial and service activities and, within each division, there are further breakdowns into 2-digit, 3-digit and, in some instances, 4-digit headings. For example, Division 3 covers the manufacture of metal articles, mechanical and precision engineering while the 2-digit heading 32 in this division covers the mechanical engineering group. A further 3-digit breakdown, 323, relates specifically to machinery for the textiles, clothing, leather and footwear industries and a further 4-digit heading, 323.1 includes just textile industry machinery and accessories. **CNAE** is based on the European **NACE** classification but few of the Spanish headings correspond exactly with **NACE** headings.

The Spanish also have a specific product and service classification known as the **National Classification of Goods and Services**, usually abbreviated to **CNBS 78**.

Import and export statistics are based on the **CN** classification.

PUBLICATIONS PRODUCED BY NATIONAL ORGANISATIONS

General industry and trade

Encuesta industrial

An annual publication with the results of the survey of industrial structure, activity and investment. General statistics on Spanish industry are followed by individual sections on particular sectors, at the 2-digit level of **CNAE**. Statistics include the number of establishments by employment size, total employment, hours worked, costs of labour, capital formation, energy consumption by type, consumption of materials and value added. Figures for the latest four years are included. Regional data is also published and another table has production details, in value and quantities, for the major products in the sector although code numbers for the products are not included. An example of a production table from this publication is given in Table 16.2.

Although the published results are supposed to appear annually, there have been publishing gaps in the 1980s. Issues covering 1980–3, 1981–4 and 1982–5 were published but then nothing appeared until the 1984–7 issue. This latter volume was published in 1990.

Numeros indices de la produccion industrial

Industrial production indices are collected monthly and quarterly on approximately 600 products. Basic results are published in a monthly information bulletin, **Hoja informativa** and a quarterly publication, **Boletin informativo**.

PRINCIPALES PRODUCCIONES: valores   Sector 39

PRODUCTOS	MILLONES DE PESETAS			
	1984	1985	1986	1987
Refrigeradores y congeladores de uso doméstico	31,327	31,707	35,727	35,364
Lavavajillas, lavadoras y secadoras de ropa, de uso doméstico	31,489	33,226	37,197	43,694
Calentadores eléctricos de agua y aparatos eléctricos para la calefacción de locales	5,930	6,502	6,781	7,799
Ventiladores y acondicionadores de aire de uso doméstico	8, 078	5, 094	6,266	7,756
Aparatos eléctricos auxiliares de cocina	11,897	9,764	10,213	15,575
Aparatos eléctricos para el cuidado y conservación del hogar	7,540	7,825	10,616	12,968
Otros aparatos electrodomésticos	4,809	6,359	8,039	6,603
Accesorios, partes y piezas sueltas de aparatos electrodomésticos	8,274	9,444	20,930	20,822
Lamparas eléctricas	12,736	11,035	10,059	11,926
Luminarias para alta intensidad de descarga	8,018	9,036	7,604	8,103
Otro material de alumbrado	6,210	4,721	11,404	14,801
Accesorios, partes y piezas sueltas de lámparas y material de alumbrado	2,083	2,930	2,911	3,442
Servicios de instalaciones eléctricas (excepto en la construcción)	6,972	11,306	11,663	15,742

(1) A partir de 1,986 se incluyen Aparatos en carbón o en grafito para usos eléctricos.

Table 16.2 Spanish production data for electrical equipment, including washing machines, refrigerators etc.

La Industria Espanola

An annual review of Spanish industry from the **Ministerio de Industria y Energia**.

Boletin Economico Informacion Comercial Espanola

A weekly journal from the **Ministerio de Economia y Hacienda**, **Secretaria de Estado de Comercia Espanola**. The journal has articles and news items on industries, products and sectors and regular statistics on production, external trade, stocks, etc.

Estadistica del comercio exterior. Comercio por productos y por paises

Annual statistics on the imports and exports, by country, of specific commodities from **Direccion General de Aduanas e Impuestos Especiales**. The statistics are published in two volumes and product headings are based on the **CN** classification.

Avances de estadistica del comercio exterior

From the above office, monthly import and export statistics, by country, for 99 product chapters.

Estacom

An on-line service from the **Instituto Espanol de Commercio Exterior (ICEX)** with monthly and annual series on commodity imports and exports. The database covers the latest five years and it is updated monthly.

Construction

Industria da Construcao
Conjuntura/Construcao

The first title is published monthly and the second title is quarterly and both review trends in the construction and civil engineering sectors. The publications come from the **Associacao di Empresas de Construcao e Obras Publicas do Sul (AECOPS)**.

Food and drink

El consumo alimentario en Espana

An annual title, first published in 1987, from the Ministry of Agriculture. There are specific sections on the consumption of food and drink products and the statistics are based on a regular survey of 2,500 households and 500 'horica' (hotels, restaurants and cafes). The horica survey has been added in the last two years.

The weekly journal **Alimarket** produces an annual trade review on the food market and retailing.

FEICEV, the trade association involving producers and exporters of wines, includes some statistics in its annual report.

Chemicals and chemical products

La Industria Quimica en Cifras

Quarterly statistics from the **Federacion Empresarial de la Industria Quimica Espanole (FEIQUE)**. Included are statistics on production, consumption, imports and exports with data on specific products.

Engineering

La Industria Siderurgica Espanola
informacion siderurgica

The **Union de Empresas Siderurgices (UNESID)** publishes annual (first title) and quarterly statistics on the iron and steel industry.

Datos Estadisticos Maquinas-Herramienta

Annual statistics on the Spanish machine tool sector based on a survey by the **Asociacion Espanola de Fabricantes de Maquinas-Herramienta**. The complete survey is only available to member companies but summary data is released to others.

Marina Mercante

An annual review of shipbuilding and shipping trends from the **Asociacion de Navieros Espanola (ANAVE)**.

Informes Estadisticos

A quarterly statistical bulletin from the private shipbuilders association, **Asociacion de Constructores Navales Espanoles (CONSTRUNAVES)**. There is also an annual review.

Electronics

Informe del Sector Electronico

Annual statistics on the electronics sector in Spain from the **Asociacion Nacional de Industrias Electronicas (ANIEL)**. The volume combines official statistics with data from **ANIEL**'s own survey.

Anuario de la Industria Electronica en Espana/Yearbook of the Electronics Industry in Spain

An annual supplement to the journal, **Electronica Hoy**, published by **VNU Business Publications Espana**. It contains an English commentary and table headings with statistics for the last few years on the major electronic sectors. Included are statistics on industry, markets, external trade, investment.

Informaciones ACEMA

A bulletin published six times a year by the association for retailers of domestic electric appliances, **Federcacion Espanola de Comerciantes de Electro-domesticos (EECE)**.

Retailing and distribution

There are no regular official statistics on retail structure although there are plans for a retailing census in the next few years. There is a system of licensing companies involved in distribution but no figures from this register are published.

Important non-official sources of retailing data are the monthly journal, **Distribucion Actualidad**, which has regular figures on retailing sectors and the weekly food journal, **Alimarket**, which publishes an annual trade review. The **Instituto Tecnico de Distribucion y Libreservicio (INTED)** also publishes some statistics and market surveys.

Financial services

Conjuntura Economica

A monthly review of the savings bank sector from the **Confederacion Espanola de Cajas de Ahorros (CECA)**, and the confederation also publishes an annual report. Other statistics are published by the finance houses association, **Asociacion Nacional de Entidades de Financiacion (ASNEF)** in its annual report.

Leisure and tourism

Anuario de estadisticas de turismo

An annual publication from the **Ministerio de Transportes, Turismo y Communicaciones** with detailed statistics on tourism.

Movimiento de viajeros en establecimientos turisticos

Annual figures, from **INE**, covering travellers staying in tourist accommodation.

Transportation

Boletin Informativo: anuario estadistico general

An annual statistical bulletin from the **Direccion General de Trafico, Servicio de Estadistica** including details of the number of vehicles, nationally and by province, registrations, sales, etc.

Public sector

Anuario Gas

Annual statistics on gas supply and consumption from the **Sociedad par el Estudio y Desarrollo de la Industria del Gas**.

Advertising statistics

Repress is part of A.C. Nielsen in Spain and it produces regular statistics on advertising expenditures by brands, sector, media, etc. Another company monitoring advertising and producing regular expenditure data is **Duplo**.

17 SWEDEN
Business statistics

INTRODUCTION

In a recent survey reported in the **Economist**, 7 September (1991), a panel of statisticians from various countries was asked to rank official statistics from 10 OECD countries. Sweden's statistics came top of the list in Europe. Sweden scores well on reliability, accuracy and timeliness and most published statistics have English translations of contents and headings.

Sweden has a centralised system of official statistics under the direction of the central statistical agency, **Statistika Centralbyran or Statistics Sweden (SCB)**. There is no legislation covering statistical provision but there is a **Scientific Council** with a consultative function. The head of the **SCB**, the Director General, is appointed by the government and the **SCB** itself is responsible to the Ministry of Public Administration. **SCB** offices are based in Stockholm and the publications can be ordered from a distribution centre at Orebo:

> **Statistika Centralbyran**
> **SCB**
> Karlavagen 100
> S-11581 Stockholm
> Sweden

> **Statistika Centralbyran**
> **SCB**
> Distribution
> S-70189 Orebo
> Sweden

Arets tryck is an annual list of the previous year's publications with English translations and the statistical yearbook, **Statistisk arsbok**, also has a list of the major titles. Statistical inquiries can be dealt with in English and responses are relatively quick.

GENERAL STATISTICAL TITLES

Compilations

The annual statistical abstract of Sweden is **Statistisk arsbok** with summary statistics on the main topic areas. There is also an international section (blue pages), an alphabetical index in Swedish and English, references to other titles in individual sections and a list of Sweden's official publications. A monthly digest, **Allman manadsstatistik**, provides regular information on key areas. In both publications, contents pages and table headings are translated into English.

Fast, often preliminary information, on important subject areas is published in a series of brief reports and much of this information is later updated and expanded on in statistical yearbooks or other publications. The general series name for these brief reports is **Statistiska meddelanden** and, in the series, there are 20 sub-groups on specific subjects. Approximately 600–700 reports are published annually although some are published by individual departments rather than the **SCB**. English translations of table headings are given and a list of the individual subject groups is given below. References to some of these will be made in the sections to follow.

Statistiska meddelanden series – Subject groups

Group code

Am	Labour
Be	Population & living conditions
Bo	Housing & construction
E	Energy
F	Enterprises
Hs	Public health & medical care
I	Manufacturing
J	Agriculture, forestry & fishing
K	Capital market, banking & insurance
Ku	Culture
N	National accounts
Na	Natural resources & environment
O	Public finance
P	Prices & consumption
R	Legal statistics
S	Social welfare
Se	Service trades
T	Trade & communications
U	Education & research
Uh	Foreign trade

Economic data

Apart from the above publications, a major source of economic data is the **Sveriges Riksbank** which publishes an annual **Statistisk Arsbok** with English headings. Various sections cover economic and financial trends plus specific monetary and banking sectors. There is also a **Quarterly Review** available in English.

Konjunkturinstitutet, the National Institute of Economic Research, publishes the annual **The Swedish Economy**, in English with chapters and tables on specific economic sectors.

Demographic and social statistics

A census has been undertaken in 1980, 1985 and 1990. The results are published in various volumes in the series, **Folk-och bostadsrakningen**. **Befolkningsforandringar** is an annual review of population changes and **Folkmangd 31st December** gives the population at the end of the year nationally and by local areas.

Sector data

General industrial statistics

Industrial statistics are based on the **Svensk standard for narings-grensindelning** or **SNI** (Swedish Standard Industrial Classification of all Economic Activities) which is based on the 1968 **ISIC** classification of the UN.

The **SNI** is identical to **ISIC** 1968 up to and including the 4-digit level but an additional 2 digits have been added in the **SNI**.

Annual statistics on industrial activity and structure are published based on a survey of establishments with five or more employees in manufacturing and based on a survey of all establishments in the mining sector. In certain manufacturing sectors, notably dairies, distillers, breweries and starch manufacturers, all establishments are included irrespective of size. Data on the production of specific commodities is also collected annually and published according to the **HS** commodity classification. Approximately 6,000 product headings are covered. Monthly production indices for mining and manu-facturing cover the 1-, 2- and 3-digit headings of the **SNI**.

External trade statistics use the **HS** classification and figures are also released using the **SITC** codes.

PUBLICATIONS PRODUCED BY NATIONAL ORGANISATIONS

General industry and trade

Industri 199–.

An annual report on the manufacturing and mining sectors published in two parts. Volume 1 includes data on industrial structure and activity. Summary data and figures for specific industry sectors showing the number of establishments, value of output, value added, costs, employment, consumption of materials, capital and capital formation. The quantity and cost of raw materials consumed is published for a few industrial sectors. Volume 2 consists of production data, for the last two years, for approximately 6,000 products arranged by the HS classification. An extract showing the section on domestic electric appliances is given in Table 17.1. The results of the 1989 survey were published in 1991, with English translations of contents pages and headings. A Swedish-English vocabulary is also included.

In the **Statistiska meddelanden** series, there are a number of regular reports including:

Industriproduktionsindex

A monthly production index for mining and manufacturing with indices down to the 2- and 3-digit levels of the **SNI**.

Industrinslager

Quarterly figures on stocks in industry.

Industrins leverans- och orderlage

Preliminary monthly figures on the delivery and order book situation in industry, down to the 2- and 3-digit levels of the **SNI**.

Industrins kapacitetsutnyttjande

Quarterly data on capacity utilisation in industry.

Industristatistik. Regional redovisning

Annual industrial statistics by region.

A number of regular reports are published in the **Statistiska meddelanden** sub group 'Enterprises' and the main titles are:

Foretagen, ekonomisk redovisning

Annual statistics on the financial accounts of business enterprises with data on gross operating income, opertaing profit/loss, depreciation, labour costs, etc. with information for different industry sectors. All enterprises carried on by legal entities are included.

Produktion fördelad enligt Tulltaxa

Statistiskt nr	Avdelningar, kapitel och varuposter	Anm	Enhet	1989 Kvantitet	Saluvärde	1988 Kvantitet	Saluvärde
				används för mask- eller öglebildning:			
511	-trikamaskinsnalar			–		–	
519	-andra slag			–		–	
590	-andra			7 226		7 226	
8449 000	Maskiner och apparater för tillverkning eller efterbehandling av filt eller bondad duk som längdvara eller i tillformade stycken, inbegripet maskiner för tillverkning av filthattar; hattformar			–		–	
8450	Vattenvtättmaskiner för hushåll eller tvätterier, inbegripet maskiner som bade tvättar och torkar tvätten: maskiner för högst 10 kg torr tvätt: – helautomatiska:						
111	– för högst 6 kg torr tvätt		st	80 496	301 412	84 484	302 990
119	–andra		st	23 783	191 000	24 127	146 497
120	–andra slag, med inbyggd centrifug						
1	–hushallsmaskiner		st	–	–	–	–
9	–andra		st	–	–	–	–
190	–andra:						
1	–hushållsmaskiner		st	–	–	–	–
9	–andra		st	–	–	–	–
200	maskiner för mer än 10 kg torr tvätt				201 499		272 467
900	delar till tvättmaskiner:						
1	–hushallsmaskiner				1 193		897
9	–andra				7 087		5 504
8451	Maskiner och apparater (andra än vattentvättmaskiner enligt nr 84.50) för tvättning eller annan rengöring, vridning, torkning, strykning, pressning (inbegripet fixeringspressar), blekning, färgning, appretering, beläggning, impregnering eller annan efterbehandling av textilgarn, textilvävnader eller andra textilvaror, även konfektionerade, samt maskiner för anbringande av massa på underlag av textilvara eller på annat underlag och som används vid tillverkning av linoleummattor elller liknande golvbeläggning; maskiner för upprullning, avrullning, läggning, skärning eller tandning av dukvaror av textilmaterial:						
100	kemtvättmaskiner torkmaskiner: – för högst 6 kg torr tvätt:				–		–
211	– torktumlare				29 650		30 991
212	– andra – för mer än 6 kg men högst 10 kg torr tvätt:				71 574		59 285
213	– torktumlare				–		–
219	– andra				–		–
290	– för mer än 10 kg torr tvätt stryk- och pressmaskiner (inbegripet fixeringspressar):				471		–
301	– hushallsmaskiner				28 600		25 072
309	–andra slag				5 308		5 967
400	maskiner för vattentvätt, blekning eller färgning				12 160		12 611
500	maskiner för upprullning, avrullning, läggning, skärning eller tandning av textilvavnader e d				19 691		25 315
800	andra maskiner och apparater				–		–
900	delar				715		949
8452	Symaskiner, andra än trådhäftmaskiner enligt nr 84.40; möbler, stativ och överdrag, speciellt konstruerade för symaskiner; symaskinsnålar:						
100	symaskiner för hemsömnad				289 637		289 877
210+290	andra symaskiner				48 532		37 644
300	symaskinsnålar						
400+900	möbler, stativ och överdrag för symaskiner samt delar till sådana varor; andra delar till symaskiner				23 747		34 591
8453	Maskiner och apparater för beredning, garvning,						

Table 17.1 Swedish production statistics – extracts of entries for electrical household equipment

Industriforetagen, ekonomisk redovisning

Annual figures for a number of years on the financial accounts of enterprises in mining, quarrying and manufacturing.

Investeringar

Quarterly investment trends by Swedish industry and other sectors including distribution, financial services, real estate companies and transport and communications companies.

Basfakta

Basic facts on Swedish industry, published annually, and based on data from the Swedish Central Register of Enterprises and Establishments.

Utrikeshandel

Annual foreign trade statistics are published in two volumes. One volume, **Import och export enligt HS nomenklaturen med varutexter**, has commodity imports and exports, by country, broken down by the **HS** international classification. Approximately 6,700 products are represented by 7-digit codes with the last digit added for national purposes. An alphabetical commodity index is also included. The second volume, **Import och export. Fordelning land/vara enligt SITC**, has imports and exports arranged by country and, within each country, by **SITC** heading.

Utrikeshandel. Kvartalsstatistik

Quarterly data on the imports and exports of specific commodities with one volume for imports and one for exports. The **HS** classification scheme is used and the reports form part of the **Statistiska meddelanden** series.

Utrikeshandel. Manadsstatistik

Monthly statistics of foreign trade published as part of the **Statistiska meddelanden** series. Statistics on total imports and exports, trade with the major trading partners and trade broken down by sections and divisions of the **SITC** and the Swedish **SNI**.

Construction

Bostads – och byggnadsstatistisk arsbok

A yearbook of building and construction statistics with data on the main construction sectors and data for a number of years in many tables. A number of regular reports are also published in the **Statistiska meddelanden** series.

Fakta om Byggandet
Bygg Konjunkturen

Two regular publications from the construction federation, **Byggentre-prenorerna**. The first is an annual review of building production while the second title is published twice a year and gives short-term forecasts for the construction sector.

Food and drink

The **Dagligvaruleverantores Forbund (DLF)** produces some statistics on food consumer goods and the journal **Livs** has data on food retailing (*see* Retailing and Distribution section below.

Electrical and mechanical engineering

Machine tool statistics are available from the Foreningen **Svenska Verktygs- och Verktygsmaskintillverkare (FVM)** and regular statistics on the iron and steel industry come from **Jernkontoret**.

Electronics

Rateko

A monthly bulletin from the consumer electronics trade association, **Radio & Hemelektronik-Landelns Riksforbund (RHR)**.

Retailing and distribution

The **Statistiska meddelanden** series has a selection of reports covering distribution including:

Omsattning och lager inom varshandel och vissa tjanstenaringar

Published quarterly with data on turnover and stocks in domestic trade and certain services.

Konjunkturbarometer for varuhandeln

A quarterly business tendency survey for the wholesale and retail trades.

Livs

A monthly journal from the Swedish food retailers association, **Sveriges Livsmedelshandlareforbund (SSLF)**. An annual feature looks at the structure of food retailing and there are selected statistics in other articles throughout the year.

Financial services

Reports in the **Statistiska meddelanden** series include:

Kreditmarknaden. Kvartalsvis redovsning av kreditmarknadsstaitistik och finansrakenskaper

A quarterly report with credit market statistics and financial accounts.

Forsakringsbolagen

Quarterly preliminary data on insurance companies.

Finansbolag och andra finansforetag

Annual figures for finance houses and finance companies.

In- och utlaningen pa kreditmarknaden

Quarterly and annual publications covering deposits and advances on the credit market.

Ekonomiska Meddalenden

A monthly bulletin from the banking association, **Svenska Bankforeningen**.

Svenska Forsakrings Arsbok

The insurance association, **Svenska Forsakringsforeningen**, publishes a statistical yearbook on the sector.

Transportation

Statistiska meddelanden in sub-group 'T' cover transport and communications and titles include:

Fordon enligt bilregistret

Monthly statistics of vehicle registrations.

Fordon i lan och Kommuner den 31st December

A survey of vehicles in counties and municipalities on 31 December each year.

Motor Traffic In Sweden
New Registrations

English language publications from the **Bilindustriforeningen (BIL)** with data on motor vehicles. The first title appears annually and presents detailed current and historical data on motor vehicles and related areas. **New Registrations** is published monthly showing new registrations by make and model.

Advertising statistics

The Swedish Advertising Association, **Annonsorforeningen**, has basic statistics on advertising expenditure in Sweden.

18 SWITZERLAND

Business statistics

INTRODUCTION

Switzerland's statistical output is a mixture of data from official sources, trade associations, banks and research institutes and there are few official statistics on industry and industrial production. The importance of business and personal confidentiality is emphasised in Swiss legislation and this clearly limits the detail available in official statistics.

Official statistics are highly decentralised with the **Federal Statistical Office (FSO)** providing a co-ordinating role. The **FSO** is usually either described in German as the **Bundesamt fur Statistik** or, in French, as the **Office federal de la statistique**. It is part of the Federal Department of the Interior and this department also decides its budget. The offices of the **FSO** are located in Berne at:

Bundesamt fur Statistik/Office federal de la statistique
Hallwylstrasse 15
CH-3003 Berne
Switzerland

Publiktionsverzeichnis/Liste des publications is an occasional publications list and most official publications have both German and French titles and headings (both languages are included in the list of official titles to follow).

External trade statistics are the responsibility of the **Directorate General of Customs** with offices at:

Eidg. Oberzolldirektion/Direction generale des douanes
Monbijoustrasse 40
CH-3003 Berne
Switzerland

GENERAL STATISTICAL TITLES

Compilations

Statistiches Jahrbuch der Schweiz/Annuaire statistique de la Suisse is the annual statistical yearbook with basic data from a range of official series. A pocket-book summarising the key statistics, **Statistical Data on Switzerland**, is also available in English as well as in French and German.

Economic data

The **Swiss National Bank** produces a monthly bulletin, **Monatsbericht/Bulletin mensuel** and a statistical supplement to this bulletin has regular figures on economic trends. A quarterly bulletin, **Geld, Wahrung und Konjunktur/Monnaie et conjoncture** has mainly articles on economic and financial issues.

The **Union Bank of Switzerland (UBS)** has a number of publications and most of these are available in English. **UBS Business Facts and Figures** is produced approximately seven times a year and **Switzerland in Figures** is a compilation of basic data. **Economic Trends in Switzerland** is actually a survey of specific business sectors and this is described in the section headed 'Sector Data' below.

The **Union Suisse du Commerce et de l'Industrie** publishes an annual report, **Rapport annuel**, and a quarterly report. The annual report has a detailed commentary on the economy and specific sectors accompanied by a statistical section on the same areas.

Demographic and social statistics

Population censuses take place every 10 years with the latest ones in 1980 and 1990. Results are published in various volumes with national data on specific topics and volumes on individual cantons.

Bevolkerungsbewegung/Mouvement de la population is the annual population report while **Soziale Indikatoren/Indicateurs sociaux** is a series of titles on living conditions, families, employment and income.

Sector data

General industrial statistics

No detailed production statistics are published but a census of enterprises is carried out approximately every 10 years and financial statistics on Swiss enterprises are published annually. Results are published in the Statistical Yearbook. The latest census was in 1985 with the previous census in 1975.

Economic activities are arranged according to a general classification of economic activities known as the **Allgemeine Systematik der Wirtschaftszweige**.

External trade statistics are collected and based on the **CN** classification.

PUBLICATIONS PRODUCED BY NATIONAL ORGANISATIONS

General industry and trade

Gewerbliche Betriebszahlung/Recensement des enterprises

The results of this 10-yearly census of enterprises are published in several volumes with data at national, canton and municipal level.

Aktiengesellschaften in der Schweiz/Societes anonymes suisses

Annual statistics on Swiss joint stock companies.

Buchhaltungsergebnisse schweizerischer Unternehmungen/Les resultats comptables des enterprises suisses

Aggregate annual statistics on the financial position and performance of Swiss enterprises.

Economic Trends in Switzerland

An annual publication covering business performance and trends in specific sectors. The report covers both manufacturing and services and is based on a survey by the **UBS** in association with **St Gall Center for Future Research**. In the latest survey, 2,400 enterprises responded.

Jahresstatistik des Aussenhandels der Schweiz/Statistique annuelle du commerce exterieur de la Suisse

Annual external trade statistics published in three volumes by the Directorate General of Customs. Products are classified according to the **CN** classification at the 8-digit level.

Construction

Jahrbuch

The building federation, **Schweizerischer Baumeisterverband (SBV)**, has a yearbook with statistics on construction activity in Switzerland. The federation also publishes an annual report and a twice-monthly journal.

Food and drink

Statistiche Erhebungen und Schatzungen uber Landwirtschaft und Ernahrung

Annual statistics on food and agriculture from the **Schweizerischer Bauernverband (SBV)**. The report includes production and trade figures. The association also publishes an annual report on the dairy products sector, monthly reports on agriculture and quarterly reports on the international dairy products market.

Jahresbericht

Commentary and statistics on the fruit industry and markets with data on specific fruits. Published annually by the **Schweizerischer Obstverband**.

Schweizerische Tiefkuhl-Wirtschaft

Annual statistics from the association for the frozen food sector, **Schweizerischer Tiefkuhl – Institut (STI)**. Data on specific foods. There is also an annual report and selected statistics on European frozen food trends.

Geschaftsbericht

Annual statistics covering production, sales and imports and exports of Swiss cheese. The report also has a review of the cheese market. Published by **Schweizerische Kaseunion**.

Statistiques de l'Industrie Chocolatiere Suisse

Annual figures covering the chocolate confectionery industry and market published by **Verband Schweizerischer Schokoladefabrikante (CHOCO-SUISSE)**. There are also general figures in an annual report.

Chemicals and chemical products

Jahresbericht

The Swiss chemicals trade association, **Schweizerische Gesellschaft fur Chemische Industrie**, has a statistical section in its annual report. Tables and graphs cover production and trade by sector plus other data including prices, turnover, consumption, energy use, etc.

Textiles and clothing

Jahresbericht

An annual report, with statistics, from the **Gesamtverband der Schweizerischen Bekleidungsindustrie**, the Swiss clothing industry association. The association also publishes quarterly import and export statistics.

Jahresbericht

Some statistics on the textiles sector are included in the annual report from **Gemeinschaftsverband Textil**.

Electrical and mechanical engineering

L'Industrie Suisse des Machines et des Metaux en 199–

Annual statistics relating to the metals and machine tools sectors published by **Verein Schweizerischer Maschinen-Industrieller (VSI)**.

Annual statistics on the Swiss watch industry are available from **Federation de l'Industrie Horlogerie Suisse (FH)**.

Services – general

Some information on specific service sectors is included in **Economic Trends in Switzerland** described in the section headed 'General Industrial Statistics' on page 188.

Retailing and distribution

Detailhandelsumsatze/Chiffres d'affaires du commerce de detail

Monthly statistics covering general trends in the retail trade.

Financial services

The reports from the **Swiss National Bank** and the **Union Bank of Switzerland**, noted in the section headed 'Economic Data' on page 188, plus the annual reports of these banks have statistical information on Swiss banking and financial services.

Leisure and tourism

There are various monthly, semi-annual, annual and occasional publications on tourism and travel plus regular press releases and details of all these can be obtained from the **FSO**. A general title is:

Schweizer Tourismus in Zahlen/le tourism Suisse en chiffres

An annual compilation of tourism statistics.

Swiss Tourism in Figures

An annual statistical review, published in English and French, from the tourism organisation, **Schweizerischer Fremdenverkehrsverband (SFV)**.

Transportation

Schweizerische Verkehrsstatistik/Statistique suisse des transports
An annual compilation of Swiss transport statistics with data on specific transport sectors.

Verkaufsstatistik Personenwagen
Figures for the monthly deliveries of new cars based on data supplied by member companies of the **Vereinigung Schweizerischer Automobil Importeure (VSAI)**. The association also publishes annual figures on commercial vehicles.

Statistiches Jahrbuch
Annual statistics for the public transport sector from **Schweizerische PTT – Betriebe**.

Jahresbericht der ASTAG
An annual review of transport and road haulage developments with selected statistics on traffic, vehicles, prices, etc. Published by the **Schweizerischer Nutzfahrzeugverband (ASTAG)** which also publishes annual data on transport costs and prices.

Public sector

VSG/SVGW – Schweizerische Gasstatistik
Annual statistics on gas supply and demand from the **Schweizerischer Verein des Gas- und Wasserfaches**.

Advertising statistics

Advertising expenditure statistics and monitoring services are available from **Media Focus** and from **Internationaler Argus der Presse**.

19 UNITED KINGDOM

Business statistics

INTRODUCTION

After the establishment of the **Central Statistical Office** in 1941, government statistical activity expanded considerably but, in 1980, a review of government statistical services, known as the Rayner review, recommended various cutbacks, efficiency measures and changes in the way statistics should be published.

During the 1980s, the frequency and coverage of many official surveys were reduced and less data was available in traditional published form. The number of people employed in official statistical activities also fell from a high of 7,000 in 1979 to 4,228 in 1989.

Industrial surveys and product sales statistics are no longer as comprehensive as before but the news is not all bad for the statistical user. In some areas, such as the services sector, the amount of published data has actually increased and to speed up the publication of useful topical data, more statistical information is being published in the form of press releases and statistical bulletins. There is also a relatively strong non-official sector with many well established series from trade associations and other organisations.

The **Government Statistical Service (GSS)** is the collective name given to all the statistical activities carried out in Central Government and the co-ordination of these activities is the responsibility of the **Central Statistical Office (CSO)**. The Head of the GSS is also the Director of the **CSO**. Despite its title, the **CSO** is only involved directly with a small percentage of the official statistical series and publications although its responsibilities were expanded in 1989 when it became a new department directly responsible to the Chancellor of the Exchequer. Its main areas of interest are general statistical compilations, economic and related press releases, the compilation of national accounts and the collection of data from businesses. This latter area was previously the responsibility of the **Business Statistics Office (BSO)** at Newport, which was part of the Department of Trade and Industry, but the **BSO** is now part of the **CSO**.

The majority of official statistical work is decentralised with individual departments responsible for the collection, processing and dissemination of statistics in their areas of interest. A specialist statistical unit, **Office of Population, Censuses and Surveys (OPCS)** is concerned with demographic data and the constituent geographical areas of the United Kingdom – Wales, Scotland and Northern Ireland – also have their own statistical offices.

CSO addresses are given below and a list of the major departments involved in statistical activities is given in Table 19.1.

Central Statistical Office
CSO
Great George Street
London SW1P 3AQ
United Kingdom

Central Statistical Office
CSO
(Business Statistics)
Cardiff Road
Newport NP9 1XG
United Kingdom

Central Statistical Office (CSO)

Office of Population, Censuses & Surveys (OPCS)

Selected government departments:

Department of Employment
Department of Trade & Industry
HM Customs & Excise
Department of the Environment
Ministry of Agriculture, Fisheries & Food (MAFF)
Department of Transport
Department of Energy

Welsh Office
Scottish Office
Northern Ireland Departments

Table 19.1 Official statistics – Key departments and units

Government Statistics: a brief guide to sources can be obtained from CSO and it offers an annual guide to the major official titles. It also lists departmental contact points for particular statistical series. A more detailed guide to all official statistical publications is the **Guide to Official Statistics** which is only published every few years. The 6th edition became available in

1990. The quarterly **Statistical News** has news items and articles on statistical publications and developments.

Most of the publications themselves can be purchased from the **HMSO Publications Centre** in London or from **HMSO** bookshops around the country:

HMSO Publications Centre
PO Box 276
London SW8 5DT
United Kingdom

While HMSO is responsible for most of the traditional statistical publications, some of the newer titles, particularly statistical press releases and bulletins, are only available from the departments responsible for their collection. Details of some of these publications along with the department responsible are given in the sections to follow.

The **CSO**'s office in Newport has a collection of all the official industrial and service sector statistics, plus a selection of non-official titles, and the library is open to the public. Telephone inquiries can also be dealt with. **OPCS** has a library of international demographic data, open to the public, and the **Export Market Information Centre (EMIC)**, part of the library service of the DTI, has an extensive collection of statistics from around the world. The centre's library is open to the public during office hours.

On-line services

CSO Databank

Official statistical series on the main economic indicators and financial statistics are also available in machine readable format. The **CSO Databank** stores data on the index of output of production industries, national accounts, balance of payments, prices, earnings, employment, financial statistics and cyclical indicators. It is available on magnetic tape or in computer print-out form from the **CSO** and accessible on-line via a number of host systems including **DRI**, **WEFA**, **Datastream International** and **IP Sharp**.

CSO Statcall is a telephone service providing up-to-the-minute information on the main economic series, such as retail prices, unemployment and GDP. Each series has its own telephone number and, when dialled, a message provides the latest statistics. Details are available from the **CSO**.

GENERAL STATISTICAL TITLES

Compilations

The annual source bringing together a range of official statistics is the **Annual Abstract of Statistics** and many of the series in this title are updated in the **Monthly Digest of Statistics**.

Economic data

The starting point for UK economic data is the monthly **Economic Trends** with a brief commentary on the economic situation and tables and charts on specific economic indicators. An Annual Supplement presents very long runs of quarterly figures for all the main series. The CSO publishes various monthly, quarterly and annual **CSO Press Releases** on specific economic indicators, usually with a short commentary and basic statistics. **Financial Statistics**, published monthly, has the main financial and monetary statistics.

The **Bank of England Quarterly Bulletin** has articles and comment on the economic and financial situation with a statistical annex. Most tables are also available on tape or disc. The **Confederation of British Industry** publishes a monthly **Economic Situation Report** with an economic survey and short-term forecasts and a number of economic research organisations and academic institutions publish regular economic surveys and forecasts. These include the **London Business School's** monthly **Economic Outlook**, a quarterly **National Institute Economic Review** from the **National Institute of Economic and Social Research** and monthly **Framework Forecasts for the UK Economy** from the **Henley Centre**.

Demographic and social statistics

A population census is currently being undertaken every 10 years with the latest one in 1991. The first results from the 1991 census were published in 1991 and more reports will appear in the early part of the 1990s. A full set of reports is available for the previous census in 1981.

Regular demographic statistics are published by **OPCS** in a series of titles with the generic name of **OPCS Monitors**. These monitors are designed for the quick release of demographic data and are available, on subscription, from **OPCS**. **Population Trends** is a quarterly publication with articles on population issues and a regular statistical section.

Through a combination of short commentaries and graphs and tables, the annual **Social Trends** provides general data on social topics and issues. The annual **Key Data** is a summary version of **Social Trends**. Two regular surveys, **Family Expenditure Survey** and the **General Household Survey**, provide more detailed information on household characteristics, spending patterns and behaviour patterns and the results of these two surveys are published annually.

Sector data

General industrial statistics

The **CSO**, through its offices in Newport, regularly collects and publishes statistics on industrial structure and activity and the sales of specific commodities and products. The **Standard Industrial Classification (SIC)** provides the framework for these statistics.

The **SIC** is a classification of economic activities which includes the production industries, energy, construction, services, agriculture, forestry and fishing. The first **SIC** was published in 1948 and the latest version is **SIC (1980)** which has been in use since 1983. This latest version corresponds closely to the European **NACE** classification. The classification is made up of 10 general divisions (1-digit code), listed in Table 19.2, and these are divided into 60 'classes' (2-digit code), 222 'groups' (3-digit code) and 334 'activity headings' (4-digit code).

0	Agriculture, forestry & fishing
1	Energy & water supply industries
2	Extraction of minerals & ores other than fuels; manufacture of metals, mineral products & chemicals
3	Metal goods, engineering & vehicle industries
4	Other manufacturing industries
5	Construction
6	Distribution, hotels & catering; repairs
7	Transport & communications
8	Banking, finance, insurance, business services & leasing
9	Other services

Table 19.2 Standard industrial classification divisions (see Appendix 3)

An example of the breakdown within the **SIC** is as follows:

Division 3	Metal goods, engineering & vehicle industries
Class 34	Electrical engineering
Group 345	Miscellaneous electronic equipment
Activity	
Heading 3452	Gramophone records and pre-recorded tapes

The **CSO** at Newport holds a register of businesses in the United Kingdom and this provides the basis for the regular surveys of the production sector. For the construction sector, a register of businesses is produced annually from the Builders Address File held by the **Department of the Environment (DOE)**.

The Census of Production is a statutory inquiry undertaken annually although the number of companies questioned has fallen in recent years and the amount of information collected has changed. From 1980 onwards, there has been a new series of 'slimline' censuses every year with a detailed 'benchmark' census every fifth year.

Businesses with 20 employees or more are covered by the Census of Production. The sampling methods are reviewed each year but, in the 1988 census, all businesses with 100 employees or more were surveyed. A 1 in 2 sample was used for businesses in the 50 to 99 employment band and a 1 in 4 sample for businesses with between 20 and 49 employees. In total, 16,050 businesses were contacted and estimates made for non-respondents and businesses not selected, including those employing fewer than 20 people. In the construction sector, questionnaires were sent to all establishments employing 50 or more people and a 1 in 2 sample was used for those employing between 20 and 49 people. In 1988, a total of 4,225 construction companies were contacted. The sectors covered by reports from the census of production (3-digit level of the **SIC**) are shown below in Table 19.3.

111	Coal extraction & manufacture of solid fuels
120	Coke ovens
130	Extraction of mineral oil & natural gas
140	Mineral oil processing
161	Production & distribution of electricity
162	Public gas supply
170	Water supply industry
210	Extraction & preparation of metalliferous ores
221	Iron & steel industry
222	Steel tubes
223	Drawing, cold rolling & cold forming of steel
224	Non-ferrous metals industry
231	Extraction of stone, clay, sand, gravel
239	Extraction of miscellaneous minerals
241	Structural clay products
242	Cement, lime & plaster
243	Building products of concrete, cement or plaster
244	Asbestos goods
245	Working of stone and other non-metallic minerals
246	Abrasive products
247	Glass & glassware
248	Refractory & ceramic goods
251	Basic industrial chemicals
255	Paints, varnishes & printing ink
256	Specialised chemical products mainly for industrial & agricultural purposes
257	Pharmaceutical products
258	Soap & toilet preparations

Table 19.3 SIC groups covered by Census of Production reports

259	Specialised chemical products mainly for household & office use
260	Production of man-made fibres
311	Foundries
312	Forging, pressing & stamping
313	Bolts, nuts, washers, rivets, springs, non-precision chains, metal treatment
314	Metal doors, windows, etc.
316	Hand tools & finished metal goods
320	Industrial plant & steelwork
321	Agricultural machinery & tractors
322	Metal working machine tools & engineers' tools
323	Textile machinery
324	Machinery for the food, chemical & related industries, process engineering contractors
325	Mining machinery, constructional & mechanical handling equipment
326	Mechanical power transmission equipment
327	Machinery for the printing, paper, wood, leather, rubber, glass & related industries, laundry & dry cleaning machinery
328	Miscellaneous machinery & mechanical equipment
329	Ordnance, small arms & ammunition
330	Manufacture of office machinery & data-processing equipment
341	Insulated wires & cables
342	Basic electrical equipment
343	Electrical equipment for industrial use, batteries & accumulators
344	Telecommunication equipment, electrical measuring equipment, electronic capital goods & passive electronic components
345	Miscellaneous electronic equipment
346	Domestic-type electric appliances
347	Electric lamps & other electrical lighting equipment
351	Motor vehicles & their engines
352	Motor vehicle bodies, trailers & caravans
353	Motor vehicle parts
361	Shipbuilding & repairing
362	Railway & tramway vehicles
363	Cycles & motor cycles
364	Aerospace equipment manufacturing & repairing
365	Miscellaneous vehicles
371	Measuring, checking & precision instruments & apparatus
372	Medical & surgical equipment and orthopaedic appliances
373	Optical precision instruments & photographic
374	Clocks, watches & other timing devices
411	Organic oils & fats
412	Slaughtering of animals & production of meat & by- products
413	Preparation of milk & milk products
414	Processing of fruit & vegetables
415	Fish processing
416	Grain milling
419	Bread, biscuits & flour confectionery
420	Sugar & sugar by-products
421	Ice cream, cocoa, chocolate & sugar confectionery
422	Animal feeding stuffs

Table 19.3 SIC groups covered by Census of Production reports (*cont.*)

423	Starch & miscellaneous foods
424	Spirit distilling & compounding
426	Wines, cider & perry
427	Brewing & malting
428	Soft drinks
429	Tobacco industry
431	Woollen & worsted industry
432	Cotton & silk industries
433	Throwing, texturing, etc. of continuous filament yarn
434	Spinning & weaving of flax, hemp & ramie
435	Jute & polypropylene yarns & fabrics
436	Hosiery & other knitted goods
437	Textile finishing
438	Carpets & other textile floor coverings
439	Miscellaneous textiles
441	Leather (tanning & dressing) & fellmongery
442	Leather goods
451	Footwear
453	Clothing, hats & gloves
455	Household textiles & other made up textiles
456	Fur
461	Sawmilling, planing, etc. of wood
462	Manufacture of semi-finished wood products & further processing & treatment of wood
463	Builders' carpentry & joinery
464	Wooden containers
465	Miscellaneous wooden articles
466	Articles of cork & plaiting materials, brushes & brooms
467	Wooden & upholstered furniture & shop & office fittings
471	Pulp, paper & board
472	Conversion of paper & board
475	Printing & publishing
481	Rubber products (incl. retreating & specialist repair of tyres)
483	Processing of plastics
491	Jewellery & coins
492	Musical instruments
493	Photographic & cinematographic processing laboratories
494	Toys & sports goods
495	Miscellaneous manufacturing industries
500	Construction industry

Table 19.3 SIC groups covered by Census of Production reports (*cont.*)

Up until the middle of 1989, quarterly statutory inquiries collected data on the sales of specific products by UK manufacturers but, since 1989, only a few quarterly surveys remain and most are now annual. Questionnaires are sent to a sample of companies above a specified employment size in each sector and this employment size varies from sector to sector.

PUBLICATIONS PRODUCED BY NATIONAL ORGANIATIONS

General industry and trade

Business Monitor PA Series, Census of Production Reports

The main results of the annual Census of Production are published in 113 separate sector reports and each report corresponds to a 3-digit heading from Divisions 1, 2, 3, 4 and 5 of the **SIC** (a list of the reports is given in the preceding section). There is also a summary volume with basic data on all sectors included in the census (PA 1002) and an introductory volume (PA 1001).

The sector reports include statistics on the number and size of companies, employment, output, costs, capital expenditure, stocks, work in progress and operating ratios. Summary data is given for the last five years and detailed statistics for the latest census year. There is an inevitable delay in the publication of Census of Production reports with the results of the 1988 census published from 1990 onwards.

Business Monitor PQ and PAS Series, Production Monitors

Regular statistics on the sales of specific products by UK manufacturers plus general import and export statistics for these products are published in a series of 170 separate Business Monitor titles. Each Business Monitor corresponds to a 4-digit heading of the **SIC** and over 3,000 product headings are covered by the complete series. Up until the middle of 1989, all these Business Monitors were quarterly and each one had the prefix 'PQ' but, from 1989 onwards, most of the monitors have become annuals with the prefix 'PAS'. Forty-one monitors remain quarterly. A sample page from a typical Business Monitor is shown in Table 19.4.

Industrial Economic Indicators Database

The private company, **Business & Trade Statistics Ltd**, produces a disc version of the official statistics relating to sectors and products. Their database has information on economic activity, production, sales, prices, exports, imports, home consumption and employment based on data from the above sources and others. The statistics can be supplied in total or for specific products and sectors and the data is produced on disc or as a computer print-out.

Industrial Trends Survey

Published quarterly by the **Confederation of British Industry (CBI)**, the survey shows trends in 50 individual industry groups arranged by the **SIC**.

ANNUAL SALES OF DOMESTIC ELECTRICAL APPLIANCES BY UNITED KINGDOM (a)

PAS 3460

UNITS IN SCOPE OF THE ANNUAL SALES INQUIRIES: (a)	No of enterprises (b) 1990	Units	1985	1986	(c)1987	1988	1989	(d)	1990
Cooking apparatus:									
Cookers	6	£millions	115.6	134.4	139.9	172.0	149.9E		127.7
		Thous	602	701	688	755	702		557
Parts and accessories		£millions	15.3	15.1	17.4	27.2	21.1	DP	
Microwave cookers (f)	10	£millions	(g)	44.6	77.1	154.8	115.3		104.6
		Thous	(g)	358	643	1,409	919		976
Parts		£millions		3.6	3.9	12.3	12.6	DP	
Kettles:									
Automatic	4	£millions	49.1	47.1	56.6	58.6	50.0		41.2E
		Thous	4,662	4,528	5,434	5,364	4,608		3,657E
Standard	..	£millions	2.7	3.0	1.7	1.5	1.4		..(i)
		Thous	335	366	235	..	206		..
Other domestic electric cooking apparatus and parts	7	£millions	63.5 (h)	35.4	42.4	46.1	35.1		37.8
Electric flat irons:									
Dry	..	£millions	3.5	2.5	2.1	1.7	1.0		..(i)
		Thous	508	348	296	271	153		
Steam	..	£millions	9.0	11.6	17.5	18.1	12.4		..(i)
		Thous	935	1,068	1,639	1,634	1,119		..
Electric heating apparatus:									
Space heating (incl portable electric fires, thermal storage and electrical units, etc)	6	£millions	97.4	130.8	144.1	140.0	122.5		110.4
Water heaters	7	£millions	54.1	58.2	58.2	73.9	58.0E		71.5
Blankets		£millions	17.4	20.5	19.8	14.0	10.0		-
		Thous	1,377	1,498	1,431	1,034	718		-
Other domestic electrical heating apparatus	..	£millions	3.7	4.1	4.0	5.5	3.4		..(i)
Parts and accessories		£millions	18.7	13.2	17.2	19.8	22.8	DP	
Fans complete and parts	..	£millions	8.2	8.3	..(i)	..(i)	..(i)		..(i)
Vacuum cleaners	3	£millions	102.7	86.2	102.2	132.5	136.7		147.9
		Thous	2,326	1,703	1,934	2,189	2,101		2,295
Parts		£millions	6.2	13.5	23.2	22.0	10.3	DP	

(DP – Discontinued Product)

Table 19.4 United Kingdom manufacturers' sales statistics – extract from publication covering domestic electrical appliances

Approximately 1,700 companies are surveyed in each quarter and asked for their opinions on likely trends in orders, stocks, output, capital expenditure, exports, costs, labour, etc. Summary data is included in a monthly publication **Monthly Trends Enquiry**.

Business Monitor MM20, Overseas Trade Statistics of the United Kingdom

Published monthly, plus an annual volume, it contains detailed data on the imports and exports of specific commodities, by country, arranged by the **SITC** international trade classification. Tables also cover the imports and exports of specific commodities arranged by the **HS** trade classification but here there is no country breakdown. Value and volume figures are included with data for the latest month and the cumulative year-to-date.

Monthly Review of External Trade Statistics

General data on imports and exports arranged by major product groups and geographical areas. It also has tables on the current account of the Balance of Payments, derived statistics of UK trade and international comparisons.

UK External Trade: Area Commodity Analysis

A quarterly publication showing UK trade with each of the Western European countries, the United States, Japan and various area groupings such as the OECD, Latin America, etc.

More detailed trade statistics than those published in the above titles are available from various companies acting as agents for **HM Customs & Excise**. Statistics are usually available in hard copy format and on disc, tape, and microfiche. Standard services and customised services are available from:

> **Abacus Data Services (UK) Ltd**
> **Business & Trade Statistics Ltd**
> **Data-Star**
> **Interactive Marketing Systems (UK) Ltd**
> **Overseas Trade Data**

The addresses of these companies are given in the organisation index.

Construction

Construction companies are included in the Census of Production and the results are published annually in the above report.

Housing and Construction Statistics

The results of regular surveys of the construction industry, including both private and public sectors, by the Department of the Environment are published in the above publication which has annual and quarterly versions. The annual publication has data for the last 10 years and includes a section on industry structure with other sections on the value of work, output, labour, materials, investment and housing. The quarterly version is published in two volumes each quarter. Part 1 looks at house building performance, housing finance and building materials. Part 2 is concerned with construction activity, employment, local authority loans and sales plus various ad hoc tables.

Department of the Environment Press Notices

A series of regular press notices are published throughout the year with individual notices on specific topics. Monthly notices include house building, new orders, new orders by type of work and building materials and components. Quarterly press releases cover construction output and employment.

Construction Forecasts

Published twice a year by the **Joint Forecasting Committee of the NEDC, Construction Industry Sector Group** and published by **NEDO**. Current and forecasted output and work of the construction sector is included.

Various other organisations are involved in the preparation of construction statistics, forecasts and opinion surveys including: the **Building Employers Confederation** with a quarterly state of trade inquiry, the **National Council of Building Material Producers** with three forecasts a year and a monthly bulletin, the **Building Services Research and Information Association (BSRIA)** which produces a quarterly statistical bulletin and the **National House Building Council** publishing quarterly statistics.

Food and drink

Official data on food and drink comes from reports and press releases produced by the **Ministry of Agriculture, Fisheries and Foods (MAFF)**.

Household Food Consumption and Expenditure: Report of the National Food Survey Committee

The annual report of the **National Food Survey Committee** with commentary and statistics on specific food groups and products.

UK Food and Drink Market Size Data Sheets

Regular information and statistics on specific product markets compiled from various sources. Published by the **British Food Manufacturing Industries Research Association** usually referred to as **Leatherhead Food R.A.** The association also has a series of market reports on specific foods and drinks and a database of food information.

Dairy Facts and Figures

An annual compilation of data from the **Milk Marketing Board** based on a combination of the Board's own data and official statistics. Other statistical services provide detailed information on milk production and yields.

British Frozen Food Yearbook

The yearbook includes a section of frozen food statistics with data on the consumption of and expenditure on specific foods. Published by the **British Frozen Food Federation**.

Statistical Yearbook

The yearbook from the **Biscuit, Cake, Chocolate & Confectionery Alliance (BCCCA)** has data on the deliveries of products to home and export markets. The results are based on a survey of member companies. There are more regular reports on specific product areas.

UK Statistical Handbook

Details of the production and consumption of beer with additional data on areas such as brewing materials, licensing, drunkenness, duties, incomes and industry structure. Published by the **Brewers Society** and mainly based on official data. Monthly data on beer production is also available.

Chemicals and chemical products

UK Chemical Industry Facts

An annual compilation of chemical industry statistics from the **Chemical Industries Association**. The association also publishes a quarterly **Economics Bulletin** showing general trends in the sector. One quarterly issue has the results of an investment intentions survey.

UK Petroleum Industry Statistics

Annual statistics on the deliveries, end use and production of petroleum products based on data collected by the **Institute of Petroleum**. The Institute also produces a series of press releases on petroleum products deliveries and various other reports and surveys.

Textiles and clothing

Annual Report and Review

A review of trends in the textile industry with supporting statistics. Published by the **British Textile Confederation** which also publishes quarterly external trade statistics.

Quarterly Statistical Review

Statistics on textiles production, imports, exports broken down into specific sectors plus employment information. Published by the **Textile Statistics Bureau** which also produces a series of monthly reports on exports and imports of textiles and another monthly report on production, employment and machine activity.

Monthly Bulletin of Statistics

Production statistics for the wool textile industry broken down into specific sectors and based on a survey by the **Confederation of British Wool Textiles**. Employment data is also included. The Confederation also publishes a quarterly review of external trade statistics.

Statistical Report on the British Clothing Industry

An annual report with statistics on clothing production, imports, exports, prices, employment, wages and salaries and consumer spending on clothing. The report is largely based on official statistics. Published by the **British Clothing Industry Association**.

Knitstats

Annual statistics for the knitting industry are published by **HATRA** based on a combination of official and non-official sources.

Footwear Industry Statistical Review

The **British Footwear Manufacturers Federation** publishes annual statistics covering industry structure, production, imports, exports, materials, employment, earnings, prices, expenditure, wholesaling and retailing. Some comparative EC data is also included. There are also quarterly and monthly statistics from the Federation.

Electrical and mechanical engineering

Engineering Economic Trends

Published twice a year by the **Engineering Employers Federation (EEF)**, there are graphs, tables and commentary on engineering output, sales, imports and exports. The statistics are broken down into specific **SIC** headings and forecasts are included.

Machine Tool Statistics

Key statistics for the machine tools sector published annually by the **Machine Tool Trades Association (MTTA)**. Includes statistics on production, orders, foreign trade, machine population, prices and employment.

UK Iron and Steel Industry: Annual Statistics

Detailed statistics on iron and steel production, consumption and trade broken down by product and end use. Additional information on the use of raw materials, foundries and employment. Based on data collected by the **UK Iron and Steel Statistics Bureau**. The Bureau also publishes a series of reports on the steel industry and market in specific countries.

Electronics

AMDEA Statistical Yearbook
AMDEA Quarterly Statistics

The yearbook contains information on the deliveries and imports of various electrical appliances plus additional information on prices and employment. The data is mainly based on a survey by **AMDEA**, the **Association of Manufacturers of Domestic Electrical Appliances**. Similar information on specific products is contained in the quarterly reports.

Deliveries of Selected Audio and Video Products to the UK Market

Quarterly statistics with a commentary covering trade deliveries of televisions, videos, music centres and compact disc players. Based on a survey of members of the **British Radio & Electronic Equipment Manufacturers Association (BREEMA)**. The association also publishes some annual reports on specific products such as televisions, audio equipment and video equipment.

Services – general

Business Monitor SDA 29 Services

From 1985 onwards, an annual sample inquiry of the services sector has been undertaken by official statisticians. The 1985 survey only gave total figures for the services sector but later inquiries have included data on specific service sectors and the number of sectors covered is increasing. A sample of 23,000 businesses was contacted for the 1988 inquiry. Information is published annually on the number of businesses, turnover and capital expenditure and information on a rotating topic appears in selected years.

Retailing and distribution

The last census of distribution took place in 1971 and there were annual retailing inquiries between 1976 and 1980 with other inquiries in 1982, 1984 and 1986. Now, there are annual sample inquiries covering retailing and wholesaling.

Business Monitor SDA 25 Retailing

From 1987 onwards, there has been a new style of 'intermediate' retailing inquiry which is held every year. Every fifth year, a full inquiry is carried out. These inquiries provide information on stocks, capital expenditure, total turnover, turnover by commodity sales, retail sales by special forms of trading, purchases, outlets and employment. This data is published on the main retailing sectors but it excludes petrol filling stations and motor vehicles and accessory sales which are covered by a separate inquiry. The results of the 1987 inquiry were published in 1990.

The inquiry is based on a sample of businesses taken from the VAT register and, in the 1987 inquiry, 12,000 businesses were contacted. All businesses with a turnover of £2 million or more a year are included but a sample of other businesses is taken and estimates are made for businesses with a turnover of less than £44,000 a year.

Business Monitor SDA 26 Wholesaling

An annual sample inquiry of the wholesaling sector provides the same general information as the retailing inquiry described above.

Food Industry Statistics Digest

A monthly update service, in a loose-leaf binder, with statistics on food retailing. Individual sections cover areas such as shops, expenditure, consumers, companies, products, etc. plus there is additional data on costs, prices, employment, stocks, capital and profits. The service is published by the **Institute of Grocery Distribution (IGD)** which publishes various other reports on the food retailing sector.

Financial services

The **Bank of England Quarterly Bulletin**, already mentioned in the section headed 'Economic Data' on page 196, has statistical tables on banking and finance. The **CBI/Coopers Deloitte Survey of Financial Services** is a quarterly opinion survey of the financial services sector.

Other sources covering specific financial services sectors include:

Major British Banking Groups' Monthly Statement

A monthly press release from the **British Bankers Association** with commentary and statistics on bank lending, deposits and liabilities. The association also produces quarterly statistics covering mortgage loans.

Building Society Factbook

An annual report on the activities of societies with statistics on numbers, loans, assets, mortgages, commitments, finances, etc. Published by the **Building Societies Association** which also publishes press releases with statistics and various occasional reports.

Housing Finance

A regular journal from the **Council of Mortgage Lenders** with a statistical section and tables and graphs in specific articles.

Insurance Statistics
Market Statistics

The **Association of British Insurers (ABI)** publishes various insurance statistics including the two annuals above. The first title is a compilation of data on general insurance and life insurance based largely on the association's own figures. The second title provides an estimate of the size of the UK insurance market. Other regular statistics include a quarterly report on new business, twice-yearly figures on new life business and annual long-term business statistics.

Monthly Unit Trust Sales Statistics

Monthly sales figures from the **Unit Trust Association** which also produces quarterly figures on the performance of unit trusts.

Leisure and tourism

Tourism Intelligence Quarterly

The **British Tourist Authority (BTA)** produces a number of regular statistical publications and one-off reports. The above quarterly brings together the major statistics on UK and overseas tourism and interprets these. Other publications include an annual report, an **Overseas Visitor Survey**, the annual **Visits to Tourist Attractions** and a **Digest of Tourist Statistics** published every few years.

Britain's Tourism

The **English Tourist Board (ETB)** also publishes a range of regular and one-off titles on tourism. **Britain's Tourism** is an annual series of fact sheets covering the main tourist topics and other publications include **British Holiday Intentions** and **English Heritage Monitor** published annually, an annual report and the **English Hotel Occupancy Survey** produced monthly.

Transportation

Transport Statistics Great Britain

Articles followed by statistics on transport and traffic trends by type of transport. Many tables give historical series of figures.

Quarterly Transport Statistics

One of a regular series of bulletins available from the **Department of Transport**. This bulletin has general statistics on transport trends but there are other monthly and quarterly bulletins with data on specific transport areas.

SMMT Monthly Statistical Review
Motorstat NR2

The **Society of Motor Manufacturers and Traders (SMMT)** publishes a number of regular statistics on motor vehicles. The monthly review includes production and registration figures, by manufacturer and model, and external trade data for products of the motor industry. Special tables are published in certain issues and there is also a summary annual forecast. **NR2** is a monthly summary of new registrations, by make and model, based on the Society's own figures. Other publications include **Motorstat Express** with monthly summary production and registration data for key countries and the annual **World Automotive Statistics**.

Basic Road Statistics

Annual statistics on roads and road transport from the **British Road Federation**. Most of the data comes from official sources.

Port Statistics

Annual figures on UK ports and imports and exports going through the ports. Published by the **British Ports Federation** which also produces quarterly external trade statistics.

UK Airports
UK Airlines

Both the above titles are published monthly and annually by the **Civil Aviation Authority (CAA)**. The first contains information on passengers, plane movements, cargo, etc. and the second has data on operating, traffic, personnel and financial trends. Both are based on data collected by the **CAA**.

Public sector

CIPFA Statistical Service

One of the main publishers of statistical data, outside official sources, is the **Chartered Institute of Public Finance & Accountancy (CIPFA)** which publishes a series of annual titles on local government finance and local government activities. Two compilations of data are **Local Government Comparative Statistics**, with basic statistics on services for specific local authorities, and **Local Government Trends**, with commentary and aggregate statistics on services. Both titles are published annually and most other **CIPFA** titles cover specific service areas.

Handbook of Electricity Supply Statistics

Annual statistics on the electricity supply system from the **Electricity Council**. Other figures are published annually on sales, performance and disconnections.

   British Gas publishes regular statistics on gas supply and demand.

Advertising statistics

Advertising Statistics Yearbook

Published by **NTC Publications** on behalf of the **Advertising Association**. Statistics on advertising expenditure, in total and by general product area and media type, plus data on agencies, top advertisers, attitudes to advertising and complaints. The association also produces a quarterly **Survey of Advertising Expenditure** and advertising forecasts.

An advertising monitoring service, with data on specific products, brands and media types, is available. The company, **Register – MEAL**, produces a quarterly bulletin of the same name.

LIST OF ORGANISATIONS

Abacus Data Services (UK) Ltd
Causeway House, 24 South Drive
Coulsdon
Surrey CR3 2BG
UK
Tel: 081 7631000
Fax: 081 6812440

Advertising Association
Abford House, 15 Wilton Road
London SW1V 1NJ
UK
Tel: 071 8282772
Fax: 071 9310376

Advertising Audit Services
28 avenue du Barbeau
1160 Brussels
Belgium
Tel: 02 6722385

Advertising Statistics Ireland
Willowbrook House
Balheary Road,
Swords
Ireland
Tel: 405173

AGB Gallup
Marina Park, Sundkrogsgade 10
2100 Copenhagen 0
Denmark
Tel: 39 272727
Fax: 31 182466

Agra Alimentation
29 rue du General Foy
75008 Paris
France
Tel: 1 43873959
Fax: 1 43870463

Agra Europe (London) Ltd
25 Frant Road
Tunbridge Wells
Kent TN2 5JT
UK
Tel: 0892 533813
Fax: 0892 524593

Alan Armstrong
2 Arkwright Road
Reading
Berkshire RG2 0SQ
UK
Tel: 0734 751855
Fax: 0734 755164

Algemeen Verbond Bouwbedrijf
Benoordenhoutseweg 21
PO Box 90603
2509 LP Den Haag
Netherlands
Tel: 70 262021

Algemene Nederlandse Bond van Binnenlandse Groothandelaren in Groenten en Fruit
Bezvidenhoutseweg 82
PO Box 90410
2509 LK Den Haag
Netherlands
Tel: 70 850100

Algemene Nederlandse Bond van Frisdrankenfabrikanten en Groothandelaren in Dranken
Heemraadssingel 167
3022 CG Rotterdam
Netherlands
Tel: 010 4774033
Fax: 010 4259025

Alimarket SA
O'Donnell 18, 20G
28009 Madrid
Spain
Tel: 1 5778225
Fax: 1 4313727

Annonsorforeningen
PO Box 6810
11386 Stockholm
Sweden
Tel: 08 302575

Arbeidsgiverforeningen for Skip og Offshorefartoyer
Raadhusgata 25
PO Box 1452 Vika
0116 Oslo 1
Norway
Tel: 02 416080
Fax: 02 415021

Arbeitsgemeinschaft Deutscher Verkehrsflughafen
PO Box 230108
7000 Stuttgart 83
Germany
Tel: 0711 79011
Fax: 0711 7901746

Arbeitsgemeinschaft Deutscher Wirtschaftswissenschaftlicher Forschungsinstitute
Konigin Luise Strasse 5
1000 Berlin 33
Germany
Tel: 030 829910

Asociacion de Constructores Navales Espanoles
Orense 11
28020 Madrid
Spain
Tel: 1 5560458
Fax: 1 5566091

Asociacion Espanola de Fabricantes de Maquinas-Herramienta
Avda. de Zaruaz 82
20009 San Sebastian
Spain
Tel: 43 219011
Fax: 43 218036

Asociacion Nacional de Entidades de Financiacion
Paseo de la Castellana 128–5
28046 Madrid
Spain
Tel: 1 4115465
Fax: 1 2621230

Asociacion Nacional de Industrias Electronicas
Principe de Vergara 74,4
28006 Madrid
Spain
Tel: 1 4111661
Fax: 1 4114000

Asociacion de Navieros Espanola
Plaza de la Lealtad 4–5
28014 Madrid
Spain
Tel: 1 2322109
Fax: 1 5319209

Associacio do Comercio Automovel de Portugal
Rua da Palmeira 6
1200 Lisbon
Portugal
Tel: 01 370040–9
Fax: 01 320064

Associacao di Empresas de Construcao e Obras Publicas do Sul
Rua Antonio, Enes 9–5
1000 Lisbon
Portugal
Tel: 01 53319315

Associacao dos Industriais de Construcao Civil e Obras Publicas do Norte
Rua Alvares Cabral 306
4099 Porto
Portugal
Tel: 02 2000082

Associacao dos Industrias Metalurgicos e Metalomecanicos do Norte
Rua Guedes de Azeudo 233–1
4000 Porto
Portugal
Tel: 02 320809
Fax: 02 2005019

Associacao Industrial Portuguesa
Praca das Industrias
1399 Lisbon
Portugal
Tel: 01 3620100
Fax: 01 3639047

Associacao Nacional dos Industriais de Material Electrico e Electronico
Avenida Guerra Junqueiro 11–2–E
1000 Lisbon
Portugal
Tel: 01 894521

Associacao Nacional de Supermercados
Campo Grande 286–5
1700 Lisbon
Portugal
Tel: 01 7580524
Fax: 01 7599508

Associacao Portuguesa de Seguradores
Avenida Jose Malhoa 1674 5
1000 Lisbon
Portugal
Tel: 01 7268123

Association Belge des Banques
rue Ravenstein 36, Bte 5
1000 Brussels
Belgium
Tel: 02 5076811

Association of British Insurers
Aldermary House, Queen Street
London EC4N 1TT
UK
Tel: 071 2484477
Fax: 071 4891120

Association Generale de l'Industrie du Medicament
Square Marie-Louise 49
1040 Brussels
Belgium
Tel: 02 2389711
Fax: 02 2311164

Association Internationale de la Savonnerie et de la Detergence
Square Marie-Louise 49
1040 Brussels
Belgium
Tel: 02 2308371
Fax: 02 2308288

Association of Manufacturers of Domestic Electrical Appliances
8 Leicester Street
London WC2H 7BL
UK
Tel: 071 4370678

Association Nationale de la Meunerie Francaise
66 rue La Boetie
75008 Paris
France
Tel: 1 43594580
Fax: 1 45637102

Association of European Airlines
350 avenue Louise
Box 4
1050 Brussels
Belgium
Tel: 02 6403175
Fax: 02 6484017

Association of West European Shipbuilders
An der Alster 1
2000 Hamburg 1
Germany
Tel: 40 246305
Fax: 40 246287

Associazione Cotoniera Italiana
Via Borgonuovo 11
20121 Milan
Italy
Tel: 02 8692141–6

Associazione dell'Industria Laniera Italiana
Via Borgonuovo 11
20121 Milan
Italy
Tel: 02 808641
Fax: 02 72623700

Associazione Industrie Siderurgiche Italiana
Piazza Velasca 8
20122 Milan
Italy
Tel: 02 860351

Associazione Italiana Industriali Abbigliamento
Viale Sarca 223
20126 Milan
Italy
Tel: 02 66103566
Fax: 02 66103667

Associazione Italiana Lattiero Casearia
Corso di Porta Romana 2
20122 Milan
Italy
Tel: 02 72021817
Fax: 02 72021838

Associazione Nazionale Aziende Ordinarie di Credito Assbank
Via Domenicmino 5
Milan
Italy
Tel: 02 48010296
Fax: 02 48010137

Associazione Nazionale Calzaturifici Italiani
Via Dogana 1
20123 Milan
Italy
Tel: 02 809721

Associazione Nazionale Cooperative fra Dettaglianti
c/o Borgo San Spirito 78
00193 Rome
Italy
Tel: 06 650861

Associazione Nazionale Costruttori Edili
Via Guattani 16–18
00161 Rome
Italy
Tel: 06 84881
Fax: 06 8444364

Associazione Nazionale fra le Imprese Assicuratrici
Piazza S. Babila 1
20122 Milan
Italy
Tel: 02 77641
Fax: 02 780870

Associazione Nazionale fra Industrie Automobilistiche
Corso Venezia 43
20121 Milan
Italy
Tel: 02 27301462
Fax: 02 27301454

Associazione Nazionale dell'Industria Chimica
Corso Venezia 47–49
20121 Milan
Italy
Tel: 02 7750236–7

Automobil Importorernes Sammenslutning
Rysangs Alle 68
2900 Hellerup
Denmark
Tel: 3162 3999
Fax: 3162 3977

Banca d'Italia
Via Nazionale 91
00184 Rome
Italy
Tel: 06 47921

Banco de Espana
Alcala 50
28014 Madrid
Spain
Tel: 1 4469050

Banco de Portugal
Rua do Ouro 27
1100 Lisbon
Portugal
Tel: 01 3462931
Fax: 01 540516

Bank of England
Threadneedle Street
London EC2R 8AH
UK
Tel: 071 6014444

Bank of Greece
21 Venizelos Avenue
10250 Athens
Greece
Tel: 01 3201111
Fax: 01 3232239

Bank Mees & Hope NV
PO Box 293
1000 AG Amsterdam
Netherlands
Tel: 20 5279111
Fax: 20 5274592

Banque de France
39 rue Croix des Petits
BP 140–01
75049 Paris Cedex 01
France
Tel: 1 42924297
Fax: 1 42960423

Banque Nationale de Belgique
boulevard de Berlaimont 5
1000 Brussels
Belgium
Tel: 02 2213101
Fax: 02 2212111

Benelux
Rue de la Regence 39
1000 Brussels
Belgium
Tel: 02 5193811
Fax: 02 5134206

Bilindustriforeningen
Storgatan 19
Box 5514
11485 Stockholm
Sweden
Tel: 08 7838000
Fax: 08 6619679

**Biscuit, Cake, Chocolate &
Confectionery Alliance**
11 Green Street
London W1Y 3RF
UK
Tel: 071 6298971
Fax: 071 4934885

Board of Customs (Tullihallituus)
Uudenmaanktu 1–5
Nylandsgatan
PO Box 512
00101 Helsinki
Finland
Tel: 90 6141

**Bond van Detaillisten in de
Parfumeriehandel**
Nassauplein 37
PO Box 85906
2508 CP Den Haag
Netherlands
Tel: 70 609915

Brewers Society
42 Portman Square
London W1H 0BB
UK
Tel: 071 4864831

British Bankers Association
10 Lombard Street
London EC3V 9EL
UK
Tel: 071 6268486
Fax: 071 2837037

British Clothing Industry Association
7 Swallow Place
London W1
UK
Tel: 071 4080020

**British Footwear Manufacturers
Federation**
Royalty House
72 Dean Street
London W1V 5HB
UK
Tel: 071 4375573
Fax: 071 4941300

British Frozen Food Federation
Honeypot Lane
Colsterworth
Grantham NG33 5LX
UK
Tel: 0476 860914

British Gas
152 Grosvenor Road
London SW1V 3JL
UK
Tel: 071 8211444
Fax: 071 7241317

British Ports Federation
Commonwealth House
1–19 New Oxford Street
London WC1A 1DZ
UK
Tel: 071 2421200

**British Radio & Electronic Equipment
Manufacturers Association**
Landseer House
19 Charing Cross Road
London WC2H 0ES
UK
Tel: 071 9303206

British Road Federation
Cowdray House
6 Portugal Street
London WC2A 2HG
UK
Tel: 071 2421285

British Textile Confederation
24 Buckingham Gate
London SW1E 6LB
UK
Tel: 071 8285222

British Tourist Authority
Thames Tower
Blacks Road
London W6 9EL
UK
Tel: 081 8469000

Brogger & Nygart/IM
Valkendorfsgade 16
1151 Copenhagen K
Denmark
Tel: 33 154444
Fax: 33 151509

Bryggeriforeningen
Frederiksberggade 11
1459 Copenhagen
Denmark
Tel: 33 126241
Fax: 33 142513

Building Employers Confederation
82 New Cavendish Street
London W1M 8AD
UK
Tel: 071 5805588

**Building Services Research and
Information Association**
Old Bracknell Lane West
Bracknell
Berkshire RG12 4AH
UK
Tel: 0344 426511
Fax: 0344 487575

Building Societies Association
3 Savile Row
London W1X 8AD
UK
Tel: 071 4379655
Fax: 071 7346416

**Bundesamt fur Statistik/Office federal
de la Statistique**
Hallwylstrasse 15
3003 Berne
Switzerland
Tel: 031 619111
Fax: 031 617856

**Bundesarbeitsgemeinschaft der Mittel-
und Grossbetriebe des Einzelhandels**
Lindenallee 41
5000 Cologne 51
Germany
Tel: 0221 376790
Fax: 0221 3767988

**Bundesverband Vertriebsunternehmen
Buro, Informations – und
Kommunikationstechnik**
Dietrich-Bonhoeffer-Strasse 4
6380 Bad Homburg
Germany
Tel: 6172 31010

**Bundesvereinigung der Deutschen
Ernahrungsindustrie**
Rheinallee 18
5300 Bonn 2
Germany
Tel: 0228 351051–53
Fax: 0228 351992

**Bundesverband der Deutschen
Fleischwarenindustrie**
Schedestrasse 11
5300 Bonn 1
Germany
Tel: 0228 224666
Fax: 0228 261597

Bundesverband der Deutschen Gas und Wasserwirtschaft
Josef-Wirmer Strasse 1
PO Box 140154
5300 Bonn 1
Germany
Tel: 0228 520010

Bundesverband der Deutschen Industrie
PO Box 510548
5000 Cologne 51
Germany
Tel: 0221 37080–0

Bundesverband der Deutschen Spirituosen Industrie
Urstadtstrasse 2
5300 Bonn 1
Germany
Tel: 0228 238061/3
Fax: 0228 234351

Bundesverband der Deutschen Susswarenindustrie
Schumannstrasse 4–6
5300 Bonn 1
Germany
Tel: 0228 26007–22
Fax: 0228 26007–89

Bundesverband Deutscher Eisenbahnen
Hulchrather Strasse 17
5000 Cologne 1
Germany
Tel: 0221 77206–0
Fax: 0221 77206–66

Bundesverband Deutscher Stahlhandel
Graf-Adolf-Platz 12
PO Box 200128
4000 Dusseldorf 1
Germany
Tel: 0211 38423–0

Bureau National Interprofessionel du Cognac
5 rue Georges Briand
16100 Cognac
France
Tel: 45820888

Business and Trade Statistics Ltd
Lancaster House
More Lane
Esher
Surrey KT10 8AP
UK
Tel: 0372 463121
Fax: 0372 469847

Byggentreprenorerna
Box 27308
10254 Stockholm
Sweden
Tel: 08 6653500
Fax: 08 6627032

CAOBISCO
194 rue de Rivoli
75001 Paris
France
Tel: 1 42664014

CECED
Leicester House, 8 Leicester Street
London WC2H 7BN
UK
Tel: 071 4370678
Fax: 071 4941094

CECIMO
Rue des Drapiers 21
1050 Brussels
Belgium
Tel: 02 5102351
Fax: 02 5102301

Central Bank of Ireland
PO Box 559
Dame Street
Dublin 2
Ireland
Tel: 01 716666
Fax: 01 716561

Central Bureau of Statistics
Prinses Beatrixlaan 428
PO Box 959
2270 AZ Voorburg
Netherlands
Tel: 070 3694341
Fax: 070 3877429

Central Bureau of Statistics
Kloosterweg 1
PO Box 4481
6401 CZ Heerlen
Netherlands
Tel: 045 736666

Central Statistical Office
PO Box 504
00101 Helsinki
Finland
Tel: 90 17341

Central Statistical Office
Great George Street
London SW1P 3AQ
UK
Tel: 071 2706363

Central Statistical Office
Cardiff Road
Newport NP9 1XG
UK
Tel: 0633 812973
Fax: 0633 812599

Central Statistics Office
St Stephen's Green House
Earlsfort Terrace
Dublin 2
Ireland
Tel: 01 767531
Fax: 01 682221

Centro de Cooperacao dos Industrias de Maquinas-Ferramentas
Rua Manuel Pinto de Azevedo 439
4100 Porto
Portugal
Tel: 02 6175071
Fax: 02 670589

CERVED
Via Appia Nousa 696
00179 Rome
Italy
Tel: 06 793901

Chambre de Commerce et d'Industrie de Paris
27 avenue de Friedland
75008 Paris
France
Tel: 1 42897000

Chambre Syndicale des Constructeurs d'Automobiles
2 rue de Presbourg
75008 Paris
France
Tel: 1 47201150
Fax: 1 47235405

Chambre Syndicale des Constructeurs de Navires
47 rue de Monceau
75008 Paris
France
Tel: 1 45619911
Fax: 1 42892532

Chambre Syndicale Nationale du Commerce Chimique
8 rue de Rome
75008 Paris
France
Tel: 1 45229617
Fax: 1 43871816

Chambre Syndicale Nationale de Motocycle
251 boulevard Pereire
75852 Paris
France
Tel: 1 45749748

Chambre Syndicale des Producteurs de Fer-Blanc et de Fer-Noir
5 rue Paul Cezanne
75008 Paris
France
Tel: 1 45631710

Chambre Syndicale de la Siderurgie Francaise
19 Le Parvis imm Elysees
92072 Paris La Defense
Cedex 35
France
Tel: 1 47678588
Fax: 1 47678577

Chartered Institute of Public Finance & Accountancy
3 Robert Street
London WC2N 6BH
UK
Tel: 071 8958823
Fax: 071 8958825

Chemical Industries Association
King's Buildings, Smiths Square
London SW1P 3JJ
UK
Tel: 071 8343399
Fax: 071 8344469

Chemical Intelligence Services
39A Bowling Green Lane
London EC1R 0BJ
UK
Tel: 071 8333812
Fax: 071 8331563

CHOBISCO
Rue de la Bourse
22 Bte 3
1000 Brussels
Belgium
Tel: 2 5110030

Civil Aviation Authority
45–59 Kingsway
London WC2B 6TE
UK
Tel: 071 3797311
Fax: 071 3794784

CMT Ltd
Teddington House, 67 Broad Street
Teddington
Middlesex TW11 8QZ
UK
Tel: 081 9778737
Fax: 081 9433697

Comite Belge de la Distribution
Rue Marianne 34
1180 Brussels
Belgium
Tel: 02 3459923
Fax: 02 3460204

Comite Centrale de la Bonneterie Belge
Rode Beukendreef 14
9831 Deurle
Belgium
Tel: 91 822111

Comite Centrale de la Laine et des Fibres Associees
37–39 rue de Neuilly
92113 Clichy
France
Tel: 1 47563100
Fax: 1 47370620

Comite Professionel du Petrole
51 boulevard de Courcelles
75008 Paris
France
Tel: 1 47660382

Committee of the Wool Textile Industry in the EC
19 Rue du Luxembourg
Bte 14
1040 Brussels, Belgium
Tel: 02 5130620

Confederacion Espanola de Cajas de Ahorros
Alcala 27
28014 Madrid
Spain
Tel: 1 5214444

Confederation of British Industry
Centre Point, 103 New Oxford Street
London WC1A 1DU
UK
Tel: 071 3797400
Fax: 071 2401578

Confederation of British Wool Textiles
60 Toller Lane
Bradford BD8 9BZ
UK
Tel: 0274 491241
Fax: 0274 547320

Confederation Francaise de la Conserve
44 rue d'Alesia
75682 Paris Cedex 15
France
Tel: 1 43212821
Fax: 1 43216839

Confederation of Irish Industry
Confederation House, Kildare Street
Dublin 2
Ireland
Tel: 01 779801
Fax: 01 777823

Confederation Nationale de la Construction
Rue du Lombard 34–42
1000 Brussels
Belgium
Tel: 02 5104611
Fax: 02 5137004

Conseil National du Cuir
109 rue du Faubourg-Saint-Honore
75373 Paris Cedex 08
France
Tel: 1 43590569
Fax: 1 43593002

Coordinating Committee for the Textile Industries in the EC
Rue Montoyer 24
1040 Brussels
Belgium
Tel: 02 2309580
Fax: 02 2306054

Council of Mortgage Lenders
3 Savile Row
London W1X 1AF
UK
Tel: 071 4379655

Creditanstalt-Bankverein
Schottengasse 6–8
1010 Vienna
Austria
Tel: 1 53131/0

Dagligvar uleverantores Forbund
PO Box 45135
10430 Stockholm
Sweden
Tel: 08 662730
Fax: 08 6675705

Danmarks Nationalbank
5 Havnegade
11093 Copenhagen
Denmark
Tel: 33 141411

Danmarks Rederiforening
Amaliegade 33
1256 Copenhagen
Denmark
Tel: 33 114088
Fax: 33 116210

Danmarks Statistik
Sejrogade 11
2100 Copenhagen O
Denmark
Tel: 33 298222

Danske Elvaerkers Forening
Rosenorns Alle 9
DK–1970 Frederiksberg C
Denmark
Tel: 31 390111
Fax: 31 395958

Danske Pengeinstitutters Forening
Finansradets Hus, 7 Amaliegade
1256 Copenhagen K
Denmark
Tel: 33 120200
Fax: 33 930260

Danske Slagterier
Axeltors 3
1609 Copenhagen V
Denmark
Tel: 33 116050
Fax: 33 116814

Datacentralen/DC Host Centre
Retortvej 6–8
Valby
2500 Copenhagen
Denmark
Tel: 33 468122

Datastar
Plaza Suite
114 Jermyn Street
London SW1Y 6HJ
UK
Tel: 071 9305503
Fax: 071 9302581

Datastream
Monmouth House, 58–64 City Road
London EC17 2AL
UK
Tel: 071 2503000
Fax: 071 2530171

Den Danske Bank
2–12 Holmens Kanal
1092 Copenhagen K
Denmark
Tel: 33 440000

Department of the Environment
Publications Sales Unit, Building 1
Victoria Road
Ruislip HA4 0NZ
UK
Tel: 081 8413425

Department of Transport
Publications Sales Unit, Building 1
Victoria Road
Ruislip HA4 0NZ
UK
Tel: 081 8413425

Deutsche Bundesbank
14 Wilhelm-Epstein-Strasse
6000 Frankfurt am Main
Germany
Tel: 069 158–1
Fax: 069 5601071

Deutsche Zentrale fur Tourismus
Beethovenstrasse 69
6000 Frankfurt am Main
Germany
Tel: 069 7572–0
Fax: 069 751903

Deutscher Fachverlag GmbH
Schumannstrasse 27
6000 Frankfurt/Main 27
Germany
Tel: 069 74331

**Deutsches Institut fur
Wirtschaftsforschung**
Forecasting publications published in the
UK by:
Gower Publishing Company Ltd
Gower House, Croft Road
Aldershot GU11 3HR
UK
Tel: 0252 331551
Fax: 0252 344405

Dialog
PO Box 188
Oxford OX1 5AX
UK
Tel: 0865 730225
Fax: 0865 736354

Direction des Ports et de la Navigation Maritimes
244 boulevard Saint Germain
75007 Paris
France
Tel: 1 45619913

Distribucion Actualidad
Ediciones y Estudios SA
Enrique Larreta 7–7A
28036 Madrid
Spain
Tel: 1 7339512

Donovan Data Systems
Berger House, 7 Farm Street
London W1X 7RB
UK
Tel: 071 6297654
Fax: 071 4930239

DRI Europe
Wimbledon Bridge House,
1 Hartfield Road
Wimbledon SW19 3RU
UK
Tel: 081 5431234

DSI
Orsoyerstrasse 4
PO Box 1127
4131 Rheinberg
Germany
Tel: 9 28433220
Fax: 9 28433230

Duplo
Mateo Inurria 26
28036 Madrid
Spain
Tel: 1 2505604
Fax: 1 2505602

Dybfrostinstituttet
Vesterbrogade 6D4
1620 Copenhagen
Denmark
Tel: 33 339500
Fax: 33 339505

EC Mortgage Federation
avenue de la Joyeuse Entree 14/2
1040 Brussels
Belgium
Tel: 02 2302551
Fax: 02 2306411

Economic and Social Research Institute
4 Burlington Road
Dublin 4
Ireland
Tel: 01 686231
Fax: 01 760115

Economisch Instituut voor Midden- en Kleinbedrijf
Italieln 33
Zoetermeer
Netherlands
Tel: 79 415024

Eidg. Oberzolldirektion/Direction generale des douanes
Monbijoustrasse 40
3003 Berne
Switzerland
Tel: 031 616525

Electricity Council
30 Millbank
London SW1P 4RD
UK
Tel: 071 8342333
Fax: 071 8342333

Elektra Press Publications
Athens
Greece

Elektronikfabrikantforeningen
Borsen
1217 Copenhagen
Denmark
Tel: 33 123619
Fax: 33 913619

Elintarviketeollis vusliitto
Union inkats 14
PO Box 228
00131 Helsinki
Finland
Tel: 90 176220
Fax: 90 657794

Elsevier Advanced Technology
Mayfield House, 256 Banbury Road
Oxford OX2 7DH
UK
Tel: 0865 512242
Fax: 0865 310981

Engineering Employers Federation
Broadway House, Tothill Street
London SW1H 9NQ
UK
Tel: 071 222777
Fax: 071 2222782

English Tourist Board
Thames Tower, Blacks Road
London W6 9EL
UK
Tel: 081 8469000

Enosis Asfalistikon Etairon
Xenophontos 10
118 Athens
Greece
Tel: 1 218742

ENTEL SA
Paseo de la Castellana 141
28046 Madrid
Spain
Tel: 1 4509096

Euromonitor
87–88 Turnmill Street
London EC1M 5QU
UK
Tel: 071 2518024
Fax: 071 6083149

European Advertising Tripartite
28 avenue du Barbeau
1160 Brussels
Belgium
Tel: 02 6724336
Fax: 02 6720014

European Association of Clothing Industries
47 rue Montoyer
1040 Brussels
Belgium
Tel: 02 5118731
Fax: 02 5141781

European Association of Consumer Electronics
c/o Simavelic, 11 rue Hamelin
75783 Paris Cedex 16
France
Tel: 1 45057181

European Association of Multiple Retailers
17 avenue E Lacomble
1040 Brussels
Belgium
Tel: 02 7360251
Fax: 02 7360531

European Chemical Industry Federation
Avenue Louis 250
Bte 71
1050 Brussels
Belgium
Tel: 02 6402095
Fax: 02 6401981

European Construction Industry Federation
3 rue de Berry
75008 Paris
France
Tel: 1 45631144

European Direct Marketing Association
34 rue du gouvernement provisoire
1000 Brussels
Belgium
Tel: 02 2176309
Fax: 02 2176985

European Free Trade Association
9–11 rue de Varembe
1211 Geneva 20
Switzerland
Tel: 022 7491111

European Savings Banks Group
Avenue de la Renaissance 12
1040 Brussels
Belgium
Tel: 02 7391611
Fax: 02 7360955

European Society for Opinion and Marketing Research
JJ Viottastraat 29
1071 JP Amsterdam
Netherlands
Tel: 20 6642141
Fax: 20 6642922

European Union of Electrical Wholesalers
Rue Col.
Bourg 127 – Bte 3
1140 Brussels
Belgium
Tel: 02 7323050
Fax: 02 7323606

European Venture Capital Association
Keibergpark
Minervastraat 6 – Box 6
1930 Zaventern
Belgium
Tel: 02 7206010
Fax: 02 7253036

Eurostat
Commission of the European Communities
Batiment Jean Monnet
381907 Luxembourg
Tel: 010 35243011

Fabrimetal
Rue des Drapiers 21
1050 Brussels
Belgium
Tel: 02 5102311
Fax: 02 5102301

Fachverband der Chemischen Industrie Osterreichs
Wiedner Hauptstrasse 63
PO Box 325
1045 Vienna
Austria
Tel: 1 501 05/3371
Fax: 1 502 06/280

Fachverband der Erdolindustrie Osterreichs
Erdbergstrasse 72
1031 Vienna
Austria
Tel: 1 7132348
Fax: 1 7130510

Fachverband der Fahrzeugindustrie Osterreichs
Wiedner Hauptstrasse 73
PO Box 335
1045 Vienna
Austria
Tel: 1 501 05/4801

Fachverband der Maschinen- und Stahlindustrie Osterreichs
Wiedner Hauptstrasse 63
PO Box 430
1045 Vienna
Austria
Tel: 1 65053468
Fax: 1 5051020

Fachverband Metallwaren- und Verwandte Industrien
Leostrasse 22
PO 110431
4000 Dusseldorf 11
Germany
Tel: 211 572154

Fachverband der Nahrungs- und Genussmittelindustrie Osterreichs
Zaunergasse 1–3
PO Box 144
1037 Vienna
Austria
Tel: 1 7122121
Fax: 1 7131802

Fachverband der Textilindustrie Osterreichs
Rudolfsplatz 12
1013 Vienna
Austria
Tel: 1 5733726–0
Fax: 1 5333726–40

Fachvereinigung Metallhutten und Umschmelzwerke
Tersteegenstrasse 28
PO Box 8706
4000 Dusseldorf
Germany
Tel: 211 454710
Fax: 211 45447111

Farmindustria
Piazza di Pietra 34
00186 Rome
Italy
Tel: 06 650981
Fax: 06 6786494

Federacion Empresarial de la Industria Quimica Espanole
Hermosilla 31
28001 Madrid
Spain
Tel: 1 4317694
Fax: 1 2763381

Federacion Espanola de Comerciantes de Electrodomesticos
Principe de Vergara 74–2A,
28006 Madrid,
Spain
Tel: 1 2610529
Fax: 1 2610611

Federatie van Nederlandse Schoenfabrikanten
Reitseplein 1
5037 AA Tilburg
Netherlands
Tel: 13 654424

Federation Belge des Enterprises de Distribution
Rue Saint-Bernard 60
1060 Brussels
Belgium
Tel: 02 537 3060
Fax: 02 539 4026

Federation Belge des Exploitants d'Autobus et d'Autocars
Rue Leon Lepage 4
1000 Brussels
Belgium
Tel: 02 512 9399
Fax: 02 514 1943

Federation Belge de l'Industrie du Coton et des Fibres Chimiques
Building Lieven Bauwens,
Martelaarslaan 39
9000 Gent
Belgium
Tel: 91 253597

Federation Belge des Industries de l'Automobile et du Cycle
Boulevard de la Woluwe 46
Bte 6
1200 Brussels
Belgium
Tel: 02 771 0085
Fax: 02 762 8171

Federation Belge des Industries de l'Habillement
Rue Montoyer 24
1040 Brussels
Belgium
Tel: 02 230 8890
Fax: 02 230 4700

Federation Belge des Vins et Spiriteux
Rue de Livourne 13
Bte 5
1050 Brussels
Belgium
Tel: 02 53700 51
Fax: 02 537 8156

Federation des Enterprises de Metaux non Ferreux
Rue Montoyer 47
1040 Brussels
Belgium
Tel: 02 5064111
Fax: 02 511 7553

Federation des Exportateurs de Vins et Spiriteux de France
95 rue Monceau
75008 Paris
France
Tel: 1 45227573
Fax: 1 45229416

Federation Hellenique de la Maille
Sotiros 2–4
10558 Athens
Greece
Tel: 01 3220651

Federation de l'Industrie du Gaz
Avenue Palmerston 4
1040 Brussels
Belgium
Tel: 02 2371111
Fax: 02 2304480

Federation de l'Industrie Textile Belge
Rue Montoyer 24
1040 Brussels
Belgium
Tel: 02 2309330
Fax: 02 2306585

Federation des Industries Chimiques de Belgique
Square Marie-Louise 49
1040 Brussels
Belgium
Tel: 02 2304090
Fax: 02 2306585

Federation des Industries Electriques et Electroniques
11 rue Hamelin
75783 Paris Cedex 16
France
Tel: 1 45057010

Federation des Industries et Commerces Utilisateurs des Basses Temperatures
51–53 rue Fondary
75739 Paris Cedex 15
France
Tel: 1 45791049
Fax: 1 45796129

Federation Francaise de l'Industrie des Produits de Parfumerie, de Beaute et de Toilette
8 place du General-Catroux
75017 Paris
France
Tel: 1 47665101
Fax: 1 42272345

Federation Francaise des Societes d'Assurances
26 boulevard Haussmann
75311 Paris Cedex 09
France
Tel: 1 42479000
Fax: 1 42479311

Federation de l'Industrie Horlogerie Suisse
Rue d'Argent 6
2501 Bienne
Switzerland
Tel: 32 225911
Fax: 32 233197

Federation des Industries Mecaniques et Transformatrices de Metaux
Centre d'Information de la Mecanique
Cedex 72
Paris La Defense
France
Tel: 1 4563020
Fax: 45635986

Federation Nationale des Boissons
49 rue de la Glaciere
75013 Paris
France
Tel: 1 45872141

Federation Nationale du Batiment
33 avenue Kleber
75784 Paris Cedex 16
France
Tel: 1 40695100

Federation Nationale des Dentelles Tulles Broderies Guipures et Passementeries
7 rue Louis-le-Grand
75001 Paris
France
Tel: 1 42615629

Federation Nationale des Fabricants-Transformateurs de l'Industrie Cotonniere
37–39 rue de Neuilly
92113 Clichy Cedex
France
Tel: 1 47563040

Federation Nationale de l'Industries Laitiere
140 boulevard Haussmann
75008 Paris
France
Tel: 1 45629660
Fax: 1 45614977

Federation Nationale des Syndicats de Grossistes Distributeurs en Material Electrique et Electronique
13 rue Marivaux
75002 Paris
France
Tel: 1 42974625
Fax: 1 42860174

Federation Professionnelle des Producteurs et Distributeurs d'Electricite de Belgique
Avenue de Tervuren 34
1040 Brussels
Belgium
Tel: 02 733 9607

Federazione delle Associazion Italiane Alberghi e Turismo
Via Toscana 1
00187 Rome
Italy
Tel: 06 4741151
Fax: 06 463004

Federazione delle Associazioni Nazionale dell'Industria Meccanica Varia ed Affini
Piazza Diaz 2
20123 Milan
Italy
Tel: 02 721311
Fax: 02 861306

FEDERCHIMICA
Via Accademia 33
20131 Milan
Italy
Tel: 02 63621
Fax: 02 6362209

FEDERMECCANICA
Piazzale Benito Juarez 14
00144 Rome
Italy
Tel: 06 5925446

FEHA
Naverland 34
2600 Glostrup
Denmark
Tel: 4343 4646
Fax: 4353 5272

FEICEV
Martires Concepcionistas 18
28006 Madrid
Spain
Tel: 1 4012412
Fax: 1 4023387

FIMET – Federation of Finnish Metal, Engineering and Electrotechnical Industries
PO Box 10
00131 Helsinki
Finland
Tel: 90 19231
Fax: 90 624462

Finnish Petroleum Federation
Fabianinkatu 8
PO Box 188
00131 Helsinki
Finland
Tel: 90 655831
Fax: 90 171314

Finnish Tourist Board
Asemapaallikonkatu 12B
00520 Helsinki
Finland
Tel: 90 144511

Foreningen af danske Medicinfabrikker
Landamaerket 25
1119 Copenhagen K
Denmark
Tel: 33 111270
Fax: 33 321770

Foreningen Svenska Verktygs- och Verktygsmaskintillverkare
Box 5506
11485 Stockholm
Sweden
Tel: 08 7838000
Fax: 08 6603378

Gemeinschaftsverband Textil
Beethovenstrasse 20
PO Box 4838
8022 Zurich
Switzerland
Tel: 1 2015755

Gesamttextil, Gesamtverband der Textillindustriein der Bundesrepublik Deutschland
Frankfurter Strasse 10–14
6236 Eschborn
Germany
Tel: 06196 9660
Fax: 06196 42170

Gesamtverband der Deutschen Maschen-Industrie
Olgastrasse 77
PO Box 101755
7000 Stuttgart 10
Germany
Tel: 711 21031–0
Fax: 711 232807

**Gesamtverband der deutschen
Versicherungswirtschaft**
Erbetplatz 1
5000 Cologne 1
Germany
Tel: 221 730055
Fax: 221 7764153

**Gesamtverband der Schweizerischen
Bekleidungsindustrie**
Gotthardstrasse 61
PO Box 265
8027 Zurich
Switzerland
Tel: 1 2027161
Fax: 1 2020651

GIANO
Vialle dell Astronomica 30
Rome
Italy
Tel: 06 59031

Government Publications Sales Office
Bishop Street
Dublin 8
Ireland
Tel: 01 781666
Fax: 01 780645

**Groupe d'Analyse Macroeconomique
Applique**
Universite de Paris
200 avenue de la Republique
92001 Nanterre
France
Tel: 1 40977788

Groupement des Industries Electriques
11 rue Hamelin
75783 Paris Cedex 16
France
Tel: 1 45057000

**Groupement des Industries Francaises
Aeronautiques et Spatiales**
4 rue Galilee
75116 Paris
France
Tel: 1 47235556
Fax: 1 40709141

**Groupement des Industries Francaises
des Appareils d'Equipement Menager**
39 avenue d'Iena
75783 Paris Cedex 16
France
Tel: 1 47203220

Groupement de la Siderurgie
Rue Montoyer 47
1040 Brussels
Belgium
Tel: 02 5031411

**Groupement National des
Entrepreneurs Constructeurs
Immobiliers de la Federation Nationale
du Batiment**
7 rue la Perouse
75016 Paris
France
Tel: 1 40605186
Fax: 1 45535877

GSI–ECO
45 rue de la Procession
75015 Paris
France
Tel: 1 45667889
Fax: 1 47344692

HATRA
7 Gregory Boulevard
Nottingham NG7 6LD
UK
Tel: 0602 623311
Fax: 0602 625450

Hauptgemeinschaft des Deutschen Einzelhandels
Sachsenring 89
5000 Cologne 1
Germany
Tel: 0221 33980
Fax: 0221 3398119

Hauptverband der Deutschen Bauindustrie
Abraham-Lincoln-Strasse 30
PO Box 2966
6200 Wiesbaden
Germany
Tel: 6121 7720
Fax: 6121 772240

Hauptverband der Deutschen Schuhindustrie
Waldstrasse 44
D–6050 Offenbach/M
Germany
Tel: 069 816272
Fax: 069 812810

Henley Centre
2–4 Tudor Street
Blackfriars
London EC4Y 0AA
UK
Tel: 071 3539961
Fax: 071 3532899

High Technology Verlag
Leopoldstrasse 70
8000 Munich 40
Germany
Tel: 089 391011

HMSO Publications Centre
PO Box 276
London SW8 5DT
UK
Tel: 071 8739090
Fax: 071 8738200

Holborn Research Services
Grosvenor House, Grosvenor Gardens
London SW1W 0BS
UK
Tel: 071 6305033
Fax: 071 8283642

Ifo – Institut fur Wirtschaftsforschung
Postingstrasse 5
8000 Munich 86
Germany
Tel: 089 92240

Imprensa Nacional-Casa da Moeda, Livraria do Estado
Rua Marques de sa da Bandiera, 16–A
1000 Lisbon
Portugal
Tel: 01 545041

Industriradet
HC Andersens Boulevard 18
1790 Copenhagen
Denmark
Tel: 33 152233

Information and Computing Services Association
Confederation House
Kildare Street
Dublin 2
Ireland
Tel: 01 779801

Institut monetaire Luzembourgeois
63 avenue de la Liberte
2983 Luxembourg
Tel: 929203
Fax: 492180

Institut National de Statistique
rue de Louvain 44
1000 Brussels
Belgium
Tel: 02 5139650

Institut fur Selbstbedienung und Warenwirtschaft
Burgmauer 53
5000 Cologne 1
Germany
Tel: 0221 234431

Institute of Grocery Distribution
Letchmore Heath
Watford WD2 8DQ
UK
Tel: 09276 7141
Fax: 09276 2531

Institute of Petroleum
61 New Cavendish Street
London W1M 8AR
UK
Tel: 071 6361004

Instituto Espanol de Commercio Exterieor
Paseo de la Castellania 141
28046 Madrid
Spain
Tel: 1 4311240
Fax: 1 4316128

Instituto Tecnico de Distribution y Libreservicio
O'Donnell 34–4A
28009 Madrid
Spain
Tel: 1 2746904

Interactive Market Systems (UK) Ltd
Grosvenor Gardens House,
Grosvenor Gardens
London SW1W 0BS
UK
Tel: 071 6305033
Fax: 071 8283642

International Air Transport Association
PO Box 672
1215 Cointrin 15 Airport
Switzerland
Tel: 022 7992525
Fax: 022 7992683

International Road Federation
63 rue de Lausanne
1202 Geneva
Switzerland
Tel: 022 7317150
Fax: 022 7317158

IP Sharp
Heron House, 10 Dean Farrar Street
London SW1H 0DX
Tel: 071 2227033
Fax: 071 7991827

L'Institut Francaise du Libre-Service
27 rue Athenes
75009 Paris
France
Tel: 1 42804212

Institut National de la Statistique et des Etudes Economiques
18 boulevard Adolphe Pinard
75675 Paris Cedex 14
France
Tel: 1 45401212

INSEE regional offices:

Alsace
14 rue Adolphe Seyboth
67084 Strasbourg
France
Tel: 88320318
Fax: 88755737

Aquitaine
33 rue de Saget
33076 Bordeaux
France
Tel: 56918990

Auvergne
3 place Charles de Gaulle
BP 120
63403 Chamalieres
France
Tel: 73360350

Bourgogne
13 Avenue Albert 1er
BP 1509
21035 Dijon
France
Tel: 80433145

Brittany
Immeuble 'Le Colbert'
36 place du Columbier
BP 17
35031 Rennes
France
Tel: 99293366

Centre
43 avenue de Paris
BP 6719
45067 Orleans Cedex 2
France
Tel: 38545465

Champagne-Ardenne
1 rue de l'Arbalete
51079 Reims
France
Tel: 26484280

Corsica
Residence du Parc Belvedere
BP 306
20176 Ajaccio
France
Tel: 95513099
Fax: 95510407

Franche-Comte
Immeuble 'Le Major'
83 rue de Dole
25042 Besancon
France
Tel: 81524220

Ile-de-France
195 rue de Bercy
75582 Paris Cedex 12
France
Tel: 1 43457374
Fax: 1 43425843

Languedoc-Roussillon
274 Allee Henri 11 de Montmorency
'Le Polygone'
34064 Montpellier
France
Tel: 67643195

Limousin
29 rue Beyrand
87031 Limoges
France
Tel: 55792625,
Fax: 55771636

Lorraine
15 rue du General Hulot
Case officielle 3846
54029 Nancy
France
Tel: 83270327
Fax: 83404561

Midi-Pyrenees
36 rue des 36 Ponts
31054 Toulouse
France
Tel: 61366113

Nord-Pas-de-Calais
10–12 boulevard Vauban
59800 Lille
France
Tel: 20308987

Normandie-Basse
93–95 rue de Geole
14051 Caen
France
Tel: 31853570

Normandie-Haute
8 quai de la Bourse
76037 Rouen
France
Tel: 35524994
Fax: 35150632

Pays de la Loire
5 boulevard Louis Barthou
BP 2189
44204 Nantes Cedex 02
France
Tel: 40417980
Fax: 40292558

Picardie
1 rue Vincent Auriol
80040 Amiens
France
Tel: 22913939

Poitou-Charentes
3 rue du Puygarreau
86020 Poitiers
France
Tel: 49883871

Provence-Alpes-Cote d'Azur
17 rue Menpenti
13387 Marseille Cedex 10
France
Tel: 91830022
Fax: 91793936

Rhone-Alpes
165 rue Garibaldi
BP 196
69401 Lyon Cedex 03
France
Tel: 78632307
Fax: 78632525

Instituto Nacional de Estatistica
Avenida Antonio Jose de Almeida
1078 Lisbon
Portugal
Tel: 01 8470050
Fax: 01 808093

Irish Tourist Board
Baggot Street Bridge
Dublin 2
Ireland
Tel: 01 765871

Istituto nazionale di statistica
Via Cesare Balbo 16
00100 Rome
Italy
Tel: 06 46732384

Istituto Nazionale per lo Studio Della Congiuntura
Via Palermo 20
00184 Rome
Italy
Tel: 06 476871

International Office of Cocoa, Chocolate & Sugar Confectionery
172 Avenue de Cortenbergh
1040 Brussels
Belgium
Tel: 02 7351072
Fax: 02 7363623

Internationaler Argus der Presse
Streulistrasse 19
8030 Zurich
Switzerland
Tel: 1 3834983
Fax: 1 3834357

Istituto Centrale di Statistica
Via Cesare Balbo 16
00184 Rome
Italy
Tel: 06 46732380

Jernkontoret
PO Box 1721
Kungstradgardsgt. 10
11187 Stockholm
Sweden
Tel: 08 224620

Joint Forecasting Committee of the NEDC, Construction Industry Sector Group
Millbank Tower
Millbank
London SW1P 4QX
UK
Tel: 071 2174004

Kaupan Keskusualiokuntu
Kasarmikatu 44
00130 Helsinki
Finland
Tel: 90 170227
Fax: 90 654762

Kemian Keskusliitto
Hietaniemenkatu 2
PO Box 359
00101 Helsinki
Finland
Tel: 90 447122
Fax: 90 447960

Koninlijke Nederlandse Zuivelbond
Volmerlaan 7
PO Box 5831
2280 HV Rijswijk
Netherlands
Tel: 70 3953100
Fax: 70 3907897

Konjunkturinstitutet
L Nygatan 1
Stockholm
Sweden
Tel: 08 7231569

Landsforeningen for Bygg og Anlegg
Holtegaten 26
0355 Oslo 3
Norway
Tel: 02 461854
Fax: 02 695856

Leatherhead Food R.A.
Randalls Road
Leatherhead
Surrey KT22 2RY
UK
Tel: 0372 376761
Fax: 0372 386228

Liaison Committee of European Retailers
Avenue E. Lacombe 17
1040 Brussels
Belgium
Tel: 02 7360251
Fax: 02 7360542

Liiketyonantajain Keskusliitto
Etelaranta 10
00130 Helsinki
Finland
Tel: 90 172831
Fax: 90 655588

Machine Tool Trades Association
62 Bayswater Road
London W2 3PS
UK
Tel: 071 4026671
Fax: 071 7247250

Maritime & Distribution Systems
28 City Road
Chester CH1 3AE
UK
Tel: 0244 346198
Fax: 0244 348471

Media Focus
PO Box 3763
6002 Lucerne
Switzerland
Tel: 041 959555
Fax: 041 959123

METAALUNIE
Wilhelminalaan 1
3732 GJ De Bilt
Netherlands
Tel: 30 204811
Fax: 30 204899

**Metallurgisk Industris
Landsforening**
Sigurd Syrsgate 4
0273 Oslo 2
Norway
Tel: 02 448480
Fax: 02 446263

Milk Marketing Board
Thames Ditton
Surrey KT7 0EL
UK
Tel: 081 3984101
Fax: 081 3984101

**Ministere de l'Agriculture,
Administration de la Recherche
Agronomique, Institut Economique
Agricole**
Manhattan Centre Office Tower
Avenue du Boulevard 21
1210 Brussels
Belgium
Tel: 02 2117602

Ministerio de Economia y Hacienda
Almagro 34
28010 Madrid
Spain

**Ministry of Agriculture, Fisheries and
Foods**
Ergon House, c/o Nobel House
17 Smith Square
London SW1P 3HX
UK
Tel: 071 2386410

Ministry of Economic Affairs
Rue de l'Industrie 6
1040 Brussels
Belgium
Tel: 02 5065111

MITEX
Vondelstraat 172
1054 GU Amsterdam
Netherlands
Tel: 20 832201
Fax: 20 162921

Naeringslivets Houedorganisasjan
PO Box 5052
Majorstua
0303 Oslo 7
Norway
Tel: 02 603290
Fax: 02 695593

**National Council of Building Material
Producers**
26 Store Street
London WC1E 7BT
UK
Tel: 071 3233770

National House Building Council
Chiltern Avenue
Amersham HP6 5AP
UK
Tel: 0494 434477

**National Institute of Economic and
Social Research**
2 Dean Trench Street
Smith Square
London SW1P 3HE
UK
Tel: 071 2227665

National Institute of Statistics
Paseo de la Castellana 183
28071 Madrid
Spain
Tel: 1 5839100

National Statistical Service of Greece
14–16 Lycourgou Street
10166 Athens
Greece
Tel: 01 3244748

Nederlandsche Bank
Westiende 1
1017 ZN Amsterdam
Netherlands
Tel: 20 249111
Fax: 20 6203426

Nederlandse Vereniging van Makelaars in Assurantien en Assurantieadviseurs
Wilhelminalaan 12
PO Box 235
3800 AE Amersfoort
Netherlands
Tel: 33 6314141

Nederlandse Vereniging de Rijwiel- en Automobiel-Industrie
Europaplein 2
1078 GZ Amsterdam
Netherlands
Tel: 20 5491212
Fax: 20 6463857

Nederlandse Verenigung van Hypotheckbanken
PO Box 95374
2509 CJ Den Haag
Netherlands
Tel: 70 3814861,
Fax: 70 3477870

Nederlandse Veriniging van Participatiemaatschappijen
Prinses Beatrixlaan 5
PO Box 97093
2509 AB Den Haag
Netherlands
Tel: 70 3471111
Fax: 70 3819508

Nielsen Hellas Ltd
2 Charokopou Str. & 196 Sygrou Avenue
17671 Kallithea
Greece
Tel: 95 88771–4
Fax: 95 98294

Nielsen Media Research
Moeringgasse 20
PO Box 513
1150 Vienna
Austria
Tel: 0222 98110
Fax: 0222 9811077

Nielsen Werbeforschung S&P
Heidenkampsweg 74
2000 Hamburg 1
Germany
Tel: 040 2371 03–0
Fax: 040 237103–22

Nordic Statistical Secretariat
PO Box 2550
2100 Copenhagen
Denmark
Tel: 31 298222

Norges Bank
Bankplassen 2
0107 Oslo 1
Norway
Tel: 02 316000
Fax: 02 413105

Norges Kjemiske Industrigruppe
Middelthunsgata 27
PO Box 5250
Majorskiu
0303 Oslo
Norway
Tel: 02 603290
Fax: 02 695593

Norsk Forsikringsselkapers Forbund
Box 2473
Solli
0202 Oslo 2
Norway
Tel: 02 555000
Fax: 02 434456

NTC Publications Ltd
22–24 Bell Street
Henley on Thames
Oxfordshire RG9 2BG
UK
Tel: 0491 574671
Fax: 0491 571188

Oliebranchens Faellesrepraesentation
Vognmagergade 5
PO Box 120
1004 Copenhagen
Denmark
Tel: 33 113077
Fax: 33 321618

**Organisation for Economic
Cooperation and Development**
2 rue Andre-Pascal
75775 Paris Cedex 16
France
Tel: 1 45248200
Fax: 1 45248500

Ossuspankkien Keskusliitto
Arkadiankatu 23
00100 Helsinki
Finland
Tel: 90 4041

**Osterreichisches Institut fur
Wirtschaftsforschung**
PO Box 91
1103 Vienna
Austria
Tel: 0222 789386

**Osterreichisches Statistisches
Zentralamt**
Hintere Zollamsstrasse 2B
PO Box 9000
1033 Vienna
Austria
Tel: 01 71128/0
Fax: 01 711 28/7728

Oy Alko Ab
Tiedotusplalvelu
PO Box 350
00101 Helsinki
Finland
Tel: 90 6091325

Per Press
Anpartsselskab
Frederik d. VI's Alle 5
2000 Frederiksberg
Denmark
Tel: 01 868584

Points de Vente
Liaisons et Convergence
5 avenue de la Republique
75011 Paris
France
Tel: 1 47573166
Fax: 1 42968752

**Radio & Hemelektronik-Landelns
Riksforbund**
Kungsgatan 19
10561 Stockholm
Sweden
Tel: 08 7915370
Fax: 08 210738

Rakennusmestarien Keskusliitto
Rahakamarinportti 3
00240 Helsinki
Finland
Tel: 90 145611

Realkreditradet
Vesterbrogade 4A
1620 Copenhagen
Denmark
Tel: 33 124811
Fax: 33 329017

Register – MEAL
2 Fisher Street
London WC1R 4QA
Tel: 071 833 1212
Fax: 071 821 7686

Reklamebyra Foreningen
PO Box 1427 Vika
0115 Oslo 1
Norway
Tel: 02 423970

Repress (Nielsen)
Luchana 23
28010 Madrid
Spain
Tel: 1 5921100

Revue Belge des Vins et Spiriteux
Rue Auguste Leveque 37c
1400 Nivelles
Belgium
Tel: 067 215155

Schweizerische Gesellschaft fur Chemische Industrie
Nordstrasse 15
8035 Zurich
Switzerland
Tel: 1 3631030
Fax: 1 3631018

Schweizerische Kaseunion
Monbijoustrasse 45
3001 Berne
Switzerland
Tel: 31 453331
Fax: 31 461176

Schweizerische PTT-Betriebe
Engadinerweg 10
8049 Zurich
Switzerland
Tel: 1 3418282

Schweizerischer Baumeisterverband
Wienbergstrasse 49
8035 Zurich
Switzerland
Tel: 1 2588111
Fax: 1 2588335

Schweizerischer Bauernverband
Laurstrasse 10
5200 Brugg
Switzerland
Tel: 56 419241

Schweizerischer Fremdenverkehrsverband
PO Box 8275
Finkenhubelweg 11
3001 Berne
Switzerland
Tel: 31 241641
Fax: 31 243357

Schweizerischer Nutzfahrzeugverband
Weisenbuhlweg 3
3007 Berne
Switzerland
Tel: 31 452661
Fax: 31 450589

Schweizerischer Obstverband
Baarerstrasse 88
6300 Zug 2
Switzerland
Tel: 42 212712
Fax: 42 215922

Schweizerischer Tiefkuhl-Institut
Forchstrasse 59
8032 Zurich
Switzerland
Tel: 1 2511038

Schweizerischer Wasserfaches
Grutliststrasse 44
PO Box 658
8027 Zurich
Switzerland
Tel: 1 2015636
Fax: 1 2021633

Secodip Pige
2 rue Francis Pedron
BP3
78241 Chambourcy
France
Tel: 1 30746011
Fax: 1 39654697

SESSI
85 boulevard du Montparnasse
75720 Paris Cedex 06
France
Tel: 1 45564108
Fax: 1 45564071

Service Central de la Statistique et des Etudes Economiques
19–21 boulevard Royal
BP 304
2103 Luxembourg
Tel: 4794–292

SNCF
88 rue St Lazare
75436 Paris Cedex 09
France
Tel: 1 42856000
Fax: 1 42856030

Sociedad par el Estudio y Desarrollo de la Industria del Gas
Balmes 357
08006 Barcelona
Spain
Tel: 93 2472804

Society of Motor Manufacturers and Traders
Forbes House, Halkin Street
London SW1X 7DS
UK
Tel: 071 2357000
Fax: 071 2357112

Suomen Kuorma-Autoliitto
Nuijamiestentie 7
00400 Helsinki
Finland
Tel: 90 578500

Suomen Pankkiyhdistys
Fabianinkatu 8
00130 Helsinki
Finland
Tel: 90 651344
Fax: 90 6947844

Suomen Satamaliitoo
Tonien Linja 14
00530 Helsinki
Finland
Tel: 90 7711
Fax: 90 7530474

Suomen Tieyhdistys
Vironket 6
00170 Helsinki
Finland

Suomen Vakuutusyhtioiden Keskusliitto
Buleuardi 28
00120 Helsinki
Finland
Tel: 90 19251
Fax: 90 1925216

Statistika Centralbyran
Karlavagen 100
11581 Stockholm
Sweden
Tel: 08 7834335
Fax: 08 7834899

Statistika Centralbyran (Distribution)
Box 902
70189 Orebo
Sweden
Tel: 019 140320

Statistisches Bundesamt
Gustav-Stresemann-Ring 11
6200 Wiesbaden 1
Germany
Tel: 0611 75-1
Fax: 0611 724000

Statistisches Bundesamt Aussenstelle Dusseldorf
Huttenstrasse 5a
4000 Dusseldorf 1
Germany
Tel: 0211 38411-0
Fax: 0211 3841128

Statistisches Bundesamt Zweigstelle Berlin-Kurfurstenstrase
Kurfurstenstrasse 87
1000 Berlin 30
Germany
Tel: 030 260030
Fax: 030 26003734

Statistisches Landesamt (Lander statistical offices):

Schleswig-Holstein
Frobelstrasse 15-17
2300 Kiel 1
Germany
Tel: 0431 6895-0
Fax: 0431 6895498

Hamburg
Steckelhorn 12
2000 Hamburg 11
Germany
Tel: 040 3681-0
Fax: 040 36811700

Lower Saxon Land
Geibelstrasse 61/65
3000 Hannover 1
Germany
Tel: 0511 8083-1
Fax: 0511 8083210

Bremen
An der Weide 14-16
2800 Bremen 1
Germany
Tel: 0421 3611
Fax: 0421 3614310

North Rhine-Westphalia
Mauerstrasse 51
4000 Dusseldorf 1
Germany
Tel: 0211 44971
Fax: 0211 442006

Hessian
Rheinstrasse 35/37
6200 Wiesbaden
Germany
Tel: 0611 3680
Fax: 0611 378324

Rheinland Palatinate
Mainzer Strasse 15/16
5427 Bad Ems
Germany
Tel: 02603 711
Fax: 02603 71315

Baden-Wurtemberg
Boblinger Strasse 68
7000 Stuttgart 10
Germany
Tel: 0711 641-0
Fax: 0711 6412440

Bavaria
Neuhauser Strasse 51
8000 Munich 2
Germany
Tel: 089 2119-0
Fax: 089 21194 10

Saar
Hardenbergstrasse 3
6600 Saarbrucken
Germany
Tel: 0681 505–1
Fax: 0681 505921

Berlin
Fehrbeliner Platz 1
1000 Berlin 31
Germany
Tel: 030 8671
Fax: 030 8673104

Western Pomerania
Lubecker Strasse 287
2762 Schwerin
Germany
Tel: 003784 40446
Fax: 003784 41626

Saxony-Anhalt
PO Box 262
Block 081
4090 Halle/Saale
Germany
Tel: 003746 616785
Fax: 003746 641019

Brandenburg
Dortustrasse 46
1561 Potsdam
Germany
Tel: 003733 38405
Fax: 003733 22024

Thuringen
Leipziger Strasse 71
5010 Erfurt
Germany
Tel: 003761 571483
Fax: 003761 26231

Saxony
Dr-Otto-Nuschke-Strasse 20
PO Box 109
8012 Dresden
Germany
Tel: 003751 4851–0
Fax: 003751 4851–256

Statistisk Sentralbyra
Skippergata 15
PO Box 8131 Dep
0033 Oslo 1
Norway
Tel: 02 864500
Fax: 02 864973

Svenska Bankforeningen
Regeringsgatan 42
B 7603
10394 Stockholm
Sweden
Tel: 08 243300
Fax: 08 7969395

Svenska Forsakringsforeningen
Tegeluddsuagin 100
11587 Stockholm
Sweden
Tel: 08 7837000
Fax: 08 6612284

Sveriges Livsmedelshandelareforbund
Box 1311
111 83 Stockholm
Sweden
Tel: 08 141870
Fax: 08 243506

Sveriges Riksbank
103 37 Stockholm
Sweden
Tel: 08 787000
Fax: 08 210531

Swiss National Bank
15 Borvenstrasse
8022 Zurich
Switzerland
Tel: 1 2213750
Fax: 1 2211875

Syndicat General des Fondeurs de France et Industries Connexes
2 rue de Bassano
75783 Paris Cedex 16
France
Tel: 1 47235550

Syndicat General de l'Industrie Cotonniere Francaise
37–39 rue de Neuilly
92113 Clichy Cedex
France
Tel: 1 47563040

Syndicat de la Machine-Outil de l'Assemblage et de la Productique Associee
Cedex 72
92038 Paris La Defense
France
Tel: 1 47176000
Fax: 1 47176499

Syndicat National d l'Industrie Pharmaceutique
88 rue de la Faisanderie
75872 Paris Cedex 16
France
Tel: 1 45032101
Fax: 1 45044771

Teknologibedriftenes Landsforening
Oscars Gate 20
PO Box 7072 Homansbyen
0306 Oslo 3
Norway
Tel: 02 465820
Fax: 02 461838

Tekstiiliteolisuusliitto
PL50
33211 Tampere 21
Finland
Tel: 90 3132277

Textile Statistics Bureau
Reedham House
31 King Street West
Manchester M3 2PF
UK
Tel: 061 8347871

Textielpatroonsverbond
Casinoplein 10
8500 Kortrijk
Belgium
Tel: 3256 216805
Fax: 3256 200359

Textil- og Beklaedningsindustrien
Bredgade 41
PO Box 300
7400 Herning
Denmark
Tel: 97 121366
Fax: 97 122350

UK Iron and Steel Statistics Bureau
Canterbury House
2 Sydenham Road
Croydon CR9 2LZ
UK
Tel: 081 6509050

Union Bank of Finland
PO Box 160
00101 Helsinki
Finland
Tel: 90 35801831

Union Bank of Switzerland
PO Box
8021 Zurich
Switzerland
Tel: 1 2343471

**Union des Chambres Syndicales d
l'Industrie du Petrole**
16 avenue Kliber
75116 Paris
France
Tel: 1 45021120

Union de Empresas Siderurgices
Principo Vergara 74
28006 Madrid
Spain
Tel: 1 4113391

Union des Industries Chimiques
64 Avenue Marceau
75008 Paris
France
Tel: 1 47205603
Fax: 1 47204869

Union des Industries de l'Habillement
8 rue de Richelieu
75001 Paris
France
Tel: 42962415
Fax: 1 42964841

Union International des Chemins de Fer
14 rue Jean Rey
75015 Paris
France
Tel: 1 42730120
Fax: 1 42730140

**Union Professionnelle des Entreprises
d'Assurances**
Square de Meeus 29
1040 Brussels
Belgium
Tel: 02 5136845
Fax: 02 5142469

**Union Suisse du Commerce et de
l'Industrie**
Borsenstrasse 26
PO Box 235
8022 Zurich
Switzerland
Tel: 1 2212707
Fax: 1 2119092

Union des Transports Publics
5 rue Aumale
75009 Paris
France
Tel: 1 48746351

**Unione Nazionale Distributori
Automotoveicoli**
Via di Villa Albani 12A
00198 Rome
Italy
Tel: 06 8415415
Fax: 06 8541115

Unione Petrolifera
Viale della Ciuilta de Lavoro 38
00144 Rome
Italy
Tel: 06 5914841
Fax: 06 6786494

United Nations
Palais des Nations
1211 Geneva 10
Switzerland
022 7346011

Unit Trust Association
65 Kingsway
London WC2B 6TD
UK
Tel: 071 8310898
Fax: 071 8319975

VEGIN
Wilmersdorf 50
PO Box 137
7300 AC Apeldoorn
Netherlands
Tel: 55 494949

Verband der Automobilindustrie
Westendstrasse 61
PO Box 170563
6000 Frankfurt/Main 17
Germany
Tel: 069 7570–0
Fax: 069 7570–261

Verband der Chemischen Industrie
Karlstrasse 21
PO Box 111943
6000 Frankfurt/Main 11
Germany
Tel: 069 2556–0
Fax: 069 2556471

Verband der Deutschen Heimtextilien Industrie
Hams-Bockler-Strasse 205
5600 Wuppertal 1
Germany
Tel: 202 750035

Verband Offentlicher Verkehrsbetriebe
Kamekestrasse 37–39
5000 Cologne
Germany
Tel: 0221 525064–66
Fax: 0221 514272

Verband der Privaten Bausparkassen
Dottendorfer Strasse 82
5300 Bonn 1
Germany
Tel: 0228 239041
Fax: 0228 239046

Verband Deutscher Maschinen- und Anlagenbau
Lyoner Strasse 15
6000 Frankfurt am Main 71
Germany
Tel: 069 66030
Fax: 069 6603511

Verband Deutscher Reeder
Esplanade 6
PO Box 305580
2000 Hamburg 36
Germany
Tel: 40 35097–0
Fax: 40 35097–211

Verband der Lebensversicherungs Unternehmen
Eduard-Pfluger-Strasse 55
6300 Bonn 1
Germany
Fax: 0228 5300820

Verband Osterreichischer Banken und Bankiers
Borsegass 11
1013 Vienna
Austria
Tel: 1 5351771
Fax: 1 535 1771–38

Verband fur Schiffbau und Meerestechnik
An der Alster 1
2000 Hamburg
Germany
Tel: 40 246205
Fax: 40 246287

Verband Schweizerischer Schokoladefabrikante
Munzgraben 6
3000 Berne
Switzerland
Tel: 31 226494

**Verbond van Nederlandse
Ondernemingen**
Prinses Beatrixlaan 5
PO Box 93093
2509 AB Den Haag
Netherlands
Tel: 70 3497373
Fax: 70 3819508

**Verein der Baumwoll Spinner und
Weber Osterreichs**
Rudolfplatz 12
PO Box 114
1013 Vienna
Austria
Tel: 1 639751

Verein Oesterriechischer Indusrtrielle
Schwarzenbergplatz 4
1031 Vienna
Austria
Tel: 1 711350
Fax: 1 71135292

**Verein Schweizerischer
Maschinen-Industrieller**
Kirchenweg 4
PO Box 179
8032 Zurich
Switzerland
Tel: 1 3844844
Fax: 1 3844848

**Vereiningung Schweizerischer
Automobil Importeure**
Mittelstrasse 32
3012 Berne
Switzerland
Tel: 31 246565
Fax: 31 243960

**Vereniging van Confectie- en
Tricotage-Ondernemingen**
Kon Wilhelminaplein 13
Confectiecentrum 20802
1062 Amsterdam
Netherlands
Tel: 20 156811
Fax: 20 170634

Vereniging FME
Bredwater 20
PO Box 190
AD 2700 Zoetermeer
Netherlands
Tel: 79 219221

**Vereniging van de Nederlandse
Chemische Industrie**
Ulietweg 14
PO Box 443
2260 AK Leidschendam
Netherlands
Tel: 70 3200233
Fax: 70 3203903

**Vereniging Nederlandse Scheepsbouw
Industrie**
PO Box 138
2700 AD Zoetermeer
Netherlands
Tel: 79 422663
Fax: 79 423151

**Verenungung Deutscher
Elektrizitatswerke**
Stresemannallee 23
6000 Frankfurt/Main 70
Germany
Tel: 069 6304–1

Verlag Metzler-Poeschel
Herman Leins GmbH & Co KG
Holzwiesenstrasse 2
PO Box 1152
7408 Kusterdingen
Germany
Tel: 07071 33046
Fax: 07071 33653

VLEHAN
Uhlanbeckkade 9
PO Box 224
2313 Leiden
Netherlands
Tel: 71 140741

VNU Business Publications Espana
Villafranca 22
28028 Madrid
Spain
Tel: 1 5643873
Fax: 1 2459562

WEFA
Ebury Gate
23 Lower Belgrave Street
London SW1W 0NW
UK
Tel: 071 7308171

Wirtschaftsverband Erdol und Erdgasgetwinnung
Bruhlstrasse 9
3000 Hannover 1
Germany
Tel: 511 326016
Fax: 511 321172

Wirtschaftsvereinigung Stahlindustrie
Breite Strasse 69
PO Box 8705
4000 Dusseldorf 1
Germany
Tel: 0211 28291
Fax: 0211 829231

World Tourism Organisation
Capitan Haya 42
28020 Madrid
Spain

Zenith Market and Media Fact
80 Charlotte Street
London W1A 1AQ
UK
Tel: 071 6365060

Zentralverband Elektrotechnik- und Elektronikindustrie
Stresemannallee 19
700969
6000 Frankfurt/Main 70
Germany
Tel: 069 6302317

ZMP
PO Box 2569
5300 Bonn
Germany
Tel: 0228 888213

SUBJECT INDEX

GEOGRAPHICAL INDEX

APPENDIX 1

NACE classification

NACE No	Description
11	**Extraction and briquetting of solid fuels**
12	**Coke ovens**
13	**Extraction of petroleum and natural gas**
14	**Mineral oil refining**
15	**Nuclear fuels industry**
16	**Production and distribution of electricity, gas, steam and hot water**
161	Generation and distribution of electric power
162	Gasworks; gas distribution
163	Production and distribution of steam, hot water, compressed air, district heating plants
17	**Water supply; collection, purification and distribution of water**
21	**Extraction and preparation of metalliferous ores**
211	Extraction and preparation of iron ore
212	Extraction and preparation of non-ferrous metal ores
22	**Production and preliminary processing of metals**
221	Iron and steel industry (as defined in the ECSC Treaty), excluding integrated coke ovens
222	Manufacture of steel tubes
223	Drawing, cold rolling and cold folding of steel
224	Production and preliminary processing of non-ferrous metals
23	**Extraction of minerals other than metalliferous and energy-producing minerals; peat extraction**
231	Extraction of building materials and refractory clays
232	Mining of potassium salt and natural phosphates
24	**Manufacture of non-metallic mineral products**
241	Manufacture of clay products for constructional purposes
242	Manufacture of cement, lime and plaster
243	Manufacture of concrete, cement or plaster products for constructional purposes
243.1	Manufacture of asbestos-cement products
243.6	Manufacture of ready-mixed concrete
244	Manufacture of articles of asbestos (except articles of asbestos-cement)
245	Working of stone and of non-metallic mineral products

NACE No	Description
246	Production of grindstones and other abrasive products
247	Manufacture of glass and glassware
248	Manufacture of ceramic goods
25	**Chemical industry**
251	Manufacture of basic industrial chemicals and manufacture followed by further processing of such products
255	Manufacture of paint, painter's fillings, varnish and printing ink
256	Manufacture of other chemical products, mainly for industrial and agricultural purposes
257	Manufacture of pharmaceutical products
258	Manufacture of soap, synthetic detergents, perfume and toilet preparations
259	Manufacture of other chemical products, chiefly for household and office use
259.1	Manufacture of photographic chemical material (sensitized photographic film, plate, paper, etc., and auxiliary products)
259.2	Manufacture of polishes and the like for household use (shoe, furniture and floor care products, metal polishes, car polishes, etc.)
26	**Man-made fibres industry**
31	**Manufacture of metal articles (except for mechanical, electrical and instrument engineering and vehicles)**
311	Foundries
312	Forging; drop forging, closed dieforging, pressing and stamping
313	Secondary transformation, treatment and coating of metals
314	Manufacture of structural metal products (incl. integrated assembly and installation)
315	Boilermaking, manufacture of reservoirs, tanks and other sheet-metal containers
316	Manufacture of tools and finished metal goods, except electrical equipment
316.5	Manufacture of domestic heating appliances and kitchen heating appliances of all kinds
316.6	Manufacture of metal furniture (including safes)
319	Other metal workshops not elsewhere specified
32	**Mechanical engineering**
321	Manufacture of agricultural machinery and tractors
322	Manufacture of machine-tools for working metal, and of other tools and equipment for use with machines

NACE No	Description
323	Manufacture of textile machinery and accessories; manufacture of sewing machines
324	Manufacture of machinery for the food, chemical and related industries
325	Manufacture of plant for mines, the iron and steel industry and foundries, civil engineering and the building trade; manufacture of mechanical handling equipment
326	Manufacture of transmission equipment for motive power
327	Manufacture of other machinery and equipment for use in specific branches of industry
328	Manufacture of other machinery and equipment
33	**Manufacture of office machinery and data-processing machinery**
34	**Electrical engineering**
341	Manufacture of insulated wires and cables
342	Manufacture of electrical machinery (comprising electric motors, electricity generators, transformers, switches, switchgear and other basic electrical plant)
343	Manufacture of electrical apparatus and appliances for industrial use; manufacture of batteries and accumulators
344	Manufacture of telecommunications equipment, electrical and electronic measuring and recording equipment, and electro- medical equipment
345	Manufacture of radio and television receiving sets, sound reproducing and recording equipment and of electronic equipment and apparatus (except electronic computers); manufacture of gramophone records and prerecorded magnetic tapes
346	Manufacture of domestic type electric appliances
347	Manufacture of electric lamps and other electric lighting equipment
348	Assembly and installation of electrical equipment and apparatus (except for work relating to the wiring of buildings)
35	**Manufacture of motor vehicles and of motor vehicle parts and accessories**
351	Manufacture and assembly of motor vehicles (including road tractors) and manufacture of motor vehicle engines
352	Manufacture of bodies for motor vehicles and of motor-drawn trailers and caravans
353	Manufacture of parts and accessories for motor vehicles
36	**Manufacture of other means of transport**
361	Shipbuilding
362	Manufacture of standard and narrow-gauge railway and tramway rolling-stock
363	Manufacture of cycles, motor-cycles and parts and accessories thereof
364	Aerospace equipment manufacturing and repairing
37	**Instrument engineering**
371	Manufacture of measuring, checking and precision instruments and apparatus
372	Manufacture of medical and surgical equipment and orthopaedic appliances (except orthopaedic footwear)
373	Manufacture of optical instruments and photographic equipment
374	Manufacture of clocks and watches and parts thereof

NACE No	Description
41/42	**Food, drink, and tobacco industry**
411	Manufacture of vegetable and animal oils and fats
412	Slaughtering, preparing and preserving of meat (except the butchers' trade)
413	Manufacture of dairy products
414	Processing and preserving of fruit and vegetables
415	Processing and preserving of fish and other sea foods fit for human consumption
416	Grain milling
417	Manufacture of spaghetti, macaroni, etc.
418	Manufacture of starch and starch products
419	Bread and flour confectionery
420	Sugar manufacturing and refining
421	Manufacture of cocoa, chocolate and sugar confectionery
422	Manufacture of animal and poultry food (including fish meal and flour)
423	Manufacture of other food products
424	Distilling of ethyl alcohol from fermenting materials; spirit distilling and compounding
425	Manufacture of wine of fresh grapes and beverages based thereon
427	Brewing and malting
428	Manufacture of soft drinks, including the bottling of natural spa waters
429	Manufacture of tobacco products
43	**Textile industry**
431	Wool industry
432	Cotton industry
433	Silk industry
434	Preparation, spinning and weaving of flax hemp and ramie
435	Jute industry
436	Knitting industry
437	Textile finishing
438	Manufacture of carpets, linoleum and other floor coverings, including leatherclad and similar supported synthetic sheeting
438.1	Manufacture of carpets, carpeting, rugs, etc. from all types of fibres
438.2	Manufacture of linoleum and similar floor coverings (on paper, board or textile base)
439	Miscellaneous textile industries
44	**Leather and leather goods industry (except footwear and clothing)**
441	Tanning and dressing of leather
442	Manufacture of products from leather and leather substitutes
45	**Footwear and clothing industry**
451	Manufacture of mass-produced footwear (excluding footwear made completely of wood or rubber)
453	Manufacture of ready-made clothing and accessories
455	Manufacture of household textiles and other made-up textile goods (outside weaving mills)
456	Manufacture of furs and fur goods
46	**Timber and wooden furniture industries**
461	Sawing and processing of wood
462	Manufacture of semi-finished wood products
463	Manufacture of carpentry and joinery components and of parquet flooring
464	Manufacture of wooden containers
465	Other wood manufactures (except furniture)
466	Manufacture of articles of cork and articles of straw and other plaiting material (including basketware and wickerwork); manufacture of brushes and brooms
467	Manufacture of wooden furniture

NACE No	Description
47	**Manufacture of paper and paper products printing and publishing**
471	Manufacture of pulp, paper and board
472	Processing of paper and board
473	Printing and allied industries
474	Publishing
48	**Processing of rubber and plastics**
481	Manufacture of rubber products
482	Retreading and repairing of rubber tyres
483	Processing of plastics
49	**Other manufacturing industries**
491	Manufacture of articles of jewellery and goldsmiths' and silversmiths' wares; cutting otherwise working of precious and semi-precious stones
492	Manufacture of musical instruments
493	Photographic and cinematographic laboratories

NACE No	Description
494	Manufacture of toys and sports goods
495	Miscellaneous manufacturing industries
50	**Building and civil engineering**
500	General building and civil engineering work (without any particular specialization) and demolition work
501	Construction of flats, office blocks, hospitals and other buildigs, both residential and non-residential
502	Civil engineering: construction of roads, bridges, railways, etc.
503	Installation (fittings and fixtures)
504	Building completion work
	Manufacturing Industry
1/4	**Industry**
5	**Building and civil engineering**

APPENDIX 2

ISIC classification

Broad structure: tabulation categories and divisions

Tabulation categories	Division	Description
A		**Agriculture, hunting and forestry**
	01	Agriculture, hunting and related service activities
	02	Forestry, logging and related service activities
B		**Fishing**
	05	Fishing, operation of fish hatcheries and fish farms; service actitivies incidental to fishing
C		**Mining and quarrying**
	10	Mining of coal and lignite; Extraction of peat
	11	Extraction of crude petroleum and natural gas; Service activities incidental to oil and gas Extraction, excluding surveying
	12	Mining of uranium and thorium ores
	13	Mining of metal ores
	14	Other mining and quarrying
D		**Manufacturing**
	15	Manufacture of food products and beverages
	16	Manufacture of tobacco products
	17	Manufacture of textiles
	18	Manufacture of wearing apparel; dressing and dyeing of fur
	19	Tanning and dressing of leather; manufacture of luggage, handbags, saddlery, harness and footwear
	20	manufacture of wood and of products of wood and cork, except furniture; manufacture of articles of straw and plaiting materials
	21	manufacture of paper and paper products

Tabulation categories	Division	Description
	22	Publishing, printing and reproduction of recorded media
	23	Manufacture of coke, refined petroleum products and nuclear fuel
	24	Manufacture of chemicals and chemical products
	25	Manufacture of rubber and plastics products
	26	Manufacture of other non-metallic mineral products
	27	Manufacture of basic metals
	28	Manufacture of fabricated metal products, except machinery and equipment
	29	Manufacture of machinery and equipment N.E.C.*
	30	Manufacture of office, accounting and computing machinery
	31	Manufacture of electrical machinery and apparatus N.E.C.
	32	Manufacture of radio, television and communication equipment and apparatus
	33	Manufacture of medical, precision and optical instruments, watches and clocks
	34	Manufacture of motor vehicles, trailers and semi-trailers
	35	Manufacture of other transport equipment
	36	Manufacture of furniture; manufacturing N.E.C.
	37	Recycling
E		**Electricity, gas and water supply**
	40	Electricity, gas, steam and hot water supply
	41	Collection, purification and distribution of water
F		**Construction**
	45	Construction

*Not elsewhere classified

Tabulation categories	*Division*	*Description*
G		**Wholesale and retail trade; repair of motor vehicles, motorcycles and personal and household goods**
	50	Sale, maintenance and repair of motor vehicles and motorcycles; retail sale of automotive fuel
	51	Wholesale trade and commission trade, except of motor vehicles and motorcycles
	52	Retail trade, except of motor vehicles and motorcycles; repair of personal and house-hold goods
H		**Hotels and restaurants**
	55	Hotels and restaurants
I		**Transport, storage and communications**
	60	Land transport; transport via pipelines
	61	Water transport
	62	Air transport
	63	Supporting and auxiliary transport activities; activities of travel agencies
	64	Post and telecommunications
J		**Financial intermediation**
	65	Financial intermediation, except insurance and pension funding
	66	Insurance and pension funding, except compulsory social security
	67	Activities auxiliary to financial intermediation
K		**Real estate, renting and business activities**
	70	Real estate activities

Tabulation categories	*Division*	*Description*
	71	Renting of machinery and equipment without operator and of personal and houshold goods
	72	Computer and related activities
	73	Research and development
	74	Other business activities
L		**Public administration and defence; compulsory social security**
	75	Public administration and defence; compulsory social security
M		**Education**
	80	Education
N		**Health and social work**
	85	Health and social work
O		**Other community, social and personal service activities**
	90	Sewage and refuse disposal, sanitation and similar activities
	91	Activities of membership organizations N.E.C.
	92	Recreational, cultural and sporting activities
	93	Other service activities
P		**Private households with employed persons**
	95	Private households with employed persons
Q		**Extra-territorial organizations and bodies**
	99	Extra-territorial organizations and bodies

APPENDIX 3
UK SIC classification

Div. 0 Agriculture, forestry and fishing
0100 Agriculture and horticulture
0200 Forestry
0300 Fishing

Div. 1 Energy and water supply industries
1113 Deep coal mines
1114 Opencast coal working
1115 Manufacture of solid fuels
1200 Coke Ovens
1300 Extraction of mineral oil and natural gas
1401 Mineral oil refining
1402 Other treatment of petroleum products
1520 Nuclear fuel production
1610 Production and distribution of electricity
1620 Public gas supply
1630 Production and distribution of other forms of energy
1700 Water supply industry

Div. 2 Extraction of minerals and ores; manufacture of metals, mineral products and chemicals
2100 Extraction and preparation of metalliferous ores
2210 Iron and steel industry
2220 Steel tubes
2234 Drawing and manufacture of steel wire and steel wire products
2235 Other drawing, cold rolling and cold forming of steel
2245 Aluminium and aluminium alloys
2246 Copper, brass and other copper alloys
2247 Other non-ferrous metals and their alloys
2310 Extraction of stone, clay, sand and gravel
2330 salt extraction and refining
2396 Extraction of other minerals N.E.S.
2410 Structural clay products
2420 Cement, lime and plaster
2436 Ready mixed concrete
2437 Other building products of concrete, cement or plaster
2440 Asbestos goods
2450 Working of stone and other non-metallic minerals N.E.S.
2460 Abrasive products
2471 Flat glass
2478 Glass containers
2479 Other glass products
2481 Refractory goods
2489 Cermaic goods

2511 Inorganic chemicals
2512 Basic organic chemicals
2513 Fertilisers
2514 Synthetic resins and plastics materials
2515 Synthetic rubber
2516 Dyestuffs and pigments
2551 Paints, varnishes and painters' fillings
2552 Printing ink
2562 Formulated adhesives and sealants
2563 Chemical treatment of oils and fats
2564 Essential oils and flavouring materials
2565 Explosives
2567 Miscellaneous chemical products for industrial use
2568 Formulated pesticides
2569 Adhesive film, cloth and foil
2570 Pharmaceutical products
2581 Soap and synthetic detergents
2582 Perfumes, cosmetics and toilet preparations
2591 Photographic materials and chemicals
2599 Chemical products N.E.S.
2600 Production of man-made fibres

Div. 3 Metal goods, engineering and vehicles industries
3111 Ferrous metal foundries
3112 Non-ferrous metal foundries
3120 Forgings, pressing and stamping
3137 Bolts, nuts, washers, rivets, springs and non-precision chains
3138 Heat and surface treatment of metals, including sintering
3142 Metal doors, windows, etc.
3161 Hand tools and implements
3162 Cutlery, spoons, forks and similar tableware; razors
3163 Metal storage vessels
3164 Packaging products of metal
3165 Domestic heating and cooking appliances
3166 Metal furniture and sales
3167 Domestic and similar utensils of metal
3169 Finished metal products N.E.S.
3204 Fabricated construction steelwork
3205 Boilers and process plant fabrications
3211 Agricultural machinery
3212 Wheeled tractors
3221 Metal-working machine tools
3222 Engineers' small tools
3230 Textile machinery

3244	Food, drink and tobacco processing machinery, packaging and bottling machinery
3245	Chemical industry machinery, furnaces and kilns; gas, water and waste treatment plant
3246	Process engineering contractors
3251	Mining machinery
3254	Construction and earth moving equipment
3255	Mechanical lifting and handling equipment
3261	Precision chains and other mechanical power transmission equipment
3262	Ball, needle and roller bearings
3275	Machinery for working wood, rubber, plastics, leather and making paper, glass, bricks and similar materials; laundry and dry cleaning machinery
3276	Printing, bookbinding and paper goods machinery
3281	Internal combustion engines and other prime movers
3283	Compressors and fluid power equipment
3284	Refrigerating machinery, space heating, ventilating and air conditioning equipment
3285	Scales, weighing machinery and portable power tools
3286	Other industrial and commercial machinery
3287	Pumps
3288	Industrial valves
3289	Mechanical, marine and precision engineering N.E.S.
3290	Ordnance, small arms and ammunition
3301	Office machinery
3302	Electronic data processing equipment
3410	Insulated wires and cables
3420	Basic electrical equipment
3432	Batteries and accumulators
3433	Alarms and signalling equipment
3434	Electrical equipment for motor vehicles, cyles and aircraft
3435	Electrical equipment for industrial use N.E.S.
3441	Telegraph and telephone apparatus and equipment
3442	Electrical instruments and control systems
3443	Radio and electronic capital goods
3444	Components other than active components
3452	Gramophone records and pre-recorded tapes
3453	Active components and electronic sub-assemblies
3454	Electronic consumer goods and other electronic equipment N.E.S.
3460	Domestic-type electric appliances
3470	Electric lamps and other electric lighting equipment
3480	Electrical equipment installation
3510	Motor vehicles and their engines
3521	Motor vehicle bodies
3522	Trailers and semi-trailers
3523	Caravans
3530	Motor vehicle parts
3610	Shipbuilding and repairing
3620	Railway and tramway vehicles
3633	Motor cycles and parts
3634	Pedal cycles and parts

3640	Aerospace equipment manufacturing and repairing
3650	Other vehicles
3710	Measuring, checking and precision instruments and apparatus
3720	Medical and surgical equipment and orthopaedic appliances
3731	Spectacles and unmounted lenses
3732	Optical precision instruments
3733	Photographic and cinematographic equipment
3740	Clocks, watches and other timing devices

Div. 4 Other manufacturing industries

4115	Margarine and compound cooking fats
4116	Processing organic oils and fats
4121	Slaughterhouses
4122	Bacon curing and meat processing
4123	Poultry slaughter and processing
4126	Animal by-product processing
4130	Preparation of milk and milk products
4147	Processing of fruit and vegetables
4150	Fish processing
4160	Grain milling
4180	Starch
4196	Bread and flour confectionery
4197	Biscuits and crispbread
4200	Sugar and sugar by-products
4213	Ice Cream
4214	Cocoa, chocolate and sugar confectionery
4221	Compound animal feeds
4222	Pet foods and non-compound animal feeds
4239	Miscellaneous foods
4240	Spirit distilling and compounding
4261	Wines, cider and perry
4270	Brewing and malting
4283	Soft drinks
4290	Tobacco industry
4310	Woollen and worsted industry
4321	Spinning and doubling on the cotton system
4322	Weaving of cotton, silk and man-made fibres
4336	Throwing, texturing, etc. of continuous filament yarn
4340	Spinning and weaving of flax, hemp and ramie
4350	Jute and polypropylene yarns and fabrics
4363	Hosiery and other weft knitted goods and fabrics
4364	Warp knitted fabrics
4370	Textile finishing
4384	Pile carpets, carpeting and rugs
4385	Other carpets, carpeting, rugs and matting
4395	Lace
4396	Rope, twine and net
4398	Narrow fabrics
4399	Other miscellaneous textiles
4410	Leather and fellmongery
4420	Leather goods
4510	Footwear
4531	Weatherproof outerwear
4532	Men's and boys' tailored outerwear
4533	Women's and girls' tailored outerwear
4534	Work clothing and men's and boys' jeans
4535	Men's and boys' shirts, underwear and nightwear

4536	Women's and girls' light outerwear, lingerie and infants' wear
4537	Hats, caps and millinery
4538	Gloves
4539	Other dress industries
4555	Soft furnishings
4556	Canvas goods, sacks and other made-up textiles
4557	Household textiles
4560	Fur goods
4610	Sawmilling, planing, etc. of wood
4620	Manufacture of semi-finished wood products
4630	Builders' carpentry and joinery
4640	Wooden containers
4650	Other wooden articles
4663	Brushes and brooms
4664	Articles of cork and basketware, wickerwork and other plaiting materials
4671	Wooden and upholstered furniture
4672	Shop and office fitting
4710	Pulp, paper and board
4721	Wall coverings
4722	Household and personal hygiene products of paper
4723	Stationery
4724	Packaging products of paper and pulp
4725	Packaging products of board
4728	Other paper and board products
4751	Printing and publishing of newspapers
4752	Printing and publishing of periodicals
4753	Printing and publishing of books
4754	Other printing and publishing
4811	Rubber tyres and inner tubes
4812	Other rubber products
4820	Retreading and specialist repairing of rubber tyres
4831	Plastic coated textile fabric
4832	Plastics semi-manufactures
4833	Plastics floorcoverings
4834	Plastics building products
4835	Plastics packaging products
4836	Plastics products N.E.S.
4910	Jewellery and coins
4920	Musical instruments
4930	Photographic and cinematographic processing laboratories
4941	Toys and games
4942	Sports goods
4954	Miscellaneous stationers' goods
4959	Other manufactures N.E.S.

Div. 5 Construction
5000	General construction and demolition work
5010	Construction and repair of buildings
5020	Civil engineering
5030	Installation of fixtures and fittings
5040	Building completion work

Div. 6 Distribution, hotels and catering; repairs
6110	Wholesale distribution of agricultural raw materials, live animals, textile raw materials and semi-manufactures
6120	Wholesale distribution of fuels, ores, metals and industrial materials
6130	Wholesale distribution of timber and building materials

6148	Wholesale distribution of motor vehicles and parts and accesories
6149	Wholesale distribution of machinery; industrial equipment and transport equipment
6150	Wholesale distribution of household goods, hardware and ironmongery
6160	Wholesale distribution of textiles, clothing, footwear and leather goods
6170	Wholesale distribution of food, drink and tobacco
6180	Wholesale distribution of pharmaceutical, medical and other chemists' goods
6190	Other wholesale distribution including general wholesalers
6210	Dealing in scrap metals
6220	Dealing in other scrap materials, or general dealers
6300	Commission agents
6410	Food retailing
6420	Confectioners, tobacconists and newsagents; off licences
6430	Dispensing and other chemists
6450	Retail distribution of clothing
6460	Retail distribution of footwear and leathergoods
6470	Retail distribution of furnishing fabrics and household textiles
6480	Retail distribution of household goods, hardware and ironmongery
6510	Retail distribution of motor vehicles and parts
6520	Filing stations (motor fuel and lubricants)
6530	Retail distribution of books, stationery and office supplies
6540	Other specialised retail distribution (non-food)
6560	Mixed retail businesses
6611	Restaurants
6612	Take-away food shops
6620	Public houses and bars
6630	Night clubs and licensed clubs
6640	Canteens and messes
6650	Hotel trade
6670	Other tourist or short-stay accommodation
6710	Repair and servicing of motor vehicles
6720	Repair of footwear and leather goods
6730	Repair of consumer goods

Div. 7 Transport and communication
7100	Railways
7210	Scheduled road passenger transport and urban railways
7220	Other road passenger transport
7230	Road haulage
7260	Transport N.E.S.
7400	Sea transport
7500	Air transport
7610	Supporting services to inland transport
7630	Supporting services to sea transport
7640	Supporting services to air transport
7700	Miscellaneous transport services and storage N.E.S.
7901	Postal services
7902	Telecommunications

Div. 8 Banking, finance, insurance, business services and leasing
| 8410 | Banking and bill-discounting |

8150	Other financial institutions	9212	Sewage disposal
8200	Insurance	9230	Cleaning services
8310	Activities auxiliary to banking and finance	9310	Higher education
8320	Activies auxiliary to insurance	9320	School education
8340	House and estate agents	9330	Education N.E.S.
8350	Legal services	9360	Driving and flying schools
8360	Accountants, auditors, tax experts	9400	Research and development
8370	Professional and technical services N.E.S.	9510	Hospitals, nursing homes, etc.
8380	Advertising	9520	Other medical care institutions
8394	Computer services	9530	Medical practices
8395	Business services N.E.S.	9540	Dental practices
8396	Central offices not allocable elsewhere	9550	Agency and private midwives, nurses, etc.
8410	Hiring out agricultural and horticultural equipment	9560	Veterinary practices and animal hospitals
8420	Hiring out construction machinery and equipment	9611	Social welfare, charitable and community services
8430	Hiring out office machinery and furniture	9631	Trade unions, business and professional associations
8460	Hiring out consumer goods	9660	Religious organisations and similar associations
8480	Hiring out transport equipment		
8490	Hiring out other movables	9690	Tourist offices and other community services
8500	Owning and dealing in real estate		
		9711	Film production, distribution and exhibition
Div. 9	**Other services**	9741	Radio and television services, theatres, etc.
9111	National government service not elsewhere specified	9760	Authors, music composers
9112	Local government service not elsewhere specified	9770	Libraries, museums, art galleries, etc.
		9791	Sport and other recreational services
9120	Justice	9811	Laundries
9130	Police	9812	Dry clearning and allied services
9140	Fire services	9820	Hairdressing and beauty parlours
9150	National defence	9890	Personal services N.E.S.
9190	Social security	9900	Domestic services
9211	Refuse disposal, street cleaning, fumigation, etc.	0000	Diplomatic representation, international organisations, allied armed forces